20 Strategies for Increasing Student Engagement

WILLIAM N. BENDER

LSi LEARNING SCIENCES INTERNATIONAL

Copyright © 2017 by Learning Sciences International

Materials appearing here are copyrighted. With one exception, all rights are reserved. Readers may reproduce only those pages marked "Reproducible." Otherwise, no part of this book may be reproduced or transmitted in any form or by any means (electronic, photocopying, recording, or otherwise) without prior written permission of the publisher.

1400 Centrepark Blvd, Suite 1000
West Palm Beach, FL 33401
717-845-6300

email: pub@learningsciences.com
learningsciences.com

Printed in the United States of America

22 21 20 19 18 17   1 2 3 4 5 6

Library of Congress Control Number: 2017947359

Publisher's Cataloging-in-Publication Data
provided by Five Rainbows Cataloging Services

Names: Bender, William N., author.

Title: 20 strategies for increasing student engagement / William N. Bender.

Description: West Palm Beach, FL: Learning Sciences, 2017. | Includes bibliographical references and index.

Identifiers: ISBN 978-1-941112-79-3 (pbk.) | ISBN 978-1-941112-89-2 (ebook)

Subjects: LCSH: Engagement (Philosophy) | Learning, Psychology of. | Students--Psychology. | Classroom management--Psychological aspects. | Teacher-student relationships. | BISAC: EDUCATION / Educational Psychology. | EDUCATION / Classroom Management.

Classification: LCC LB1065 .B43 2017 (print) | LCC LB1065 (ebook) | DDC 370.15/4--dc23.

Acknowledgments

Learning Sciences International would like to thank the following reviewers:

David Bosso, EdD
2012 Connecticut Teacher of the Year
Berlin High School
Berlin, CT

Stephanie Day-Young
Assistant Principal
KIPP DC
Washington, DC

Victoria Truman
Seventh-Grade English Teacher
Watson B. Duncan Middle School
Palm Beach Gardens, FL

Table of Contents

About the Author... xiii

Introduction
Student Engagement and Learning 1
What Is Student Engagement?... 1
Engagement Strategies and Teaching Tips 3
How to Use This Book... 6

Section I
Instructional Organization for Increasing Engagement 9

1 Differentiated Instruction 11
Four Models for Differentiation 12
Modification of a Traditional Lesson Plan 12
A Classroom Example: A Differentiated History Lesson 13
Guidelines for Differentiated Instruction............................. 18
Research on Differentiated Instruction................................ 19
Summary 20

2 The Flipped Class Strategy............................. 21
Development of the Flipped Class Concept 22
Four Pillars of Flipped Learning 22

Advantages of Flipping the Class 23
A Classroom Example: Inside a Flipped Science Class 24
Steps for Flipping Your Class 26
A Case Study: Flipping the History Class 28
Research on Flipped Learning 30
Summary 30

3 Project-Based Learning 31
Project Scope in PBL Instruction 32
Structure and Components of PBL Instruction 34
PBL Project Phases 37
Research on PBL Instruction 42
Summary 42

4 Makerspace and Genius Hour 43
Materials and Tools for Your Makerspace 45
Virtual World Support for Makerspaces 50
Guidelines for Setting Up a Makerspace 50
Research on Makerspace and Creative Time 52
Summary 53

Section II
Tech Strategies to Increase Engagement 55

5 Augmented Reality 57
A Classroom Example: AR Making History Come Alive 58
Setting Up Your AR Classroom 60
Research on AR 61
Summary 62

6 Games, Gamification, and Simulations 63
Educational Games for Teaching 64

A Classroom Example: Gaming in Mathematics 66
Virtual Worlds as Complex Gaming 67
Beginning Gaming in the Classroom 72
Research on Games and Virtual Worlds 73
Summary 74

7 Virtual Field Trips 75
New Tech Tools for Virtual Field Trips 76
Case Study: Virtual Field Trips in Science Class 77
Guidelines for Teaching With Virtual Field Trips 79
Guidelines for Creating Virtual Field Trips 81
Research on Virtual Field Trips 84
Summary 84

8 Coding and Robotics 87
Coding in the Classroom 89
A Classroom Example: First Time Coding in Grade 1 91
Robotics: The Next Step 94
Steps for Teaching Coding/Robotics 97
Research on Coding and Robotics 98
Summary 99

9 Individualized Computer-Driven Instruction: Khan Academy 101
Khan Academy 104
Steps in Implementing Khan Academy 106
Research on Khan Academy 108
Summary 110

10 Storyboarding for Comprehension: Comic Life 111
Comic Life 112
A Classroom Example: Using Comic Life 114
Steps in Using Comic Life 114
Research on Storyboarding With Comic Life 117
Summary 117

11 Animation 119
Animation in the Classroom 120
A Case Study: Animation to Increase Student Engagement 123
Creating an Avatar Animation.. 124
Research on Animation 127
Summary 127

Section III
Collaborative Instruction to Increase Engagement 129

12 Blogging 131
Using a Classroom Blog... 132
A Classroom Example: Using Blogs for Differentiated Instruction........ 133
Guidelines for Beginning a Blog... 134
Research on Classroom Blogging 137
Summary 137

13 Social Networking for Learning: Twitter 139
Using Twitter in the Classroom... 140
Guidelines for Using Twitter 143
Research on Social Networking in the Classroom 145
Summary 145

14 Wikis to Enhance Student Engagement 147
What Is a Wiki?... 148
Using a Class Wiki 148
A Classroom Example: Using a Wiki..................................... 149
Setting Up a Class Wiki... 151
Research on Wikis in the Classroom 156
Summary 156

15 Peer Tutoring to Enhance Student Engagement ...157
A Case Study: Classwide Peer Tutoring in Health Class. ...158
Classwide Peer Tutoring. ...160
Steps in Classwide Peer Tutoring ...161
Research on Classwide Peer Tutoring. ...162
Summary ...163

16 The Role-Play Instructional Strategy ...165
A Classroom Example: Using Role-Play ...166
Steps for Implementing Role-Play ...167
Research on Role-Play ...173
Summary ...173

Section IV
Personal Responsibility and Student Engagement ...175

17 Mindfulness to Increase Engagement ...177
A Classroom Example: Mindfulness in High School ...178
Implementing Mindfulness ...179
Research on Mindfulness Training ...181
Summary ...182

18 Reward and Response Cost: ClassDojo ...183
ClassDojo to Increase Student Engagement ...185
A Classroom Example: ClassDojo for Positive and Negative Behavior ...186
Research on ClassDojo ...187
Summary ...188

19 A Growth Mindset Strategy 189
Understanding the Concept of Growth Mindset 190
Lessons to Foster a Growth Mindset 193
A Case Study: Teaching Growth Mindset 197
Research on Growth Mindset 199
Summary 200

20 Goal Setting and Self-Monitoring for Increasing Attention Skills 201
Teaching Goal Setting and Self-Monitoring 202
Research on Goal Setting and Progress Monitoring 205
Summary 205

Appendix
Meta-Analysis and Effect Size 207
Advantages of Meta-Analyses 208
Disadvantages of Meta-Analyses 209
Use of Meta-Analyses 210

References 211

Index 225

About the Author

William N. Bender, PhD, is a national leader on the general topic of instructional tactics for the classroom, with special interests in discipline, project-based learning, technology in the classroom, differentiated instruction, and response to intervention. He has written twenty-five books in education, many of which are leading sellers in their respective topics.

He currently presents numerous workshops each year for educators around the country and in Canada, using humor and his down-to-earth personal style. His focus is always on practical strategies and tactics that will work in real classrooms, and his work is firmly based on his experience teaching public school special needs students in eighth and ninth grades. After earning his PhD from the University of North Carolina, he spent a career teaching educators at Rutgers University and the University of Georgia.

Introduction

Student Engagement and Learning

Teachers have long realized that student engagement is absolutely essential for student learning; if students are not engaged with the content to be mastered, they will not learn it. I wrestled with this reality during my teaching days, working with eighth- and ninth-grade students with mild to moderate disabilities. I saw students with learning disabilities or emotional problems struggling to pay attention for more than two or three minutes to their assignments. A few years later, my dissertation focused on the attention skills of students with learning disabilities in high school (Bender, 1985), so student engagement is one issue on which I have a long-standing interest. In many ways, this book stems from that work.

However, this book is not just a theory on attention or student engagement. In this book, I'll not present brain structures that facilitate arousal or attention, nor will the attention–memory connection be discussed herein. Rather, this book is focused on specific strategies for engaging students in the classroom, based on the simple fact that as student engagement with the educational content increases, academic achievement also increases.

What Is Student Engagement?

Definitions of student engagement vary somewhat and have changed over the years, as have the methods for measuring student engagement. For example, engagement or attention used to be measured in terms of eye contact. That is, if a student's eyes were directed toward the academic content in the book or on the board, the student was believed to be paying attention and engaged with the learning content (Bender, 1985). However, this eye contact definition of engagement was never satisfactory because, with a moment's thought, all teachers will quickly realize that students can easily stare at a book without being engaged with the content.

More recent thought on student engagement has identified particulars, and even included emotional reactions, in the definition of engagement. For example, engagement is frequently defined today as students' cognitive investment in, active participation with, and emotional commitment to learning particular content (Zepke & Leach, 2010). A limited body of research investigates student engagement by measuring actual brain activity during various tasks, but this type of research is rare.

> Engagement may be defined as students' cognitive investment in, active participation with, and emotional commitment to learning particular content.

In my workshops with teachers around the country, I often use an example from an old movie called *Teachers*. That movie presented a teacher in the late 1970s who "taught" exclusively using worksheets. The students and other teachers all called this worksheet-crazed teacher "Ditto," a name derived from the ditto machines that were used at that time to make copies of worksheets. Students came into Ditto's class, took the ditto worksheet copies off one side of his desk, passed them out, and worked on them all period. Meanwhile, Ditto himself sat at his desk and read the newspaper, never making eye contact with a student or talking to anyone! At the end of each class when the bell rang, the students collected all the completed worksheets and put them on the other side of Ditto's desk prior to leaving the classroom.

As presented in the movie, Ditto died one day in third period, still holding his newspaper, seated behind his desk. No one noticed!

His fourth-period class came into the room, collected their ditto worksheets, completed them, put them on the other side of the desk, and left, as did the fifth- and sixth-period classes. Ditto merely sat there, dead, behind his newspaper. The janitor found Ditto, cold as a stone, later that night, still seated behind the desk holding up the newspaper. In the context of this book, Ditto, this fictional teacher, can provide a useful lesson:

> If a dead guy can do it, it ain't teaching!

There is at least one important corollary to that guideline that is somewhat more relevant for this book:

> If a dead guy can do it, it ain't learning!

Learning must be active. For students to be engaged with their learning, they must be invested, they must be involved. As both the definition and this movie example illustrate, student engagement is more than merely a passive response to a lecture or even a halfhearted attempt to pay slight attention and complete a worksheet. Rather, student learning—student engagement—is an active, involved, cognitive, and emotional investment in the content to be learned. While teachers have long understood that cognitive involvement was necessary for learning to take place, the more recent insight herein is that students must be emotionally invested in their learning activity. Teachers who plan their lessons with that in mind might find that they begin to plan different types of lesson activities.

In fact, using this concept of student engagement provides teachers with a goal for lesson development, a general direction for planning lesson activities. For student engagement to be maximized, it becomes the teacher's task to delineate learning activities that will foster cognitive involvement in and emotional connection with the learning content. To the degree that we educators can provide such activities, students are much more likely to be engaged and also more likely to learn.

There is one additional caveat to this discussion of student engagement. As shown previously, engagement is very hard to measure in an academic setting. Further, student engagement is not a targeted or direct goal of education. Rather, engagement is most frequently discussed as a precursor and essential cause for increased student achievement. For that reason, there is not a great deal of research proving that any given instructional strategy increases student engagement. Rather, most efficacy research involves documenting how a strategy impacts students' achievement, rather than student engagement itself. Therefore, in each following strategy, the research discussed will emphasize improving academic achievement.

Engagement Strategies and Teaching Tips

At the outset, I should describe the distinction between a strategy to enhance student engagement and a simple teaching tip. A teaching tip involves a simple, easily implemented practice or teaching habit that will typically enhance the instruction for all teachers. For example, Ripp (2015) recommends a number of teaching tips that teachers might employ to keep students engaged. These include things like:

- Change it up—varying instructional practices from time to time
- Find a new way—seeking ways for students to present their knowledge
- Get up and move—using movement in class to keep students from getting bored

- Stop the train wreck—stopping and discussing educational activities on which students lose interest and then discussing why they lost interest while seeking another way to do the same thing

All of these teaching tips are effective ways to increase student engagement, but they are merely teaching tips, suggestions on how to teach. These are not highly involved strategies to implement in the classroom. A quick look at the literature on student engagement reveals many articles that provide teaching tips or suggestions of this nature (Cochrane Collegiate Academy, 2014; Marzano, 2015; McCarthy, 2015; Ripp, 2015; Tizzard, 2010; Zepke & Leach, 2010), and many of these suggestions have merit. A list of tips from these sources, along with a very brief explanation of each, is presented in Box 1.

> **Box 1: Teaching Tips to Enhance Student Engagement**
>
> **Hold a meaningful conversation:** When students are not engaged, stop the lesson and ask why. Talk about what might interest them more, and let them know you are willing to try activities they suggest.
>
> **Turn on some music:** Sometimes playing soft background music can help motivate them. However, take care to note the impact of background music on every student; for some students, any noise merely creates a distraction.
>
> **Make learning content personal:** Personalizing the learning by showing how content is meaningful and relevant to students will help them remain focused on the content.
>
> **Use technology:** Students today use technology in almost every aspect of their lives, and integrating this into learning will help hold the attention of many students.
>
> **Give students some choices:** By making different choices among lesson assignments available to students, we are sharing control of the class with them. Students will often focus on the content more when they have chosen one of several activity options.
>
> **Create collaborative learning that fosters relationships:** Students will often engage more in collaborative working situations than in individual situations.
>
> **Create challenging activities:** Students will often engage more when working on activities that challenge their knowledge, particularly in team or learning-pair types of activities.
>
> **Use movement to make learning active:** High-energy activities always seem to increase retention compared to more passive types of learning activities, so teachers should create learning environments that build energy.
>
> **Make it a game:** Games and competitive activities foster higher student engagement more readily than simple practice-the-learning activities.

> **Focus on clearly stated goals:** Teachers should identify specific essential questions or lesson objectives and stress the importance of them for the students.
>
> **Use an activating task:** A brief high-interest activity at the beginning of a lesson will help students focus actively on the content. Competitive activities or interesting brief video clips can add interest to the content.
>
> **Limit the lecture:** Teachers have long recognized that lectures make students passive learners, and as a rule, the only lectures used in classrooms today should be brief highly focused mini-lessons (eight to fifteen minutes, as suggested by research on brain functioning; Sousa & Tomlinson, 2011).
>
> **Use graphics and illustrations:** Graphic organizers or simple student drawings that highlight aspects of the content can greatly aid in remembering that content. Having the students create these graphics and illustrations using either simple drawings or digital creative tools will enhance learning.
>
> **Focus on higher-order thinking:** Questions that focus on the bigger picture or the more complete task will often engage students more than simple factual or memory questions.
>
> **Summarize the work at the end:** Summarization is a great closure activity for the end of a lesson, and having students discuss the summary in partners for the last five minutes of class will increase memory for the content.

Teachers should certainly employ some or most of these teaching tips, but again, these are not specific instructional strategies designed to increase student engagement. In contrast to the brief teaching tips, a strategy in this context is a more involved instructional procedure that will be more likely to foster student engagement. Strategies will take some time for teachers to plan and implement and may involve in-depth modification of long-standing instructional practices. Strategies to increase student engagement may involve how instruction is organized or how teachers facilitate students' taking personal responsibility for learning. Alternatively, some strategies involve learning about and employing new teaching tools, many of which involve modern teaching technologies, in the classroom.

Teachers who have chosen to purchase this book typically have explored and implemented many of the teaching tips that one can find in the literature or in Box 1. However, many teachers, having implemented those teaching tips and habits, are still seeking substantive ideas to increase engagement. These teachers need practical, proven strategies that engage the students we find in the classroom today, the tech-savvy students who know and utilize all of the most modern phone apps and in their spare time focus on highly engaging computer games with sophisticated graphics, games that are highly interactive and demand near-instantaneous responses. These students routinely engage with their friends in various social networks.

Today's students are not likely to be highly engaged in a traditional "lecture, discuss, test" type of instructional format. These students demand and expect intensive, attention-grabbing instructional practices. This book is intended to fulfill that need.

How to Use This Book

Specifically, this book is intended for teachers across the grade levels who are seeking ways to meaningfully engage students with the curricular content. Herein, I present a variety of instructional strategies that are known to foster high levels of student engagement. These are presented in four broad areas—instructional organization strategies, technology strategies, collaborative strategies, and personal responsibility strategies—with multiple strategies shared for each broad area.

In various strategy sections, I have included classroom examples and case studies, which include examples in various subjects across the grade levels. In order to ensure the practicality of this work, I have also invited several educators to write teacher contributions in which they note how they use specific strategies to enhance student engagement in their classes. In various sections, I've included some specific related information in boxed form that should generally be considered as sidebar information. I've also included various figures and data charts throughout the text to show how teachers might evaluate the efficacy of the strategies described.

This book also provides many specific instructional guidelines or step-by-step instructions for various strategies. Each of these text features is clearly identified in the book and should help the reader in understanding the strategies.

This book is structured such that teachers should feel free to skip around. While research evidence is cited throughout the book, the primary purpose here is to provide teachers with practical, effective, and time-efficient instructional strategies, and given that teachers' time is always at a premium, teachers should feel free to select individual strategies that they wish to consider for their own classroom and read those sections of the book first.

Teachers should realize that, for most of these strategies, there are a variety of ways they may be implemented, and guidelines for implementation presented are exactly that—guidelines. I realize that the primary audience for this book is veteran teachers just like you! You are probably already an effective teacher who is exploring ways to become more effective. Thus, you should feel free to adapt these ideas, to merge these strategies, or to modify them in any reasonable or ethical manner that works in your classroom. Talk with your colleagues and reflect on these teaching strategies in order to make them your own.

With that noted, I would also make one additional request: drop me a line or two via email (my direct email is williamnbender@gmail.com) and let me know how any of these strategies worked for you. Let me know of your modifications, adaptations of these ideas, and how and why they worked, if they did, in your classroom. Please understand that this is more than merely a polite invitation. I truly enjoy interacting via email with teachers who have used my work to further their own, and I seriously invite you to contact me about the topics included herein. I sincerely hope that this work is useful for you, and as a classroom teacher myself, I understand your time constraints, as well as the job you are doing. Further, I recognize the importance of that job.

Finally, with that in mind, let me join the many parents and students who, I'm sure, have told you in the past: Thanks for what you do! You are making a difference!

SECTION I

Instructional Organization for Increasing Engagement

Student engagement, as defined previously, involves many facets, but one of the most important involves structuring the curriculum and delivery of instruction specifically to maximize engagement. When the traditional "lecture, discuss, test" instructional approach is considered, an effort to increase engagement will be, in essence, an effort to decrease lectures and whole-class discussion. This does not mean that these traditional teaching approaches have no place in the modern classroom; it does mean that these instructional activities should be fairly rare, since it has long been recognized that lecture is one of the least effective ways to teach, forcing students into a passive role. Student engagement is often quite low during lecture types of classes. This section focuses on several ways to organize instruction to minimize those traditional forms of teaching.

Differentiated instruction is one instructional approach that fosters varied instructional activities. This concept is now nearly two decades old, and we educators should give credit where credit is due. The concept of differentiated instruction developed by Carol Tomlinson (1999) represents one of the first, and certainly one of the most effective, efforts to vary how instruction was delivered in order to address individual learning styles and the needs of specific students and to increase their engagement with the subject content. As such, a discussion of differentiated instruction is warranted here.

In addition, several more recent instructional organization approaches have likewise been developed in recent years, including project-based learning, the flipped classroom, and genius hour / makerspace. The impact of each of these instructional organization strategies on student engagement is presented in this section.

Strategy 1

Differentiated Instruction

Differentiated instruction is an excellent instructional strategy for keeping students engaged in an intensive, meaningful way with the learning content. Differentiation involves varying the instructional activities in the class by selecting specific types of activities for each individual student, based on his or her individual learning characteristics and learning style preferences (Bender, 2013a; Sousa & Tomlinson, 2011; Tomlinson, 2003, 2010). Tomlinson originally developed this teaching strategy in 1999, and since then, much work has been done to further this concept, with Tomlinson herself leading this effort (Sousa & Tomlinson, 2011; Tomlinson, 2003, 2010).

> Differentiated instruction involves varying the instructional activities in the class by selecting specific types of activities for each student, based on his or her individual learning characteristics and learning style preferences.

Over the last decade, the differentiated instruction approach has moved away from a dependence on only one learning style theory to embrace a variety of student differences and appropriate curricular modifications (Bender, 2013a, 2013b; King & Gurian, 2006; Lee, Wehmeyer, Sookup, & Palmer, 2010). Further, the concept has been applied in a variety of subjects and a variety of ways across the grade levels (Bender, 2013a; King & Gurian, 2006). Because student learning differences are more directly addressed in differentiated classes, students are more likely to be engaged with the learning content, and limited research evidence does show increased academic achievement resulting from increased differentiation (King & Gurian, 2006; Lee et al., 2010; Sousa & Tomlinson, 2011; Tomlinson, Brimijoin, & Navaez, 2008).

Four Models for Differentiation

At least four different models for differentiation have been developed and promoted (Bender, 2013a, 2013b; Tomlinson, 2010; Tomlinson, Brimijoin, & Narvaez, 2008), including: modification of a traditional lesson plan, learning centers, project-based learning, and the flipped classroom. All of these teaching approaches are, in essence, various ways to differentiate instruction, because each of these approaches fosters use of a wide variety of lesson activities and also allows students to use their preferred learning style to maximum effect (Bender, 2013a).

Because the differentiated instruction concept has been around since Tomlinson's initial work in 1999, many teachers have already explored various approaches to differentiating instruction. Still, because differentiation does increase student engagement and provides a very viable alternative to more traditional approaches, such as lectures in content classes, it must be presented here. This section focuses primarily on the original approach to differentiated instruction, modification of the traditional whole-group lesson plan.

Modification of a Traditional Lesson Plan

The traditional lesson plan format was developed in the late 1960s and is typically described as phases of instruction within a single-day whole-class lesson. The five phases of instruction are presented in Box 1.1. Of course, variations of the phases in that traditional lesson plan vary from one author to another, but in most cases, that plan looks something like this.

Box 1.1: Phases in a Traditional Whole-Class Lesson Plan

Orientation to the topic: Teacher gives a three- to five-minute orientation using an essential question, objective, or real-world example.

Teacher-led instruction: Teacher presents additional examples and shows the content as the students' first exposure to the topic.

Teacher-led practice: Students practice a few problems, under teacher supervision.

Independent practice: Students practice problems independently, often as homework and sometimes as small-group work.

Check and reteach: Teacher checks student understanding on a few problems and reteaches the content as necessary.

In this lesson plan, students' attention often wanes either because the content is too difficult and they cannot keep up or they are advanced and get bored listening to initial instructional examples that they do not need. Thus, traditional lessons typically lose students at both ends of the ability spectrum—gifted students and students with learning challenges. Still, in traditional classes, the whole class proceeds through all of these steps simultaneously, and if small-group instruction is provided, it comes following the initial instruction led by the teacher.

In order to increase student engagement with learning content and to optimize achievement, Tomlinson recommended varying the instructional activities for different class members, based on their individual learning styles. While her first book (Tomlinson, 1999) was based largely on Howard Gardner's multiple intelligences theory, most of her later books have moved beyond that one theory to focus on many learning style preferences and achievement differences (Tomlinson, 2003, 2010; Sousa & Tomlinson, 2011).

After teachers became familiar with Tomlinson's work, many began to modify the traditional whole-group lesson plan to allow for more differentiated activities. The differentiated classrooms of today present a much wider array of activities, targeted at individual learners, in order to address the issues of more varied learning styles, learning preferences, and the wider academic diversity in today's schools.

A Classroom Example: A Differentiated History Lesson

Imagine a traditional history lesson in Ms. Kimball's fifth-grade class, a class of twenty-four students, five of whom are students with special needs. Several of those five students have learning disabilities or ADHD, and five students, including one student with ADHD, are academically advanced. In other words, Ms. Kimball's class is a typical fifth-grade class. Ms. Kimball is teaching a history lesson in a one-week history unit concerning Manifest Destiny and the Texas Revolution. Box 1.2 (page 14) shows the phases of a traditional whole-group lesson plan on the left and a series of differentiated lesson activities on the right for the same lesson.

> ### Box 1.2: Traditional and Differentiated Lesson Plan
>
> | **Traditional Lesson** | **Differentiated Lesson** |
> |---|---|
> | **Orientation** ||
> | Ms. Kimball introduces the Alamo. | Same activity for all students. |
> | **Teacher-Led Instruction** ||
> | Ms. Kimball begins discussion of what caused the Texas Revolution with eighteen students in the mainline group who receive increased teacher attention. | Ms. Kimball assigns a group to write a role-play on causes to fight. The Omega group is formed to begin that work. |
> | **Teacher-Led Practice** ||
> | Ms. Kimball gives student groups an assignment to look up how their chosen character perceived the fight. Ms. Kimball is now working with eleven students in the mainline group. | Omega group continues its work, while Ms. Kimball forms a second group—the Beta group—for another differentiated assignment, perhaps seeking online information on the Runaway Scrape in the Texas Revolution. |
>
> **Independent Practice and Check Reteach Phases**
>
> Whole group comes back together for further activities.

To begin this lesson with an attention-grabbing orientation activity, Ms. Kimball shows a three- to ten-minute segment of the movie *The Alamo* and asks students to identify their favorite historic figure from among five figures. That movie presents many historic figures (Davy Crockett, Jim Bowie, Colonel William Travis, Juan Seguin, General Santa Anna). She then asks them to list three reasons for their choice. She announces that there will be a popularity vote on who is the best-loved historic character at the end of the week-long unit but that each student has to know the history of the whole Texas Revolution. After that brief introduction activity for the whole class, the students are interested in learning more about their choices.

At that point, Ms. Kimball has captured the interest of the students and set up a competition among them for that week. In a traditional whole-class lesson, she would proceed to the next phase—teacher-led instruction—by saying, "Let's look at why these men fought in the revolution," and in many cases, that is exactly where many students lose interest in the lesson. Students with disabilities or limited attention simply wander away mentally, and while interesting orientation activities can hold students' interest for a brief time, moving into teacher-led instruction is often where they mentally check out. Further, some of the more advanced students may have already understood the idea and may be looking in the text for information on their chosen historic figure. Thus, like their less successful classmates, they too have mentally checked out. In this example, both advanced students and students with learning problems have become unengaged with the lesson content during the whole-group lesson format. Further, when five students with disabilities and five advanced or gifted students cease to pay attention, Ms. Kimball has effectively lost ten of her twenty-four students. In this example of a traditional lesson plan, ten students have stopped participating in the lesson simply because Ms. Kimball taught the traditional whole-group lesson plan, just as recommended in the teacher's manual!

Forming Differentiated Groups

The differentiated lesson plan on the right side of Box 1.2 provides a set of modified lesson activities that are much more likely to keep all or most of these learners actively engaged with the lesson. Rather than begin the second phase of the traditional whole-group lesson, Ms. Kimball selects a group for a different activity while she continues the traditional lesson with the other students. To do this, Ms. Kimball identifies several students at the end of the orientation activity who can work independently and several who can't in order to have a heterogeneous ability group. She selects students who work well together and have a similar learning style—perhaps learning through collaborative role-play and movement. She then forms a differentiated instructional group for a different learning activity on these characters that is directly tied to their learning style preference.

For example, she assigns an activity of planning a one-act role-play in which three or four of the historic figures debate their perspective on the Texas Revolution. There is considerable debate on what the defenders of the Alamo were fighting for. They may not have known that Texas independence had been declared by other Texans at the time of the battle, and most, like the Mexican Juan Seguin, who fought with the Alamo defenders, were probably fighting for the restoration of the Mexican constitution, which Santa Anna had defied. Jim Bowie and Davy Crockett were both rough and tumble Americans and were probably fighting for total independence, while the Alamo commander, Colonel Travis, may have been fighting for the restoration of the Mexican constitution. Clearly Santa Anna perceived all the defenders as "pirates" or revolutionaries with no legal basis for their claims.

Thus, these students are assigned to present a role-play of these historic figures meeting in a frontier tavern and discussing their perspectives before the fight. The students work relatively independently, while Ms. Kimball works with others in the class in a traditional lesson plan format, as shown in Box 1.2. We'll call that differentiated group the Omega group.

Ms. Kimball knows that as long as some students in the Omega group get the overall concept of what is needed, the group should be able to work on its own in this differentiated learning activity, while Ms. Kimball continues the traditional lesson format with others in the classroom. Note that while small-group instruction in traditional lessons is typically used much later in a traditional lesson plan, after the teacher has taught the content, in a differentiated lesson plan students are doing different activities within five or ten minutes of the beginning of the class, even before the teacher-led instructional phase of the lesson. Thus, fewer students get mentally lost during instruction, and fewer get bored than in a traditional lesson.

The names used for differentiated groups in the class should be nonsequential and should not indicate a quantitative or qualitative judgment on the skills or the intellect of the group. However, as teachers differentiate more, the class will grow to understand that different groups are frequently formed to complete alternative learning activities and that not all students in the class do the same activities.

In this example, Ms. Kimball has previously developed an assignment sheet for the Omega group presenting a scenario for a secret meeting in a neutral place, a guarded frontier tavern, where participants gather to discuss their positions and hopefully prevent the coming battle. The Omega group students are instructed to explore the perspectives of these historic figures using the text and Internet sources and then begin to write dialogue formulating these positions. The final step is ordering and structuring the dialogue such that each participant speaks in response to the others. Thus, rather than merely listening to Ms. Kimball discuss the Texas Revolution, these students are engaged at a deeper, more creative level. As the Omega group students work, they become one with their characters, which is why role-play can be so effective in history classes.

Of course, Ms. Kimball and other teachers rarely have to create these alternative differentiated activities. Most modern curricula include instructional alternatives in the teacher's manual, so Ms. Kimball need only preselect an appropriate activity and provide any necessary materials to the Omega group.

The Mainline Instructional Group

In this example, Ms. Kimball has provided an orientation and then differentiated the lesson activities based on individual learners' characteristics by forming two groups: the Omega group and the mainline group. As the Omega group does its work, Ms. Kimball engages in the next phase of the lesson, teacher-led initial instruction, for the mainline group. She makes certain that the activity provided for that group is at least as engaging as the work the Omega group is doing. However, we should note that, with fewer students working directly with Ms. Kimball, the efficacy of her teaching is likely to go up. In a smaller mainline group, she can make better eye contact with the students and give each student more attention than in a whole-class lesson. This tends to increase the engagement of both groups, which is why differentiated instruction is very effective; more students are more highly engaged with the history content. Also, in order to focus the attention of the mainline group, Ms. Kimball considers reorienting the class. For example, if the Omega group is working in the right front of the classroom in a small-group workspace, she has the mainline group turn their desks to face the left rear corner of the room. In that way, Ms. Kimball can increase student engagement in two critical ways:

1. She has oriented the mainline instructional group to have their backs to the Omega group, and both groups are more likely to pay attention to their own assigned task.
2. She has placed herself in a position to lead instruction for the mainline group and still visually monitor the Omega group with ease.

The Beta Group

At the end of the teacher-led instructional phase, several things happen at once. First, if the students in the Omega group happen to finish their assignment, they are told to rejoin the mainline group. Otherwise, they simply continue their group work. Next, prior to beginning the next phase of the traditional lesson, the teacher-led practice phase, Ms. Kimball selects another group for a second differentiated activity. We'll refer to it as the Beta group. Again, Ms. Kimball takes care to include both students who have grasped the content and a few who haven't. The Beta group is then given some type of assignment on the history lesson. As shown in Box 1.2, this involves seeking information on the Runaway Scrape, which was the second part of the Texas Revolution. Note that when the two differentiated groups are doing separate, small-group assignments, Ms. Kimball is instructing a group of only ten or twelve students in the mainline group, resulting in even more direct teacher attention for every learner and increased student engagement.

In this classroom example, Ms. Kimball is providing highly fluid differentiated instruction, targeted at individual students based on their learning styles and individual needs. In a differentiated class, small groups are frequently formed from the very beginning of the lesson and then rejoin the mainline instruction, as appropriate. Not all groups do all the activities, but all receive small-group work tied to their learning preferences and direct teacher attention in a smaller mainline instruction group. Meanwhile, during almost all of the class, Ms. Kimball is working with smaller numbers of students and instructional efficacy is very likely to increase.

As this example indicates, rather than lecturing to the whole class, differentiated lessons offer an option to all teachers for replacing lecture with brief, intensive small-group and teacher-led instruction. In the differentiated class, students tend to be much more engaged with the learning content, and therefore, learning is likely to increase.

Guidelines for Differentiated Instruction

Know Your Students

The concept of differentiated instruction has always focused on knowing the learning styles and abilities of each student in the class. Some students learn best through movement-based instruction; others learn verbally or from reading texts or from computer-based study. Some students learn best in small-group discussions. Knowing the individual learning characteristics of every student, along with that student's overall achievement level, will allow teachers to form effective small groups virtually instantly, and matching the instructional activity to individual learning characteristics is the very essence of differentiated instruction.

Take Time to Plan Differentiated Lessons

When teachers first consider differentiated lessons, they are often very concerned with the time it takes to plan multiple activities. Clearly, relying on the traditional lecture-based lesson plan is easier than planning a dynamic, differentiated lesson. However, teachers must understand that the main emphasis of differentiated instruction is the presentation of lesson activities that actively engage the learners in new and dramatic ways. At least initially, such lesson planning will take a bit more time.

We should also note that effective differentiated instruction takes place well before the class begins. Differentiation is based on well-planned, highly focused, small-group lessons for learners with similar learning styles and needs. Teachers will need to select these activities in advance of the lesson and prepare for them. In the previous example, Ms. Kimball might have continued to differentiate the lesson throughout the period by forming additional groups as necessary. In most cases, however, differentiated lessons rarely involve more than three small groups in the class, because as students finish a differentiated assignment, they frequently rejoin the teacher-led instruction for a brief time.

Prepare Students for Differentiated Group Work

Increased collaborative work and small-group work are emphasized in most state curricular standards, so teachers are seeking ways to increase these learning activities. Differentiated lessons provide an excellent vehicle for doing exactly that. However, effective small-group work doesn't just happen! To prepare students for these small groups, all teachers moving into more differentiation should also plan to teach small-group learning skills such as brainstorming, active listening, timelining, and providing constructive criticism. Of course, these skills are also critical in the modern world and directly transfer to later life experiences.

Invite Students to Plan and Prepare Differentiated Activities

As shown in Box 1.2, it is possible on many occasions to have one small group prepare an educational activity for the class. In this example, the role-play should be performed for the whole class, followed by a discussion of the differing perspectives of these historic figures. With a strong focus on the specific historical content, students can often prepare an activity for others to subsequently use.

Trust Students to Learn From Each Other

Differentiated instruction is working in classrooms because students can and do learn from each other, and teachers must learn to trust that. Some students might even learn more effectively from each other than from a teacher, because some students pay more attention to their peers than to the teacher. If the small groups are selected carefully by the teacher, students will learn from others in the class.

Replace Lectures With Differentiated Lessons

Educators have long realized that lecture is the least effective way to teach, and for that reason, many teachers have already moved to differentiated lessons rather than exclusive use of traditional, whole-group lecture-based lesson plans. However, not every whole-group lesson needs to be highly differentiated. There are many whole-group activities that can and do actively engage almost all learners. These include gaming activities, project-based work, video/computer-based presentations, debates and role-play, interactive simulations, and other whole-class activities. When a teacher is using these types of high-engagement activities, little differentiation will be necessary to keep all students focused on the learning content, and many of these are discussed later in this book. As an initial goal for teachers moving into differentiated instruction, I suggest that teachers use those types of whole-group activities for one or two periods weekly and implement a highly differentiated lesson on other days.

Research on Differentiated Instruction

The research support base for differentiated instruction is neither particularly strong nor extensive, and this lack of a strong, broad research base may stem, in part, from the assumption that differentiated instruction is a broad instructional approach rather than a specific teaching strategy. Nevertheless, teachers have responded quite strongly to the differentiated instruction concept, and many teachers report improved student satisfaction and increased academic performance resulting from increased differentiation (King & Gurian, 2006; Lee et al., 2010; Sousa & Tomlinson, 2011). In fact, educators generally seem to believe that differentiated instruction represents an expectation for all teachers in the future. Marzano, as one example, includes differentiated instruction in his book on excellence in teaching (Tomlinson, 2010).

Further, case-study research does suggest increased academic performance when differentiated instruction is widely employed at the school level (Bender, 2013a; King & Gurian, 2006; Tomlinson, 2010; Tomlinson, Brimijoin, & Navaez, 2008). Tomlinson, Brimijoin, and Navaez (2008), for example, describe the implementation of differentiated instruction at two schools, an elementary school and a high school. These researchers documented rates of proficiency in core subjects of reading, writing, and mathematics prior to and after implementation of differentiated instruction. The faculty was provided an implementation period of one year, which included significant professional development focused on the differentiated instruction concept. Those proficiency-score pre/post comparisons showed that after differentiated instruction was implemented schoolwide, students' proficiency jumped up in each subject, between 10 percent and 30 percent. That is a very significant jump in achievement scores schoolwide!

Summary

Teachers who are not already providing differentiated instruction should certainly begin to do so, because this instructional strategy will increase student engagement rather drastically. Further, while research results here are limited, this teaching strategy does represent the future of instruction simply because of the increased academic and learning style variance in the typical classroom today. At the very least, replacing most lectures with differentiated instruction assignments will increase academic engagement and performance. Also, this emphasis on differentiated instruction will provide an opportunity for both students and teachers to enjoy learning in new and novel ways.

Personally, I've become committed to this differentiated instruction strategy. This strategy represents a drastic improvement over the "teacher in front lecturing" approach, coupled with little to no classroom activity and resulting in very bored students. For that reason, I like to see highly fluid, differentiated groups in every classroom in the school.

Strategy 2

The Flipped Class Strategy

Many teachers today are experimenting with flipping the classroom, and most report increased student engagement in class as well as increased academic performance (Bergmann & Sams, 2014; Green, 2012, 2014; Tucker, 2012). In order to understand this flipped class phenomenon, teachers must begin with the traditional whole-class lesson plan presented previously in Box 1.1 (page 12). In the flipped classroom, several phases in that traditional lesson plan are "flipped" such that the teacher-led initial instruction phase, which is usually completed in class, becomes homework, while the practice activities or applications-focused project assignments usually done as homework become classwork (Bergmann & Sams, 2014; Flipped Learning Network, 2014; Green, 2012, 2014; Hamdan, McKnight, McKnight, & Arfstrom, 2013; Tucker, 2012).

> The flipped classroom is defined by instruction in which the traditional lesson plan is "flipped" such that teacher-led initial instruction becomes homework, and homework is done during class time.

In flipped classes, the initial instruction is usually made available as homework via videotaped minilessons on the content that are published over the Internet on a school or class website or simply found on a video provider such as YouTube or TeacherTube. Using those types of resources, students conduct their own initial instruction on new topics individually as homework, which frees much more class time for practice types of activities such as class projects, which are then completed in class, under direct teacher supervision.

This teaching strategy was developed only recently (Bergmann & Sams, 2014), so it has not yet been included in any of the meta-analysis reviews of effective teaching strategies (Hattie, 2012; Marzano, 2009). In fact, the concept was first articulated in 2006 (Bergmann & Sams, 2014) and came to national attention as recently as 2010. Nevertheless, many teachers today around the world are flipping their classes, with positive benefits in both student engagement and achievement.

Development of the Flipped Class Concept

Initially, Bergmann and Sams (2014), two practicing high school teachers, were reflecting on finding time in their classes to reteach topics when students didn't seem to grasp the content. They decided to record and annotate their lessons and put that video content on the class website so students could refer to those videos during the reteach phase of the lesson. They then noted that two groups of students were using that online content: those who didn't get the lesson concepts initially and those who simply needed more time to process the new content (Tucker, 2012).

In their ongoing discussions, these two teachers discussed the fact that when initial instruction was delivered in class, students tended to be much less attentive than when students were doing applications-of-knowledge types of assignments. Further, they decided that their presence as teachers was more valuable to individual students when students were doing these applications lessons or class projects, because in those class activities the teacher was there to immediately assist and offer feedback. Thus, they decided to flip the traditional lesson plan by requiring students to learn their material at home using online lesson content. They then used that extra class time—time that would usually have been taken for initial instruction—to do more applications activities in which students actually applied their knowledge. They witnessed firsthand both increased student engagement in class and increased academic performance.

Four Pillars of Flipped Learning

Today, many teachers are experimenting with flipping the classroom, and in order to help provide leadership on this concept, Bergmann and Sams (2014) published their own guidance on how to do flipped learning, including a conceptual foundation for the flipped class movement. They presented these basics as the four pillars of flipped learning, presented in Box 2.1.

> **Box 2.1: Four Pillars of Flipped Learning**
>
> **Flexible Environments:** Educators in the flipped class will often physically rearrange their learning space to accommodate the lesson or unit, which may involve group work or independent study. Educators are also flexible in their expectations of student timelines for learning and how they assess students.
>
> **Learning Culture:** There is a deliberate shift from a teacher-centered classroom to a student-centered approach in the flipped class, where in-class time is meant for exploring topics in greater depth and creating richer learning opportunities through various student-centered pedagogies. Students are actively involved in their own learning in a way that is personally meaningful.
>
> **Intentional Content:** Educators believe the flipped class model is able to help students gain conceptual understanding as well as procedural fluency. They evaluate what they need to teach and what materials students should explore on their own.
>
> **Professional Educators:** During class time, teachers observe their students, providing them with feedback relevant in the moment and assessing their work. While professional educators remain very important, they take on less visibly prominent roles in the flipped classroom (Bergmann & Sams, 2014).

As these four pillars of flipped learning suggest, the flipped learning movement is more than merely restructuring the lesson format; it involves a richer perspective on the roles of teachers and students in the learning process, and in a flipped class, students are viewed as responsible for their own learning. To get a better sense of how teachers and students respond to flipping the classroom, I encourage teachers to view one of the many videos on the flipped class on YouTube. Here is a brief video I recommend, featuring a flipped fifth-grade mathematics class at Lake Elmo Elementary School in Lake Elmo, Minnesota (see the video at www.eschoolnews.com/2012/02/09/a-first-hand-look-inside-a-flipped-classroom). This video (and many others) helps teachers see a flipped class in action and get a sense of the excitement associated with flipping the class.

Advantages of Flipping the Class

There are many advantages to flipping the class (Bergmann & Sams, 2014; Horn, 2013). As discussed previously, the engaged time for most students is likely to increase both during the initial instruction completed at home and during the applications activities in class. Increasing the time that students are actually mentally engaged with the content will increase their academic performance.

Next, having lessons in a video format allows students to immediately review lesson points when they need to. Students can literally hit rewind and review content they didn't understand (Horn, 2013), or they can fast-forward through material they have already mastered. This is empowering for the students since they themselves decide what to watch and when to review. This gives them more ownership over their learning (Horn, 2013).

Next, immediate feedback is increased in the flipped class approach. Specifically, in traditional homework, the students complete drill and practice work on some type of worksheet—work which everyone would agree is not highly motivating. Should a student need help with a problem while doing that work at home, he or she would have to wait until the next day to ask the teacher a question. However, in the flipped class approach, the drill and practice work and other applications of knowledge are incorporated into in-class activities, and if a student needs help, the teacher is available to respond, to offer feedback immediately, and to guide the student as he or she applies what he or she learned the previous evening.

Finally, because flipped learning does empower students to learn for themselves and take ownership of learning, flipping the class can lead to a more robust lifelong learning perspective. In the flipped classroom, students learn that it is their job to learn what they need, and schools will become much more effective if every student exits with that understanding of his or her role. Simply put, it is the students' job to learn what they need to accomplish their task, and that is a very healthy lifelong learning attitude to take into the modern workplace.

A Classroom Example: Inside a Flipped Science Class

In order to share a real-world flipped class example, I invited Jessica Shoup, MEd, to share her experience. Shoup is a veteran mathematics and science teacher with National Board Certification. She has taught middle school classes in science and mathematics for many years in both Wisconsin and North Carolina. She is now working as a teacher and professional development facilitator at Community House Middle School, in Charlotte, North Carolina. She has been using the flipped class model of instruction in mathematics and science for several years now.

> One of my main goals as a science teacher was to have students learn through hands-on experiences and exploration. Like many teachers, I originally felt that students couldn't be successful unless I personally taught the content through lectures, discussions, notes, and examples first. My entire opinion changed several years ago when I worked at a project-based elementary school where students took charge of their own learning.

We used the flipped class approach. Flipped classrooms allow for engaging conversations and in-depth exploration of the content, and class time is no longer consumed with lecture, note-taking, and repeated examples. The students are assigned a task to complete at home in order to gain background knowledge on a particular standard or topic. Gaining background knowledge can be completed in many formats, such as filling in guided notes while watching a video, reading a passage and creating a graphic organizer, or answering questions after completing an online simulation. With each of these activities, students gain information on their own. In contrast, traditional copying of notes in class is mindless, and students often write things down without even paying attention to the meaning of the words. When I shifted to a flipped class model, I quickly found that my students were more likely to retain the information because they had completed the work on their own.

After completing the background knowledge assignment on their own, students came to class already discussing the content and excited to see what they were going to do with their new information. I frequently started class with a four-question warm-up to review the main ideas of the concept. The warm-up was completed as a team process in a whole-class format. One student read the first question and led a discussion with classmates to arrive at the answer. Throughout the discussion, I added comments to clear up misconceptions or asked questions if they were missing necessary details. The discussion continued with remaining questions.

The class then shifted to directions for the exploratory activity that would further student understanding of the concept. I always allowed students to work with others on these activities. There is so much that the students can learn from one another by struggling through a task and having conversations while doing so. As the students worked, I moved around the room listening to their conversations and providing input as needed. I was always amazed while listening to the students ask questions and help each other learn. Students worked through the activity at different rates. So as learning continued, extension activities were provided to the early finishers.

At the conclusion of the activity, students shared their findings and related them to the standard being covered. This was my favorite part of the flipped lesson. Students often argued with one another about their ideas. It is important to sit back and let the students struggle with the ideas. More is learned from these discussions than from me telling them the same information.

The class period ended with a "ticket out the door." Students had to answer questions, analyze data, write a summary, or create a list to demonstrate their understanding of the concept prior to leaving. Using that information, I was able to determine whether further teaching or enrichment should take place.

It is clear to me that my incorporation of flipped lessons increased student engagement as well as understanding of the concepts. Moreover, my students were excited to come to class and talk about what they were learning, and that might be the best payoff of all!

Steps for Flipping Your Class

Check Wi-Fi Availability for Initial Instruction Content

Shoup's class example provides a great deal of guidance for implementing flipped learning in your class. Initially, when moving to flipped learning, teachers must ensure availability of the online lesson content. Not all schools are Wi-Fi capable today, and not all students have Internet access at home. Teachers who wish to try flipping the class must therefore ensure that all students have the capability to see the initial instruction lesson online. In most cases, students do have Wi-Fi options and computers (or tablets or smartphones) at home and accessing these web-based lessons is not a problem. For other students, opportunities to review and study the video or online lesson content must be provided in a school media center or in the teacher's class itself, perhaps with several computers in the back of the room.

Create or Select Video Lessons

Next, teachers must identify a specific podcast or video-based lesson on the unit content. Some teachers videotape themselves to create video lessons for subsequent instruction and then place that video on the class or school website. However, first, teachers should explore predeveloped lessons from sources such as YouTube or TeacherTube. Video lessons from Khan Academy or TedEd are also widely used to help teachers flip a class. For example, prior to taking the time to create a video on multiplication of fractions with unlike denominators, teachers should check the free Khan Academy videos for a ten-minute lesson focused on that specific type of problem. Lessons appropriate for flipped classes tend to be highly focused on one type of problem and quite brief—perhaps six to ten minutes in length (Bergmann & Sams, 2014).

Devise a Quick-Check Tactic

Initially, most students will actually use the video or online lesson to complete the initial instruction at home, but some will not. Therefore, teachers should follow every flipped initial learning assignment with some required product or quick-check quiz by which students can demonstrate their understanding at the first of the next class (Bergmann & Sams, 2014; Horn, 2013). In the classroom example previously, the teacher used a four-question warm-up as a check on the students' independent work at home. In other cases, students might be required to do some brief follow-up activity during or after watching the video and present that work to the teacher the following day. Bergmann indicated he always required some type of work from students to demonstrate their understanding, rather than merely taking their word that they had done their initial instruction at home (Horn, 2013).

Develop Engaging In-Class Activities

One rationale for doing flipped learning is to develop deeper understanding of the content through richer practice and application work. Therefore, teachers must develop engaging and content-rich learning activities for the class to complete. These can typically be somewhat longer than in traditional lessons, since little or no class time will be invested in initial instruction in the flipped-class model. Project-based learning activities (discussed in the next chapter) certainly provide one option for these content-rich activities, but team-based investigations and even makerspace types of creative activities can also be highly effective, content-rich instructional options for the flipped class.

Differentiate In-Class Assignments

If the quick-check quiz indicates that some students in the class have either not done the initial instruction work at home or have not understood the content, those students will need time at the first of class to redo that online instruction activity. Most of the class will have completed the initial instruction at home and will be ready for an exciting application type of activity to extend their understanding. Thus, the teacher will, of necessity, differentiate the class activities. If six to eight computers are available in the rear of the classroom, the teacher might merely assign the students who didn't understand the lesson to complete it again on those computers, while the teacher begins a project-based activity with the rest of the class. This differentiation will ensure that each student is receiving what he or she needs. Further, practitioners of flipped learning have asserted that, as students get used to this learning strategy, the number of students who complete the online lesson increases to a point at which noncompletion of the lesson is virtually eliminated (Bergmann & Sams, 2014).

Document the Efficacy of the Flipped Class

When flipping the class, teachers are undertaking a new and different instructional strategy, and the effects of such experimentation should be carefully documented. I suggest that teachers devise some type of plan for documenting the impact of flipped learning. One option would be a before-and-after comparison of student performance on unit test grades or unit products. For example, the teacher might average student grades on unit tests for several units in which lessons were not flipped and compare those scores with average scores from several lessons in which students did their own initial instruction via the flipped class strategy. This would document the efficacy of flipping the class in each teacher's specific situation.

A Case Study: Flipping the History Class

Mr. Leeds was required, within his professional development plan, to undertake an action-research project using a teaching strategy of his choice. He was interested in having more time for student projects in his history class, and when he read about flipped learning, he decided to try the concept. The average unit test grades provided him with a dependent variable that could be used in his experiment, so he began by averaging the grades from the previous two unit tests in his history class, a unit on World War I and another on the interwar period and the Great Depression. Grades from tests in those units formed the baseline data in figure 2.1. In order to really assess the impact of flipped learning, Mr. Leeds also developed a three-question survey, which he decided he would use for some students who completed the initial learning work at home and for all students who did not. While not a scientific comparison, the answers to those questions combined with the charted data on student achievement might help Mr. Leeds understand students' reaction to flipped lessons.

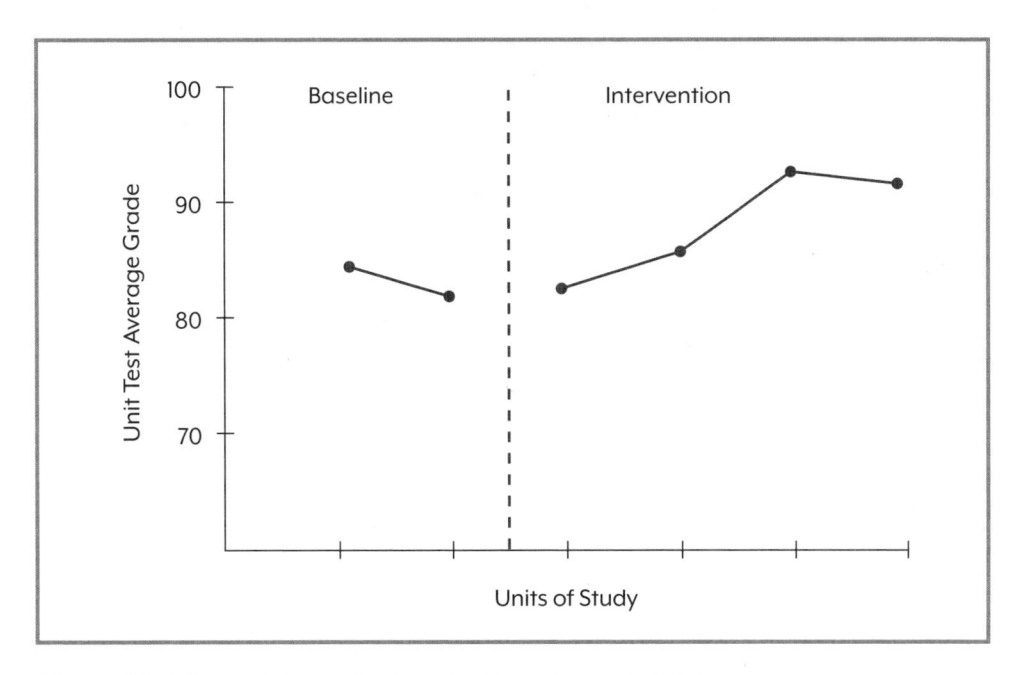

Figure 2.1: Flipped class strategy in fourth-grade history.

After ensuring that all of the students in his class had some Internet capability at home, Mr. Leeds began a flipped lesson on the history of the Second World War. He would follow that with several more units in U.S. history, including postwar America, the Cold War, and race relations and the 1960s. In each case, he ensured that appropriate video content was available. For example, on the WWII unit, he searched YouTube and TeacherTube and found video lessons on the causes of WWII, two wars in one (Pacific and Africa/Europe), D-Day and the march through Europe, the atomic bomb, and postwar America. He decided he could build a flipped class unit around those video segments, so for each video, he developed a simple ten-question sheet for students to complete as they did the assignment. Then he found appropriate video content for the subsequent unit topics.

The intervention data in figure 2.1 demonstrate that student achievement increased when flipped lessons were used. The average grades increased by over five points for the units that involved flipped learning. Also, the survey results showed that only a few students failed to undertake the at-home video work, and they then had to do the video and questionnaire at the first of the next class. However, the survey data showed that the number of students not doing that work decreased over time, such that even students with poor study habits did begin to participate more. Mr. Leeds considered the flipped learning a success in increasing student engagement and achievement.

Research on Flipped Learning

Research on the flipped class strategy is very recent and still somewhat limited, but existing anecdotal evidence does provide considerable support for the flipped class model (Bergmann & Sams, 2014; Flipped Learning Network, 2014; Green, 2012, 2014; Hamdan et al., 2013; Horn, 2013; Stansbury, 2013; Tucker, 2012). In one widely discussed example, Greg Green (2012), principal of Clintondale High School, reported his school's success with the flipped class strategy. Clintondale is a financially challenged school in Detroit, and with failure rates through the roof in that school, teachers chose to improve student academic performance across the curriculum by flipping their classes. Thus, teachers videotaped shorter versions of their own lectures on new content and posted those videos to the school website. Students were then required to access that content as the initial instructional phase of the lesson when they began a new unit of instruction. The class periods in each subject then became a practice and applications laboratory for that content.

Within eighteen months, failure rates in many core subjects had gone down drastically, according to Green (2012, 2014), the school administrator. Specifically, those failure rates dropped as follows: English failure rates dropped from 52 percent to 19 percent; mathematics failure rates dropped from 44 percent to 13 percent; science failure rates dropped from 41 percent to 19 percent; and social studies failure rates dropped from 28 percent to 9 percent.

As these impressive data from Clintondale High School indicate, flipping these classes produced a very positive impact on student achievement across the board (Green, 2014). Further, in a wide variety of other schools, student achievement has increased as a result of flipping the class (Flipped Learning Network, 2014; Hamdan et al., 2013; Horn, 2013; Stansbury, 2013). While more research is ongoing, there is sufficient anecdotal evidence supportive of flipped learning to encourage all teachers to explore this exciting new instructional strategy for increasing student engagement and academic performance.

Summary

Flipping the class has become much more common only in the last several years, and many teachers are seeing the success of this instructional strategy (Bergmann & Sams, 2014; Flipped Learning Network, 2014). For that reason, I believe that all teachers should explore this strategy, using some type of action research to show the efficacy of this approach. If our goal in the 21st century class is a more highly engaged, self-directed group of students, then those students will need to become adept at learning new content on their own. The promise of flipped learning is that all students might one day leave schools as highly experienced, self-directed, lifelong learners.

Strategy 3

Project-Based Learning

Project-based learning (PBL) in the 21st century involves much more than merely planning a class project. In fact, projects have always been a component of many units of instruction in traditional teaching. In contrast, proponents of PBL today argue that true project-based learning involves basing all of the instruction on team or individual student activities that are student-selected, real-world projects, independent of instructional unit planning or individual whole-group lesson plans that drive the curriculum (Bender, 2012; Boss & Krauss, 2007; Larmer, Ross, & Mergendoller, 2009). In that sense, while the flipped classroom discussed previously turns the traditional lesson plan upside down, PBL actually does away with the whole-class one-activity lesson altogether.

> PBL may be defined as using authentic, real-world projects as the basis for all or most instruction, with such instruction founded on student-selected, highly motivating and engaging questions, tasks, or problems and resulting in a product or project that addresses the driving question (Bender, 2013a, 2012).

Within a PBL framework, each project is likely to take considerable time—often a number of weeks or perhaps as long as a year—and should be developed jointly by the teacher and students to teach academic standards within the context of students working cooperatively to solve a real-world problem and complete a real-world project (Barell, 2007). Individual projects may, on occasion, be found in PBL classes, but most projects are undertaken by teams of students. Also, student choice and student inquiry, within a team decision-making process, are definitive components of PBL.

In the context of this book, PBL is a critical teaching strategy for increasing student engagement, because research has shown that students are more engaged in PBL than in traditional unit-based instruction (Boss & Krauss, 2007; Larmer, Ross, & Mergendoller, 2009; Mergendoller, Maxwell, & Bellisimo, 2007). Further, in PBL the increased student engagement results in higher levels of academic achievement than in more traditional instruction (Barell, 2007; Hattie, 2012; Larmer, Ross, & Mergendoller, 2010; Mergendoller, Maxwell, & Bellisimo, 2007). For this reason, PBL must be emphasized in teachers' efforts to increase student engagement.

Project Scope in PBL Instruction

In many examples, PBL is implemented by individual teachers. However, some projects are interdisciplinary and involve two or three teachers and their classes. In some cases, PBL represents a schoolwide initiative. Most projects have a class or schoolwide impact, but others may impact a much larger target audience. In one recent PBL example, North Idaho STEM Charter Academy has been selected to create a nanosatellite for the NASA CubeSat project. The nanosatellite student construction will be included in an upcoming NASA launch (Maben, 2016). The effort is headed by ten students who will be assisted by engineers living in that area. The students have a year to complete the small cubical satellite for NASA, which is one of only twenty such teams selected for this work. This project, called the Project da Vinci proposal, emphasizes the study of radio waves, aeronautical engineering, space propulsion, and geography. The satellite will use amplified radio frequencies and, when launched, will deliver a Morse code message to schools anywhere on the globe. Other schools worldwide who choose to build a small radio receiver (estimated cost is less than $100) will be able to hear that message as they study radio waves. This should help encourage students to pursue careers in science, technology, engineering, and math.

To get a quick sense of modern PBL, I urge you to review a wide array of brief introductory videos on PBL found on the Internet (check the website Edutopia.org /project-based-learning as an initial source). The YouTube video at www.youtube.com/watch?v=nMCCLB9gOag shows teachers discussing a schoolwide PBL implementation for Sammamish High School.

While not every project can involve such a broad target audience, some projects seem to grow in scope during PBL implementation. For example, Boss (2011) provides an excellent example of a single class project that became a project for the whole school. When studying deforestation resulting from erosion, one upper-elementary science teacher in Indiana made an extra effort and introduced his students to a professional colleague who was headmaster of a school in Haiti. In that locale, tree-cutting has led to flooding problems. The Indiana students explored how deforestation led to flooding just prior to the several hurricanes that hit Haiti in 2011. After one hurricane struck Haiti, the Indiana students heard stories of school students who could not get clean drinking water for days. The class decided to help their friends in Haiti obtain clean drinking water, and that became a focus for a PBL study in science. Students focused on the question, How can we get our friends in Haiti some clean drinking water?

Students then began to study water purification, factors that made water unsafe, and so forth. Several teams of students were formed to research those questions (Boss, 2011). Another group of students focused on the actual construction of simple water purification devices (Boss, 2011). That group consulted a retired local engineer and obtained a patented water purification device, which they immediately dismantled for study. They investigated its operation, testing the electrolysis device with various salts and different voltages (Boss, 2011). The team then sought ways to both simplify the device and improve it.

Another team began a campaign to invest their community in the project. They chose to refer to this as investing rather than fundraising because they wanted their community to care about and become involved in the cause of water purification for Haiti. All of these student teams presented their work each Friday to every other group, and after yet another massive earthquake struck Haiti, the whole school became involved in this exciting PBL project. Ultimately eight students, selected competitively, and eight teachers used community-generated funds to travel to Haiti along with a number of simple water purification devices, which were then given to their new friends in Haiti.

Again, few PBL projects hold this scope or involve this much time and community commitment; indeed, most projects are much more modest in scale and do not involve fundraising or international travel at all! Box 3.1 presents several brief descriptions of PBL projects of smaller scope, as well as several additional websites that feature projects from across the grade levels. Teachers are encouraged to review several of these projects and websites and specifically compare the lesson plan examples for PBL projects.

Box 3.1: Examples of PBL Projects/Websites

The Fly Me to the Moon Travel Agency is a project for kindergarten students. They study the moon environment and what they need to travel to the moon. The project culminates when they book a trip to the moon. This project is available for teachers to evaluate online (http://wveis.k12.wv.us/teach21/public/project/Guide.cfm?upid=3266&tsele1=3&tsele2=100).

Drug Movie is a project from High Tech High School tenth graders (www.hightechhigh.org/pbl/drug-movie/sitemap.html). In this project, students

> investigate over-the-counter and illegal drugs and how those drugs impact the body. The culminating project involves the creation of a short movie on drug usage and supporting materials for that video. The website presents an overview of this project and its time line and objectives.
>
> **BIE.org** stands for the BUCK Institute for Education, a very helpful must-see website devoted to PBL. Many of the projects found here include both math and science.
>
> **RealWorldMath.org** (www.realworldmath.org/project-based-learning.html) provides a selection of PBL mathematics projects.
>
> **Edutopia.org** is a must-see for teachers interested in PBL. Many resources, videos, and projects can be reviewed here, as well as information to help you develop your PBL projects.

Structure and Components of PBL Instruction

Box 3.2 presents a general lesson format for a multiweek PBL project. In this example, PBL instruction often begins with the formulation of a project narrative or problem statement. This is sometimes referred to as a project anchor since it is intended to anchor the students within their topic and to motivate them. Often, the anchor includes a driving question that can become the basis and framework of a PBL project (Bender, 2012).

> A project anchor is a brief paragraph narrative that excites students about a real-world problem and/or describes a real-world project to be developed.
>
> A driving question helps set the parameters for a PBL project.

If both teachers and students are experienced with PBL, teachers might develop the anchor and driving question and then begin the PBL process with only those components in hand. This will lend more structure to the initial PBL effort, yet still leave some choices for students to make in their PBL teams. When all are familiar with the PBL process, students should undertake more of the work.

> ### Box 3.2: A Sample PBL Project
>
> **The Project Anchor**
>
> The City of Pittsford, New York, recently created a walking trail along the historic Erie Canal within the city boundaries. The city government invited schools and community organizations to contribute signage to help make

this walking trail an educational experience. The nature trail features many places for animals and insects to live, and one of the topics they are interested in involves butterflies that are local to the area. This project will focus on developing signage about butterflies and possibility other wildlife that can be seen along the trail.

Driving Questions

What butterflies live here along this trail?

When can these butterflies be seen here?

Necessary Resources

To understand when butterflies are here, we need to understand their life. Thus, we need information on the four phases of the life cycle of the butterfly. There are several websites on the life cycle of butterflies. Begin with this one: www3.canisius.edu/~grandem/butterflylifecycle/The_Lifecycle_of_a_Butterfly_print.html

We need information on when different butterflies may be seen locally.

We need contributed treated wood, plastic, and time for construction of the actual signage. (One teacher's husband can help purchase appropriate wood and plastic and construct the actual signs.)

We also need a map of the trail with locations of the signs marked.

Artifacts

Four life cycle posters: One poster about each of the four phases of the life cycle with drawings and/or pictures and written information for each stage. One poster focused on the most common butterflies seen in our area and when.

A five-minute PowerPoint presentation of these artifacts to a committee of the city parks and recreation department.

Culminating Project/Artifact

Five finished signs using treated wood, posters developed by the class, and plastic to cover and protect the artwork. The class will do a field trip to install the signage along the trail in the spring of the academic year.

Here is a summary of this project: http://13wham.com/news/local/pittsford-2nd-graders-butterfly-project-takes-off

An early version of this sample PBL project was developed by two teachers in a workshop I recently conducted in Pittsford Public Schools near Rochester, New York. Those teachers chose to work together to help their students understand the life cycle of butterflies and the ecology that supports them, as well as to help place signage along a greenway walk beside the Erie Canal in Upstate New York. This sample PBL project shows the general framework for a PBL project, including a number of components: project anchor, driving questions, list of necessary resources, anticipated artifacts (or specific products) and rubrics for production of these artifacts, and finally, the culminating project.

PBL does involve the use of additional specific terminology. In PBL the term *artifact* is used to mean a product developed by the students. This term is used to emphasize that projects typically involve the development of a large variety of products, rather than merely a written report or presentation. Artifacts may include: video products, wikis, podcasts, written work, artwork, spreadsheets, website development, or participation in or development of computer games and simulations. In most PBL projects, a variety of preliminary artifacts are developed prior to the culminating artifact or project, and teachers can exercise some control over which educational standards are covered in the project by requiring specific artifacts.

> An artifact is any product developed within a PBL project. This may include written reports, PowerPoint presentations, spreadsheets, videos, art projects, songs, poems, or any other creative product.

The culminating project is the final, and most important, artifact of the PBL project, and it must involve some type of publication or public display beyond the classroom. In the butterfly sign project mentioned previously, students' work was presented to an outside parks and recreation department committee and ultimately displayed along a city walking trail along the Erie Canal. In the nanosatellite project, the final artifact is a satellite launched into space and sending a coded message worldwide! The ultimate publication of student work as shown in these examples often reaches far beyond the class venue, and this is the payoff for the students that dramatically increases student engagement overall (Maben, 2016). Because students realize that many people will be reviewing their work, they are much more engaged in that work. Of course, not every project results in public signage. Rather, publication of the culminating project may be a presentation published on the class or school website, a presentation to a school or community committee, a YouTube video, or any other publication option that places student work before an outside group.

> The culminating project is the final and most important artifact of the PBL project, which will be published in some form beyond the classroom.

PBL Project Phases

Box 3.3 presents a rough guide to the phases or steps within a PBL project, including indicators of the types of instruction that will be necessary as students and teachers move toward increased PBL instruction (Bender, 2012). While these can provide an indication of what PBL instruction involves, these phases should be considered quite fluid because these processes often overlap during a project, as both teachers and students respond to the real-time requirements of PBL.

Box 3.3: PBL Project Phases

Introduction of PBL Project Anchor

Brainstorming possible problem solutions
Identifying specific areas of inquiry
Developing artifact list
Dividing up research responsibilities
Developing time line for initial research

Initial Research Phase

Evaluation of web-based sources and web search
Minilessons (short whole-group lessons led by the teacher) on specific topics

Creation/Development of Initial Artifacts

Synthesizing information via collaborative decision making
Using rubrics to evaluate initial work
Beginning development of culminating artifact
Identifying additional information needed

Second Research Phase

Seeking additional information
Modifying responsibilities and time line
Developing additional artifacts as needed

Development/Evaluation of Culminating Artifact Phase

Development of culminating artifact
Team evaluation of all artifacts including culminating artifact

Presentation/Publication of PBL Project

Introductory Planning Phase

Typically, the teacher begins a project with at least the project anchor/narrative developed. The teacher then divides students into teams, usually ranging in size from four to ten students, depending on the size and scope of the project. The teams then meet and brainstorm the anchor, creating ways to attack the problem. As they brainstorm, they identify specific pieces of information they need, and these initial research areas will eventually become initial artifacts to be developed during the project.

During this phase, teachers may spend time teaching various collaborative-work activities such as the brainstorming process (including suggestions such as "Accept all possible ideas without criticism during initial brainstorming; compare/critique them later"). For students new to the PBL process, teachers might also teach teamwork skills (e.g., using *I* messages and not *you* messages when criticizing, and active listening skills). These skills have collectively been referred to as "emotional intelligence," and as Myers and Berkowicz (2015) point out, emotional intelligence should be stressed in modern instruction because these skills dramatically impact students' overall success in the world of work later in life. These skills will greatly facilitate the types of collaborative work required within the PBL experience.

> Emotional intelligence is a set of people skills including the ability to respectfully brainstorm without criticism and, later, to criticize without rancor, using *I* messages and not *you* messages. Active listening is also included.

This initial phase may take place over two or three class periods, and most of those initial days will be spent in PBL team meetings. These meetings should last between fifteen and twenty minutes and be highly focused on developing the remaining components of the PBL project, including the components in Box 3.3. Each team meeting should generate a set of team meeting notes that delineate specific artifacts to develop, the role responsibilities for each team member, a to-do list for all students, and any decisions reached by the team, and this takes time. Further, when students are first exposed to PBL instruction, the teacher will spend more time on the emotional intelligence skills discussed above, so this phase will take more time than in later PBL experiences.

This phase ends when the team has fleshed out each of the components presented in Box 3.3. Of course, during those first days, when students are not in team meetings, research should be undertaken for the remainder of the period. Finally, I recommend that teachers require a written summary from each team at the end of this phase that identifies each artifact needed and the responsibility of each team member, as well as a time line for artifact and project completion. Teachers may wish to develop forms to document individual students' responsibilities as this phase is completed. Later in the PBL process, these documents will help the teacher understand the work that has been accomplished and will also keep the team focused during their subsequent work.

Initial Research Phase

Next, teams will move into the initial research phase, and this will usually overlap with the introductory planning phase. During the initial research, teams will gather information on their proposed artifacts. This second phase will take multiple days and perhaps several weeks, depending on the nature and scope of the project, since much of the work in PBL is accomplished in this phase.

During this phase, teachers often note that students from different teams seem to be having the same problem with certain concepts. Therefore, if teachers see a need, they may offer minilessons of ten to fifteen minutes on particularly difficult concepts to help team members move forward (Bender, 2012). This resembles traditional, whole-class instruction on that particular concept and ends with some demonstration from every student that he or she has mastered that content.

> A minilesson is teacher-directed group instruction, usually lasting only ten to fifteen minutes, focused on a specific topic or concept.

When determining which students need a minilesson, teachers can use a tool like the LSI Tracker (www.learningsciences.com/?s=LSI+Tracker). The LSI Tracker is an application, developed by Learning Sciences International, that works with any mobile device. It helps teachers track individual student progress during the less-structured instructional activities that characterize the initial instruction phase of PBL. With the LSI Tracker, teachers can input specific goals and subordinate indicators for each goal to document mastery of that content. Then, during the PBL lesson, or during the minilesson, the teacher can quickly check off specific indicators for individual students as they demonstrate mastery.

Here's an example. If a teacher notes that some students are having difficulty with the brainstorming skills discussed previously, the teacher might create the following goal and behavioral indicators and input these into the LSI Tracker.

Goal: Demonstrate ability to brainstorm successfully during PBL.

Subordinate Indicators:

- Contribute ideas to the discussion without self-censoring.
- Help generate additional ideas through encouragement.
- Respond to ideas of others with a compliment.
- Do not criticize any idea during the initial brainstorming.

Using the LSI Tracker, the teacher could check off, for each individual student in the class, when that brainstorming indicator is observed. Most students will understand the behaviors of brainstorming merely by having the brainstorming process described to them, so the teacher would check off those indicators for most students during the first brainstorming session. However, other students may not follow the brainstorming guidelines and may need a minilesson on the brainstorming process.

Again, during the initial research phase, various minilessons can be provided on any content that students need help with. Strategic use of minilessons for selected groups of students helps ensure that all students reach mastery of the content, even during the less-structured instruction that characterizes the PBL classroom (Bender, 2012). Note that most minilessons are typically offered when most students are engaged in research procedures. Thus, the students who are not participating in the minilesson continue their individual research.

As an additional suggestion, I recommend that teachers instruct students in the evaluation of web-based sources during this phase of the PBL process (Bender, 2012). This may be either in a minilesson or instruction offered for the entire class. It is clear today that much research will be undertaken in the future based on Internet searches, and students should understand how to evaluate the quality of information available. For example, information from government sources and websites is, in most cases, more reliable than information from Wikipedia, and information from both of those types of sites is more likely to be accurate than the information from the website of an advocacy organization. Also, evaluation of the intentions behind the authors of various sources is critical, and PBL projects provide many opportunities to teach students critical thinking and evaluation of information quality during this initial research phase. Again, a tool like the LSI Tracker could be useful here. Teachers might input the indicators of information evaluation and check off when students demonstrate those behavioral indicators.

Creation of Initial Artifacts

The next phase in the process involves the actual development of initial artifacts. As students complete their initial research, they will share their information and synthesize that information as they begin to develop the specific artifacts required. Again, these initial artifacts may include almost anything, such as artwork, graphics, spreadsheets of data, wikis, video presentations, or PowerPoint presentations. This phase will, of necessity, overlap with the previous research phase, since students typically begin artifact development while they are still doing research and then realize they need more information. Thus, this phase is somewhat ill-defined, and students may spend considerable time here.

Rubrics can be very helpful here, and most teachers are quite fluent in developing rubrics. Since teachers can typically tell which artifacts will be necessary in a given PBL project, teachers can develop rubrics for various artifacts even before the project begins. However, the development of rubrics for various artifacts can also be undertaken by the students themselves. Finally, all rubrics can then be shared with everyone as students work on the initial artifacts. Rubrics from either source can suggest additional research areas or where additional information is needed, and in that fashion, students will instantly receive feedback on their work throughout this phase of the process.

Second Research Phase

The second research phase is a catch-up phase in which students collect additional information and perhaps design and develop additional artifacts that were not previously identified. This phase will be much shorter in general than the previous phases, but it is necessary to emphasize that during the project completion process, sometimes it is necessary to return to the research material for additional information. Also, teachers typically stress reflection and self-evaluation during this phase in order to strengthen each learner's self-reflection skills. Reflective thinking is a skill that will be necessary throughout life.

Development/Evaluation of Culminating Artifact

At some point, usually during the second phase, students begin the development of their artifacts. Because some or most of those artifacts will appear or be represented in some form in the culminating artifact, the development of the culminating artifact cuts across several phases of this process. The culminating artifact is often some type of combined presentation that utilizes various components from the previous artifacts and synthesizes them into a meaningful whole.

In addition to developing the culminating artifact, students must evaluate each artifact in the context of formative evaluation. As indicated previously, rubrics are frequently used for the development of initial artifacts and can likewise be used in this evaluation of the culminating artifact. Further, this final formative evaluation offers the opportunity for a team-based peer evaluation. Thus, this phase provides students with many opportunities to practice these skills, skills that are in demand in the 21st century workplace (Bender, 2012).

Publication Phase

The PBL project is published in the final phase. This may be a presentation of some type to an outside body or uploading the culminating project to YouTube, a school website, or another website on the Internet. At this point, parents should be informed of the availability of the project, and students should be encouraged to talk with their parents about their role in the PBL process. In this manner, the publication of the project to a larger world is a powerful student motivator that will, in most cases, drastically increase student engagement. Simply knowing that many people will see the project often spurs students to work harder to get the culminating artifact as strong as possible.

Again, these phases will vary considerably from one project to another and across the grade levels. The size of the project teams will also impact this time frame, since larger PBL teams will typically require more meeting time to complete these project phases. However, as these phases demonstrate, most PBL projects are week-long or multiweek projects, since that much time is required to cover these phases and develop a valuable and valid culminating artifact.

Research on PBL Instruction

Research on the efficacy of PBL instruction has shown this to be a very effective instructional approach (Bender, 2012; Boss & Krauss, 2007; Hattie, 2012; Larmer, Ross, & Mergendoller, 2009; Maben, 2016; Myers & Berkowicz, 2015; Vega, 2012). Hattie's (2012) research demonstrates that this type of instruction is among the twenty-five most impactful types of instruction to positively affect student achievement. PBL has been applied in virtually every subject area and grade level, and students do seem to learn more using this approach than in traditional instruction (Boss & Krauss, 2007; Larmer, Ross, & Mergendoller, 2009). Because PBL increases student engagement, motivation to learn, and collaborative skills, it is now recommended across the board as a 21st century teaching approach (Bender, 2012; Larmer & Mergendoller, 2010).

Summary

PBL is presented early in this book because it is one of the most effective instructional procedures for increasing student engagement. Further, PBL is receiving increased emphasis from educators around the world, because the PBL process emphasizes the emotional intelligence skills and collaborative skills that define the workplace of the 21st century. Because PBL incorporates real-world problems and uses team decision making from the modern workplace, this instructional procedure better prepares students for the world of work. For teachers interested in increasing student engagement with the content, PBL is one instructional strategy that must be explored.

Strategy 4

Makerspace and Genius Hour

In traditional classes, students are not often expected to create things, yet within the modern world of work, creativity is at a premium. Whether in manufacturing, developing ad campaigns, or creating software or new apps, creativity is a highly valued commodity, and schools are seeking ways to foster creativity among students. Further, embedded within the implementation of most state curricular instructional standards, there has been a concerted effort to have students practice creativity in their classroom activities in order to reach a deeper understanding of the curricular content.

This emphasis on creativity in the classroom has generated several instructional strategies designed to foster creative thinking by providing free creative time for students. These include genius hour, 20 percent time, and makerspace or the maker movement (Anderson, 2014; Miller, 2015; Rendina, 2016). While these instructional practices are slightly different in focus, they all involve the concept of encouraging student creation as a significant component of learning in the modern world. Further, advocates of these strategies argue that students are much more engaged when they are creating than when working in traditional classes, and thus educators will see increased engagement and ultimately increased achievement from providing free creation time (Anderson, 2014; De Gree, 2015; Yokana, 2015).

> Makerspaces are spaces in the classroom where students can create, explore, and make stuff. Tools, time, materials, and space to build are provided to give students freedom to creatively explore making things they choose (Anderson, 2014). Students may be allowed to go to the makerspace in the class for an

> hour three times a week or perhaps daily, and there they create a project or item based on their interests and passions (see the website MakerFaire.org for resources and ideas).
>
> Twenty percent time involves a return of 20 percent of the instructional time to the students for exploration of topics they select. During that time, students are free to creatively design and create things. This idea was first implemented in industry. For example, Google used 20 percent time (Anderson, 2014) by giving employees 20 percent of their time to work on something not related to their assigned work area. Gmail was one of many innovations to result from that 20 percent time.
>
> Genius hour is a term developed by educators that is based on the 20 percent time from industry. The website geniushour.com is helpful in understanding the genius hour strategy as are the following YouTube videos: www.youtube.com/watch?v=NMFQUtHsWhc and www.youtube.com/watch?v=FEQzKH7v0-Q.

Again, this concept of free creative time was intended to meet the demands of the modern workplace. Rachel Park, a leader in 3-D printing and additive manufacturing and former editor in chief for *Disruptive* magazine for 3-D printing, considers the maker movement critical for both industry and modern education. She states, "Presenting the opportunity and developing practical skills in designing using 3-D printers can only improve the odds of producing more designers, engineers, and manufacturers that will develop applications that remain impossible today. Even putting the potential to one side and focusing solely on the present and the clearly identified skills gap within manufacturing industries in Western nations, anything and everything that can be done to close this gap should be emphatically embraced" (Park, 2016).

Clearly these creative time strategies have captured the attention of industry, and educators would be wise to take note of this interest. There seems to be more discussion among public school teachers about the maker movement or makerspace initiative than other approaches, so this section will focus mainly on the maker movement (Flanagan, 2015; Miller, 2015; Park, 2016; Rendina, 2016). Makerspace in both industry and the classroom is based on providing space, time, and materials for employees or students to gather, invent, tinker, explore, and create things using a variety of tools and resources (Flanagan, 2015; Park, 2016).

However, the maker movement is not merely about placing students in a certain area with the instructions "Make something!" Rather, structure for the makerspace time is typically provided in both the types of materials available in the makerspace and the suggestions for possible makerspace projects from which students choose, based on their interests.

Materials and Tools for Your Makerspace

There is an array of creative makerspace materials used in classrooms today, and we have room to discuss only a few. However, this section will provide some guidelines for the types of things that may be placed in a makerspace in the classroom. Of course, those makerspace materials and resources will vary across the grade levels. In a primary class, teachers might place constructor sets, LEGOs, cardboard, tape, crayons, cardstock paper, clothespins, paste, and similar materials to encourage students to create stuff. I like to see small sections of one-half-inch PVC plumbing pipe (a white, lightweight pipe), maybe in sections that are six inches, one foot, and two feet long, along with elbow and T connectors that can be reused in various creations.

For middle and secondary classes, the makerspace materials will typically be much more sophisticated. These makerspaces typically include some of the materials mentioned but also small electric motors, wire, connections, batteries, and perhaps small robotic arms. While few teachers will have large budgets for their makerspace resources, teachers can accumulate these materials over time and encourage students to plan for reuse of them.

3-D Printers and MakerBots

As this book was written, the world was in the midst of a revolution in engineering and manufacturing, a revolution that some suggest may surpass the Industrial Revolution or the information age in terms of changing the daily lives of millions of people (Smith, 2015). This creative revolution stems from one of the most innovative developments in history since the wheel: the 3-D printer (De Gree, 2015; Smith, 2015). Many classroom makerspaces include a 3-D printer, a newly developed machine that allows for virtually unlimited creativity.

The 3-D printing process is, of course, an innovation that is very recent and is exactly what it sounds like—using the equivalent of digital printing technology and a wired manufacturing printer to print using fluid plastics or metals rather than ink. By printing and reprinting layer by layer, the machine literally builds a three-dimensional object over time. This drastically expands the options for what students and teachers can create in the classroom.

> 3-D printing is the use of digital printing technology and a manufacturing printer to print fluid plastics or metals and, layer by layer, actually create three-dimensional objects.

The MakerBot is one of the most popular 3-D printers available today (Breeden, 2015; Davis, 2015; De Gree, 2015; Epps & Osborn, 2014; Smith, 2015). Printing with fluid plastic, this 3-D printer can create virtually any object that can be imagined and digitally described, and this technology is now finding its way into public school classrooms. Breeden (2015), for example, described his use of a 3-D printer in the science classroom, noting that simple objects were created in fairly short order but that more detailed objects took time. A simple button or badge took Breeden's students about fifteen minutes to create, whereas a scale model of the U.S. Capitol was built in slightly over twelve hours. Students have printed dinosaur heads, complete with teeth, to scale and replicas of planets—virtually anything they can imagine they can create.

MakerBot has created several sites to assist teachers in using 3-D printing in their classroom makerspaces. First, Thingiverse (www.thingiverse.com) is an online repository of 3-D printing designs teachers can access. Also, Jumpstart (www.thingiverse.com/jumpstart) is a site devoted to help newcomers into the world of 3-D printing in the classroom. Jumpstart was created specifically with early learners in mind, so primary and elementary teachers should explore these resources as they create or continue to enrich their makerspaces. Also, several teachers have provided guidance for using 3-D printers in the classroom (Breeden, 2015; Davis, 2015; see also the web page of Kathy Schrock, www.schrockguide.net/3d-printing.html). Davis (2015) presents her reflections in that regard, and some of those suggestions are provided in Box 4.1.

> **Box 4.1: Teaching Tips for Using a 3-D Printer**
>
> 1. Find a video about loading the filament properly, using the printer, and planning initial print jobs.
>
> 2. Review all the material that comes with the printer and then call the printer manufacturer when you need help (don't wait).
>
> 3. Printers use heat that will burn fingers, so keep fingers (and students) away from the printer during the print process. Also, let items cool off once they are finished, since they will remain hot for some time.
>
> 4. Play with the resolution, density, and thickness, since you can control these. Resolution involves how thick the layers are, and smaller layers make for smoother printed objects. Fill density involves how full of filament the inside of a 3-D object is—hollow objects sometimes collapse, so the inside of most 3-D jobs looks like the inside of a honeycomb. Thickness involves the thickness of the outside wall of the printed object (Davis, 2015).
>
> 5. Be near the printer during all print jobs, which means you will probably do the larger print jobs during the school day.

6. Combine the smaller parts of a print job. Install print software on every computer students use, which will allow you to print smaller jobs into one print job.

7. Organize your printing, deciding in advance how students will submit work for printing, how you will approve that work or give feedback before printing, how students might revise work, and how you can organize print jobs efficiently.

8. Let students work in teams of three or four students. They will then serve as self-correcting prior to the print job, and fewer resources will be wasted.

9. Start with premade items. A variety of sources (e.g., Thingiverse.com) offer downloadable instructions for premade items for students to print. Starting with those items gives students the necessary practice.

10. Let students use 3-D print software that's comfortable for them. You should use the software that came with the printer but explore other programs as well. SketchUp (www.sketchup.com) might be easier. Let students test and compare the 3-D print programs (Davis, 2015).

11. Plan longer-term projects by giving student teams one day with the printer. It is unlikely that students will be able to finish a print job in one class period, so planning is critical.

12. Learn with your students! 3-D printers are still quite new, so teachers and students can explore applications together.

Of course, the implications of 3-D printing can hardly be imagined. Box 4.2 presents some real-world examples of the types of creativity and innovation resulting from this technology. Teachers should note that, as indicated in these examples, important real-world engineering work using 3-D printing can be and is being done by non-engineers and even elementary school students!

Box 4.2: Examples of 3-D Printing

An Indonesian man, Arie Kurniawan, participated in an open innovation design challenge to redesign a bracket that attaches a jet engine to an airplane wing (Smith, 2015). Kurniawan was not an engineer and had no experience in manufacturing. However, he used a 3-D printer to make his bracket. His design beat out over one thousand other submissions, and it worked perfectly, passing every single industrial test for durability, stress, and reliability. Further, it weighed 83 percent less than the part it replaced, and saving weight is a big deal in airplane construction! Soon, his bracket will be flying all over the world on the most modern jets in the sky, and you will be riding on one!

> A fifth-grade student used 3-D printing and created a prosthetic hand for a needy student (this example was described by Myers and Berkowicz, 2015). Sierra Petrocelli was a fifth grader in Monkton, Virginia, and was developing a project for her school science fair. Her teacher challenged her to create something to change someone's life, and Sierra decided to print an affordable 3-D prosthetic hand. She contacted a company that does that type of work, and the company sent her a tutorial. She then printed a prosthetic hand that cost only $50 for a young girl in California (http://kdvr.com/2014/07/15/11-year-old-girl-uses-science-project-to-create-prosthetic-hands-for-children/).
>
> A team at General Electric used 3-D printing to create a new fuel injection system for jet engines. The previous system included twenty-one separate parts, any one of which might fail and all of which had to be produced and shipped to the engine manufacturing factory. The new 3-D printed system had only one part and that part was many times stronger than the original. The new part increased fuel efficiency by 15 percent, thus saving over one million dollars in fuel costs per year per jet! Additional savings are soon to be realized from saving shipping costs. Rather than have the older parts shipped in, the 3-D printing process allows the company to build that new part on site (Smith, 2015).

LEGOs for the Makerspace

Most adults are quite familiar with LEGOs—the lock-together plastic bricks so frequently used as a play toy. Today, those same lock-together toys have been supplemented with various sensors, electric motors, and computer-based instructions to provide makerspace construction opportunities for students from kindergarten through grade 8 (Hicks, 2015; also see the LEGO Education podcast, www.teachercast.net/lego-education-iste-2015).

Of course, any parent who ever shared a set of LEGO blocks with his or her children has seen youngsters play with the blocks, sometimes to the near exclusion of the world around them. Certainly, many children consider such LEGO play anything but schoolwork! However, by coupling these simple construction bricks with software and several motors and sensors, LEGO Education has provided a number of tools for teachers that will make the use of LEGOs virtually a required feature in any makerspace at the primary and elementary level. For example, the LEGO Machines and Mechanisms curricular program introduces students to simple machines, including gears, levers, pulleys, wheels, and axles, and they construct various projects to demonstrate concepts such as energy, force, and motion. This LEGO program parallels much of the early science content in the elementary grades.

A range of additional products allows this to be extended past fifth grade and well into middle school. Using interdisciplinary theme-based activities, students begin to develop creative skills in the makerspace and when provided with suggested project options. Further, because LEGOs are most frequently perceived as toys, many students will undertake project work with LEGOs who otherwise might tend to be less engaged with the ongoing classroom work.

Finally, in addition to using LEGOs in the makerspace, a variety of course-focused instructional activities will be enhanced by the use of LEGOs. Hicks (2015) provides a list of ways to use LEGOs in the classroom, ranging from the use of LEGOs as counters to represent mathematics facts in operations to the LEGO More to Math program to help students visualize the mathematics problem. Hicks (2015) also notes that simple coding can be taught using LEGOs—bricks of a different size, shape, or color representing different symbols in a code that can then be used to control robots, which are in this case other students in the class. Box 4.3 presents several instructional ideas for various subjects.

> **Box 4.3: Instructional Ideas Using LEGOs**
>
> - Use LEGOs to teach math visually, including counting, comparing, and measuring.
> - LEGOs can help students visualize arithmetic problems. For example, a square piece with four studs helps students see what 2 × 2 looks like. If you connect that piece to a rectangular one with eight studs, students can count out what 4 + 8 is. By setting different pieces side by side, you can show how fractions work—this one is ½ the size of that one, which is ¼ the size of this other one (Hicks, 2015).
> - LEGOs can show patterns and symmetry. Varied colors and shapes encourage creativity and can demonstrate symmetry.
> - LEGOs can illustrate a story. History lessons involve imagining historical settings, such as the attack on Bastogne in WWII or the burning of the White House in the War of 1812.
> - LEGOs can help teach students about classification systems. Classification can be based on color, size, shape, and combinations of these (Hicks, 2015).

Other Makerspace Tools

Beyond the 3-D printer and LEGOs, a number of other tech tools can greatly facilitate student creative options in the makerspace. Le (2016) provides five suggestions for simple technologies that might be included in a makerspace.

1. **Desktop laser cutter:** Take line drawings done through Illustrator and turn them into a map for the laser to follow. Laser cutters use a very

strong, highly focused laser beam that either cuts or etches materials like wood and acrylic plastic.

2. **Conductive thread:** Also called conductive textile, conductive thread is a fabric that can conduct electricity. Threads function as thin wires that can be sewn into clothing seamlessly.

3. **Open-source software programs:** Open-source software applications allow students to take a program and make their own additions, thus creating subsequent versions.

4. **Drones:** Drones are small flying remote-controlled robots that can be used for any number of fun, educational activities. Often drones are equipped with video cameras that are used for taping outdoor activities, exploring various ecosystems, or obtaining random footage of the school or any location.

5. **Microcontrollers:** Microcontrollers are small computers that have programmable input and output options and use simple codes. Students can then program these to control LEDs, robots, or other machines.

Virtual World Support for Makerspaces

Given the previous list, most teachers quickly realize that creating a makerspace can be quite costly. For that reason, teachers should not overlook the option of setting up a makerspace to access virtual world options. As one example, Contraption Maker is a new computer app that allows students to create Rube Goldberg–type machines in the virtual world (TeachThought Staff, 2015). This app is free for schools and includes a Teacher Dashboard, allowing teachers to track individual students' progress. Curricular ideas are also included. Using hamster motors, pulleys, balls, conveyor belts, and various tools presented onscreen, students will either repair machines or make new machines and test them operationally. Students can then save and share those creations. The app is intended for students from grade 3 up through high school and makes a great addition to any teacher's makerspace.

Guidelines for Setting Up a Makerspace

Join the Maker Movement

To prepare yourself and hopefully one or more of your colleagues for implementing genius hour or makerspace, you should join a maker movement or genius hour group, either in your community or online (Graves, 2015). The most effective teachers using makerspace are familiar with the maker movement, so teachers should join a maker group along with their colleagues, who then become resources for each other. By becoming a maker yourself, you can begin the maker process with several simple maker challenges and get a sense of the lure of the maker movement, as well as begin to share workable classroom ideas with other teachers.

Make Time and Space for Makerspace

Sometimes making time within the day or space within the classroom can be a significant challenge, so teachers should consider these decisions up front. In some cases, where space was limited, teachers have created mobile makerspaces by using a cart for the maker materials. To make time for maker activities is often more of a challenge, because giving time to free creative activity means taking time from other curricular activities. Of course, most elementary teachers control the time of their students for the entire day, and these teachers can fit makerspace time into the day more easily than teachers in the higher grades who are probably teaching multiple classes throughout the day. In each case, however, finding the time for makerspace, even if it is only twenty minutes twice a week, can result in large benefits in terms of student engagement (Flanagan, 2015).

Obtain Makerspace Materials

The materials required for a makerspace might differ in various subject areas and across grade levels. Many tech tools have been briefly described, but because of the cost of many of these tools, acquisition of these tools will typically occur over a number of years. With that noted, the non-tech tools, particularly for makerspaces in primary and elementary classes, can often be obtained for little or no funds (e.g., paperclips, popsicle sticks, glue, cardboard, cardstock paper, etc.). Teachers might also ask other teachers, students, and parents for materials such as old electronics, balloons, older electronic toys, wire cutters, old wires, tennis balls, and millions of other things that can be used in creating various projects (Graves, 2015). Teachers should also check sources such as the websites mentioned previously and Pinterest for other ideas.

It is probably safe to say that virtually no makerspace includes all of the tools and options discussed previously, and that compendium only scratches the surface of what might be useful in a makerspace. In this regard, teacher creativity in stocking the makerspace is as critical as student creativity in using the makerspace!

Begin With Student Choice

Because neither teachers nor students are practiced in using unstructured time in the classroom, proponents have suggested that teachers move into the makerspace concept using several project options from which students may choose (Rendina,

2016). A variety of sources are available on the Internet for planning makerspace projects, including the following websites.

- http://makered.org/makerspaces/?gclid=CjwKEAiA0ZC2BRDpo_Pym8m-4n4SJAB5Bn4xp_PgZh31Zv0Ir6mEivVj6qTRgbs_Oa8js1YvYeFNJRoCkiPw_wcB
- www.edutopia.org/blog/starting-school-makerspace-from-scratch-colleen-graves
- www.edutopia.org/blog/creating-makerspaces-in-schools-mary-beth-hertz
- http://makezine.com/2014/01/10/makerspace-in-the-classroom
- https://eric.ed.gov/?id=EJ1042206

While beginning a makerspace strategy with previously developed projects may seem antithetical to the 20 percent time or makerspace concept, Rendina (2016) points out that project guidelines and instructions are not necessarily the enemy of creativity within the makerspace. Many students find their creative freedom within various design challenges, and as they work through guided projects, they develop the skills that they need to further explore creatively. In fact, a veteran makerspace teacher indicates that most students need a "gentle push to get them started" (Rendina, 2016). As one example, a makerspace challenge in a history class studying the Middle Ages might be: "Create a trebuchet that will launch a small rock and destroy the teacher's castle." The teacher might then have several students make a castle out of a cardboard box, some popsicle sticks, and some glue.

Collect Evidence of the Efficacy of Makerspace

Many teachers attest to the impact of genius hour and makerspace in terms of student engagement (Flanagan, 2015; Rendina, 2016). However, teachers must make the effort to document these positive impacts, because these are new ideas in education. Simple surveys of students' attitudes and excitement toward learning might be used in this context. Also, teachers should consider having students videotape successful makerspace products and putting those tapes on the class or school website. Teachers should make certain that these videos stress the curricular problems and standards that might have been addressed in the project.

Research on Makerspace and Creative Time

The makerspace concept is very recent, and research has not yet demonstrated the impact of this strategy in the classroom. With that noted, much anecdotal evidence suggests that both teachers and students love the experience of a makerspace or genius hour strategy (Anderson, 2014; Breeden, 2015; Epps & Osborn, 2014; Flanagan, 2015; Vega, 2012). There is also limited evidence documenting increased achievement based on these creative-time strategies (Epps & Osborn, 2014; Flanagan, 2015). However, there is evidence of increased student engagement based on the positive impact of student choice among assignments (Flanagan, 2015; Vega, 2012).

For example, Flanagan (2015) recently reported on the maker movement in a middle school math class. She described a middle school teacher, Elizabeth Little, who taught at Martin Luther King Jr. Middle School in Berkeley, California. In an effort to better engage her remedial mathematics students, Little instituted a hands-on maker workshop in the class, resulting in student creations such as a banana piano and bongos made from lemons. Mathematics problems were embedded within all the maker projects, and by the end of the school year, Little reported that all her math students were clamoring for more math! Little even reported being surprised by the changes she saw among her students. By instituting maker-based projects, she transformed the class social hierarchy. Kids who had been ostracized for being deficient in math were suddenly valuable when their strengths, such as problem solving or brainstorming, were clearly needed.

Epps and Osborn (2014) present evidence on the positive impact of using a 3-D printer in math class. In their project, forty-six students in North Carolina used a 3-D printer to build models that they created mathematically. The Interactive Project-Based Learning Using 3D Grant Results (Epps & Osborn, 2015) presents very positive academic achievement results from that 3-D printing project in Richmond County Schools (www.youtube.com/watch?v=bfT1AqO1qi8). Using math modeling and a 3-D printer together engaged and motivated these lower achieving students much more than traditional instruction, and over time, these students' achievement increased by 44 percent.

Summary

Genius hour and makerspace are remaking classrooms around the world, and clearly there seems to be increased student engagement and academic improvement based on these innovative strategies. While we may well expect more structured research on this instructional strategy in due time, there is significant anecdotal evidence now, and teachers should explore this creative-time idea in their classes. It is a virtual certainty that our methods of teaching many subjects are about to change, as the influence of the makerspace movement grows. Teachers today are increasingly embracing these concepts because they realize that they are preparing their students for a new and different world in which creative construction is at a premium.

As usual, teachers will have to move quickly to stay ahead of that curve, and effective teachers have always embraced such a challenge. Still, the payoff for implementing a makerspace strategy is virtually limitless. Perhaps one of your students will find a way to impact the world as did the fifth grader Sierra Petrocelli. Her construction of an artificial hand changed the life of a girl in California, and few learning experiences could be more memorable or more important than that!

SECTION II

Tech Strategies to Increase Engagement

Nothing seems to capture students' attention quite as well as modern technology in the classroom. With students engaged with modern communications virtually every minute they are not in school, educators simply must embrace the modern tech tools that students prefer to use in order to hold students' attention.

Of course, with literally hundreds of apps and educational software programs being published virtually every day, no teacher can stay current with the available options. With that noted, this section will present a variety of technology tools that enhance student engagement with the academic content. These include augmented reality; games, gamification, and simulations; virtual field trips; coding and robotics; computer-driven individualized instruction; storyboarding with Comic Life; and animation.

Strategy 5

Augmented Reality

Augmented reality (AR) is one of the most interesting and innovative ways to make classrooms highly stimulating and engaging for the digital natives we currently teach. Every child in the class today is inundated with digital games, social networking, and videos, and almost all students find these activities quite exciting. Educators must make certain that their classes reflect the expectations of today's students in this regard, and AR can facilitate that task.

Basically, AR involves the use of computers, tablets, or other communications technologies to augment or supplement the real world by providing additional information about objects, events, and concepts under study. This technology holds the potential to make classroom learning much more interactive and engaging than ever before (Class Tech Tips, 2014; Politis, 2015). In most educational settings, AR involves using one of several apps that allow the teacher to tag information to a specific object or location in the classroom or school. Then, the student, using a tablet, can read that digital overlay of information (Klopfer, 2008; Walsh, 2011). In that sense, each image, picture in the text, poster in the classroom, model, or any other object or location becomes a tutor for further information (Bharti, 2014; Dunleavy, Dede, & Mitchell, 2009; Holland, 2014).

From the teacher's perspective, AR allows students access to extended and expanded information via a virtual overlay of information. The mobile device (e.g., iPad or smartphone) will scan the tag (sometimes called a trigger or marker) associated with an object, image, or location. When scanned, the device shows a new layer of information such as informative text, images, video or audio recording, or a 3-D model (Politis, 2015). For example, AR can assist students in understanding chemistry by helping them visualize the internal structure of a molecule using a dynamic 3-D model of the molecule that appears when they scan a picture of a molecule in the text or a poster of the molecule on the wall of the class. Here is a video example from an elementary mathematics class teaching students how to calculate the area of different two-dimensional shapes: www.youtube.com/watch?v=8Zb2spZvHFQ.

> Augmented reality involves using technology to overlay digital information onto real-world objects, images, or locations. In that sense, each image or object becomes a tutor for information on itself.

A Classroom Example: AR Making History Come Alive

Imagine a history class in which a poster of Washington crossing the Delaware River is tagged with additional information. The teacher can seek a video (YouTube is a great source) or even record himself or herself portraying Washington, while talking about the difficulty of crossing that river in a winter storm and then discussing how important that subsequent victory in Trenton, New Jersey, on Christmas Day was for the morale of the colonists during the American Revolution. History can come alive in a real sense using AR (Politis, 2015).

A more complex AR option is construction of an AR trail around the school (sometimes referred to as progressive AR content). In this application of AR, the final information presented with one triggered object must include either specific travel instructions or hints for where students might find additional AR content associated with other objects in the class.

Imagine a social studies teacher who wants to use exploratory learning involving an AR trail around the building that mimics the construction of the interstate highway system. Using an AR trigger affixed to a poster of a road construction site from the 1950s when the interstate highway system was built, the teacher can have students begin the trail at that location by holding a mobile device up to the poster. Then the trigger affixed to that poster will present the initial plan and perhaps the legislation for that highway system from the Eisenhower administration. Next, the information associated with that first trigger should give instructions to "follow the interstate to the door," where another trigger presents a video news story from 1956 showing a work crew on the interstate highway system. The final information at that site might suggest that students "follow the highway" down the hallway to the media center doorframe, where another trigger presents tabled information on miles of interstate built on a year-by-year basis (Bharti, 2014; Politis, 2015). For additional video examples of AR in the class, teachers can visit this site: www.educatorstechnology.com/2013/10/excellent-videos-onthe-use-of-augmented.html.

A number of AR creation options are utilized in schools today, and from the perspective of engaging students, few teaching strategies can have the impact of AR. I strongly urge all teachers to work together, select one of these tools for the school, and begin to create targets around their classes and the school. Of course, once such triggers are created, they can be used during subsequent years and by other teachers in the building. Teachers today are using all of the options presented in Box 5.1.

> **Box 5.1: AR Options for Teachers**
>
> **Aurasma** (www.aurasma.com): This AR option works with either iOS or Android mobile devices, allowing teachers or students to create their own 3-D overlays that will trigger based on an image. This will greatly extend and enhance the learning context. A free iBook on using Aurasma in the classroom is available from teacher Paul Hamilton. His website also presents several videos on AR (http://augmentedrealityeducation.blogspot.com/).
>
> **Daqri** (http://daqri.com): This site, like many AR sites, is primarily devoted to the business and industrial sector but is being used by educators to create augmented reality options for the classroom. This does involve the use of a helmet for AR rather than tablets or mobile devices. For some students, this might be a more engaging format for AR.
>
> **Layar** (www.layar.com): This is one of the most popular AR tools used by teachers and works with both iOS and Android mobile devices. Using a drag-and-drop system, this site allows teachers to enhance pictures with interactive content such as photo slideshows, videos, or 3-D projections. Users are offered an option of free creation for their first-time experience.
>
> **Build AR** (http://buildAR.com): This platform is for teachers and others who want to create augmented reality without the need for coding or development. Teachers and students can create AR experiences in a standard web browser for multiple devices (including smartphones, tablets, or even wearable devices like Google Glass).
>
> **BouncePages:** Pearson Education is working quickly to bring AR to every classroom. For example, Pearson's BouncePages app presents engaging animations that bring any text page to life, with enhanced information, animation, and video. BouncePages even includes brief practice items for students to demonstrate the skill they just learned.
>
> **LangAR:** This is an app that can overlay a picture of any city with information desired by a traveler, such as hotels nearby, restaurants, or other locations of interest. It also provides phrases in any foreign language that might be used in that selected AR environment (an order for coffee, for example). This is an excellent way to enrich any foreign language class.

Setting Up Your AR Classroom

Work Together

I always suggest that two or more teachers in the same subject or grade level work together to create AR environments. For example, if one fifth-grade teacher is teaching about dinosaurs, the other fifth-grade teachers are likewise teaching that content. If three such teachers work together to acquire five dinosaur models for each class, then information on those creatures can be tagged to each, for all of the fifth-grade classrooms. Thus, three teachers can divide up the work of writing those informational paragraphs.

View Several AR Tutorials

Teachers might begin their AR experience by viewing videos that are provided on several of the websites in Box 5.1. These can give teachers a sense of what the process is when setting up AR triggers for objects or posters in the classroom. However, teachers should remember that the flashiest video portrayal of an AR option does not necessarily mean that teachers will find that option easy to use. Also, cost is a factor, and while some AR sites offer a free option for initial AR development, others do not, so teachers must choose wisely.

Select the AR Tool

This initial exploration will take some time, but after viewing several videos, and prior to using AR, teachers should consider cost factors, ease of use by students, what other teachers in the school might be using, and what seems to feel most comfortable for the teacher. There are many advantages to all teachers in the school using the same AR tool, because that makes everyone's tagged items sharable! For example, if one teacher creates tags for the interstate highway system around the school, then other teachers can use that AR teaching tool. After several hours of video viewing and exploration of the websites mentioned previously, teachers can make their selection of an AR platform.

Select Initial Objects for Triggers

Teachers should consider what items they might want to use as trigger options. These might include posters in the class, pictures in the text, or simply a location in the classroom. For example, a physical science class might have a poster of the solar system, or a biology class might have a picture or diagram presenting the parts of a cell. Each of those posters would be great locations for a marker. Also, a teacher may wish to associate markers with pictures throughout a text. Of course, this does not mean that all texts in the class would be marked, but even five or ten triggers around the classroom can greatly enhance an instructional unit. The teacher's initial goal is not to mark every picture or poster but to have a few AR options for each planned topic. Again, those markers can be permanently associated with the objects or locations and used again the next year.

Select or Write the AR Content for Each Trigger Object

For each trigger around the class, the teacher must determine what supplemental information to provide. While text material or table material provides additional information, video and 3-D presentations are typically much more engaging for the students. Using YouTube, TeacherTube, and other similar open resources, teachers can often find excellent video clips for use with AR triggers. You should select video clips that range from a minute to three or four minutes for these AR locations rather than longer videos. Of course, knowing what content will be presented will help determine where to place the triggers around the class. Therefore, this content selection step and the previous step on trigger location are often undertaken together.

Surprise the Students

I encourage teachers to surprise the students the first time they use AR content in the class. By merely holding their mobile devices near a poster, students may suddenly find additional, highly engaging information on the topic under study. This can excite students and motivate them to further explore the class, seeking additional triggers for content.

Hand the AR Responsibility to Students

Teachers in many elementary, middle, and high school classes are having students develop the markers in the class, write the supplemental information, and tag the objects, with teacher approval (Klopfer & Sheldon, 2010; Noonoo, 2012). In fact, using students to develop additional AR content in the classroom not only enriches the classroom for future classes, but also prepares the students with a high-level 21st century communications skill that they can take with them long after they leave school.

Research on AR

AR in the educational setting is relatively new, and efficacy research is limited and ongoing. However, the available research shows a number of benefits in using AR in the classroom (Bharti, 2014; Dunleavy, Dede, & Mitchell, 2009; Holland, 2014; Klopfer, 2008), including increased student engagement. For example, Dunleavy, Dede, and Mitchell (2009) conducted case studies of AR implementation in classes in two middle schools and one high school to investigate teachers' and students' reactions to AR implementation. Both teachers and students reported that they found AR to be highly engaging, particularly for students who had previously presented behavioral and academic challenges. Teachers indicated AR potentially held transformative value for middle and high school teaching.

Several researchers have reported that students enjoy working with AR and even creating AR options in the classroom (Klopfer, 2008; Klopfer & Sheldon, 2010; Noonoo, 2012). Noonoo (2012), for example, indicated that during AR implementation, students were highly aware that teachers were as new to AR as they themselves were, and this caused the students to consider themselves as co-researchers in the AR transformation. Students often suggested to teachers what objects or locations might be enhanced with AR. Clearly that level of engagement should be one goal in every classroom today.

Summary

With research ongoing, it is very difficult to guess how AR technologies might impact classrooms over the next decade. This enhanced reality allows students to actually experience the academic content in new and novel ways, and this can result in profound learning experiences. Also, the creative options involved when students themselves are creating AR tags in various subjects are virtually endless. In fact, all a teacher has to do is complete enough AR generation to understand the process, and then turn this process over to the students! This is clearly a teaching strategy that all teachers should soon begin to explore.

Strategy 6

Games, Gamification, and Simulations

Educational games and simulations have become increasingly important components in many classrooms around the world. Of course, teachers have used stand-alone board games for decades, but more recently, technology-based games have appeared in classrooms (Anderson, 2014; Maton, 2011; Schwartz, 2014, 2015; TeachThought Staff, 2015; Wolpert-Gawron, 2015). In some cases, students actually create games for teaching content. Clearly, gaming has now become an important instructional strategy, rather than merely an after-class activity or reward for other work. Further, proponents suggest that the use of games seems to be increasing exponentially (Ash, 2011; Hattie, 2012; ISTE, 2010).

In fact, billions of dollars worldwide are spent on commercial games yearly by students and adults, so educators have justifiably taken note of the excitement many students show for gaming or simulation scenarios. It is no surprise that educators have harnessed this powerful tool for motivational purposes (Miller, 2012; Shapiro, 2014). Also research data has shown that gaming and simulation scenarios are highly effective for increasing student engagement and academic performance (Ash, 2011; Hattie, 2012; ISTE, 2010; Maton, 2011; Miller, 2012; Short, 2012).

Proponents of games in the classroom often differentiate between use of specific games for learning content and gamification. Gamification refers to use of various game attributes such as competition, rewards, or accumulation of points to transform non-game curricular activities into some type of competitive game or simulation. Gamification may be used for either practice activities or initial instruction activities for teaching new content. Further, gamification may also involve teachers or students actually authoring digital games or creating virtual-world game-like learning experiences for others.

> Gamification refers to use of various game aspects such as competition, rewards, or the accumulation of points to turn non-game curricular activities into some type of game or simulation.

Educational Games for Teaching

Computer-based games, such as *Age of Empires*, *Civilization*, and *SimCity*, have long been used to teach how civilizations come into existence and develop over time or how cities might be organized (Bender & Waller, 2013). The decades-old *Oregon Trail* taught generations of Americans what the settlers of the western frontier faced as they traveled across the continent in the 1800s. Today, both educational games and simulations, as well as many other games that were originally developed for personal entertainment, are being used in the classroom. As an example, one teacher uses the popular game *Angry Birds* to teach physics principles, while others use popular, commercially available games such as *SimCity* to teach how complex systems interact (Sheely, 2011).

These games are generally considered stand-alone game applications when used in the classroom, and such stand-alone games represent the simplest class of games used in education today. These are simple games or apps that can generally be played individually, often in one sitting, while teaching specific predesignated content. While students make choices in these games, there is less creativity required for most of them than in the games discussed later in this section. Of course, some stand-alone games do allow multiple players, so several players might work together to accomplish the game objectives while mastering various targeted educational standards. Today many, if not most, teachers are familiar with gaming sites such as BrainPop, a site filled with educational games in a variety of subject areas. These stand-alone games and associated websites grow in popularity among educators each year (Shapiro, 2014; Short, 2012; Wolpert-Gawron, 2015).

For a better understanding of the use of games for learning, teachers might wish to view a brief video on gaming in the classroom from Edutopia.org: www.edutopia.org/blog/games-for-learning-community-resources-andrew-miller. Also, Box 6.1 presents additional information on several of the more popular gaming websites for stand-alone educational games.

Box 6.1: Educational Gaming Sites

BrainWare Safari (www.mybrainware.com/how-it-works) is a set of game scenarios that are intended to strengthen certain cognitive skills, including skills in the areas of attention, memory, visual and auditory processing, thinking, and sensory integration. This educational software program is currently being used by teachers and homeschooling parents alike (Shah, 2012). The game is a cloud-based program (user performance data is stored on computers of the publisher) and operates like a video game. Over twenty different games are included, and each offers many levels of play and focuses on multiple skills. These games are sequenced and intended to help the student develop automaticity in the targeted cognitive skills. The developers recommend that students access the games three to five times weekly and spend thirty to sixty minutes on the game each time they play in order to improve those targeted cognitive skills.

Public Broadcasting System (www.pbs.org) offers many mathematics and science games. At that site, parents or teachers can pick an age range from kindergarten through upper elementary and find a variety of free games.

Mangahigh.com has games that are targeted for students ranging in age from seven to sixteen. The games all stipulate a goal for students to achieve by repeatedly practicing the core learning concept, and teachers can track the progress of their students using their logins and passwords. Teachers report anecdotally that these games result in students playing their math games long after school is over and sometimes well into the night (see www.mangahigh.com for several teacher reviews). Certainly any mathematics teacher should take advantage of this website to access educational games that will motivate most students.

BrainPop (www.brainpop.com) is one of the most popular stand-alone gaming sites and is used in over 20 percent of schools in the United States. It features many games in various subjects across the primary and elementary grade levels including science, mathematics, technology, engineering, social studies, health, and many other courses. These games work well on computers, tablets, and other mobile devices, and this site offers animation options for the classroom. This site is also home to GameUp, an educational portal for the classroom, and Make-a-Map, a map generation tool for the classroom that can be very useful in geology, history, and social studies. Teachers can customize assessments or participate in professional development. Many teachers explore this website first for educational games. At this site, teachers can also view many videos of how other teachers are using games in classroom instruction (http://educators.brainpop.com/whygames).

A Classroom Example: Gaming in Mathematics

Stephanie Bowling is a five-year veteran of the classroom and teaches mathematics at Scott Middle School in Denison, Texas. She has seen the benefits of gaming in the STEM classroom.

> I believe that if the students aren't having a positive experience in class, then they will not be as engaged, so I try to make mathematics as fun as possible. I don't use games every day and also try to gamify other exercises. I try to create ways for students to practice concepts while having fun at the same time. For example, I often have them practice their work in either teams or with partners in a friendly competition.
>
> One idea is to incorporate whiteboards into the lesson. I often split the class into teams of two, three, or four students. Each student uses a whiteboard, an erasable pen, and an eraser. I print out a worksheet that all students can use on an individual basis, or I project the problems on the board. Next, I call out the number of one of the problems on the page, and they get to work solving that problem. They have to work together to get the correct answer before the time is up, and the time allowed varies with the difficulty of the problem. To create a game environment in the class, I use an online timer (www.online-stopwatch.com), downloaded to my desktop. That is easy to use and has several different timer options. The team with the first correct solution wins!
>
> One game that I have used came from the Secondary Math Activities Middle School Math Workshop by Susan Scott (www.secondarymathactivites.com). Scott presents many awesome ideas that can help every teacher find ways to incorporate games of all types in the classroom. One of my favorites is "Pin the ghost on the graveyard" (or "Pin the arrow on the heart"). Basically, the teacher prints out ghosts, arrows, or pumpkins, based on the holiday that is closest, along with the "board" (graveyard or heart, etc.). The graveyard has a hidden prize underneath. Teachers need task cards presenting the concept or problems under study. Then the teacher hands one card out to each group, and they all work a problem on the card individually. They then must show all their work, and they raise their hand when everyone on the team is finished. The

teacher then checks the cards, and if they have them all right, they get a ghost for the group. They put their group number on the ghost and pin or tape it to the graveyard. The team with the most ghosts on the graveyard wins that prize at the end of the game. My students absolutely love this game!

For all of the games in my class, I use the same ground rules, including: (1) everyone has to do the problem; (2) everyone has to show their work; (3) everyone has to have the correct answer to get points; (4) when the timer goes off, I say, "Three, two, one," and when that countdown ends, everyone must raise their boards in order to earn their points; and (5) everyone must show good sportsmanship. In that sense, my games are teaching the content but also emphasizing good citizenship. I often award prizes for these games, but I've discovered that middle school students will work just as hard and be just as engaged without prizes.

Finally, it is exciting for me to teach this way. During the games, I see my students talking math, working together to get the right answer, and helping each other succeed. I think that is the most rewarding part. While we don't necessarily complete thirty math problems like we would had I merely used a practice worksheet, the fact is, using games, every single student is participating and gets something from the experience.

Virtual Worlds as Complex Gaming

One type of complex educational game is the alternative reality game, or virtual world, in which students explore, interact with, and/or create an alternative digital world online, forcing them to utilize and ultimately master educational content (Anderson, 2014; Ash, 2011; Shapiro, 2014; Short, 2012; Rapp, 2008; Wolpert-Gawron, 2015). Virtual worlds might offer either the option of creating a digital world or using a digital online environment created by others. Such virtual worlds are multiple player and may be used over a long period of time, rather than used for only one class period. Not all virtual worlds feature all gaming components. That is, some virtual worlds are collaborative rather than competitive, and some involve the completion of a quest or assigned task rather than an accumulation of points. However, these virtual worlds are similar enough to games to facilitate high levels of student engagement, so these tools must be considered as options in the modern classroom (Ash, 2011; Shapiro, 2014; Short, 2012; Rapp, 2008).

> A virtual world is a digitally created online environment in which students create, explore, or interact within an alternative digitally created reality either on a single computer or online.

Kevin Ballestrini, as one example, created a virtual world for his Latin class that placed the students' characters in the alternative virtual world of ancient Rome in order to teach them Latin (Maton, 2011). Each student created an online character (called an avatar) to represent them in the online gaming environment. These avatars were required to work in the ancient city of Rome, wandering the streets and interacting with other avatars in Latin. To successfully play, the students had to plan, act, create, and write like a Roman citizen. Also during the game, the students were given the assignment of rebuilding the city of Pompeii. Students sought inscriptions on stones and solved mysteries during that process, thus learning the language and applying their knowledge in ways that are simply not possible in standard Latin classes. That particular virtual world is now being used experimentally in classrooms across the United States (Maton, 2011).

In this example, students were actually interacting in an ancient city online, using their knowledge of the language and culture to accomplish a task. Virtual worlds such as this can be used for high-level instruction in virtually any subject. In the virtual world, students can tour the inside of a nuclear reactor, look one mile deep in the Earth along a fault line during an earthquake, travel inside a volcano, fly inside a hurricane, or travel inside the human bloodstream. The possibilities are limitless, and that is one reason educators have become so enamored with virtual world instruction.

Minecraft in the Classroom

One virtual world that has captured the imagination of educators worldwide is *Minecraft* (https://minecraft.net; Schwartz, 2015a; Sheely, 2011; Short, 2012). This is one of the most popular virtual worlds with over 30 million players worldwide, and while this was not originally intended as an educational tool, thousands of teachers have used this tool to increase student interest in, and enthusiasm for, their content-area studies.

In *Minecraft*, students either explore existing content within a precreated world or they construct a virtual world, with which they then interact. Like most virtual worlds, *Minecraft* environments can be used across the curriculum. For example, students might create a North Pole world and then visit that environment with the early explorers. They might see a to-the-death struggle between a Neanderthal and a Cro-Magnon man or experience a Civil War battlefield. They might construct a pirate ship that includes various details that document the life of male and female pirates from the golden age of piracy along the eastern coast of the Americas. The city of London in the days of the Black Plague can be recreated in order to explore the spread of disease, or a Mars colony might be used to depict how early explorers could support themselves in a Martian environment.

Both students and teachers can visit existing worlds or create their own worlds in *Minecraft*. Students can work independently or together in collaborative, longer-term projects. In fact, any world that one wishes to imagine and create is possible in *Minecraft*, and both students and teachers find this work absorbing, resulting in a total immersion learning experience (Schwartz, 2015; Shah, 2012; Sheely, 2011; Short, 2012). For some students who do not respond to traditional instruction, game-based instruction using *Minecraft* will often result in increased engagement with the content.

Minecraft has been used as a teaching tool in many subjects. Because *Minecraft* worlds are structured with square shapes, the program lends itself nicely to mathematics instruction, geometry problems dealing with volume, and even structuring equations in algebra (Schwartz, 2015). In science, teachers have used *Minecraft* to help students tour inside an animal cell, watch as a single DNA strand is transcribed into mRNA, or even measure gravity in a virtual world and then transfer the discussion to the real world (Schwartz, 2015).

Joel Levin initially used *Minecraft* in a second-grade class to teach his students computer skills (Sheely, 2011). He was a gamer himself who was experienced with this virtual world, and he believed it would engage his students in a profound way, so he began to use it in the class. Results were impressive in terms of students' excitement with the activity. Levin reported that his students loved the experience while they learned computer skills, online etiquette, Internet safety, and even conflict resolution in a gaming context (Sheely, 2011). He then decided to share that experience with other teachers, so after his own use of *Minecraft*, Levin helped found MinecraftEDU (http://minecraftedu.com; see also Levin's personal blog, http://minecraftteacher.tumblr.com/), a company that provides precreated *Minecraft* worlds for teachers to utilize in the classroom. I suggest that teachers who wish to explore using *Minecraft* in the classroom begin with this site rather than *Minecraft* itself, since much of the early creation work has been done for you, thus saving considerable time.

Many other resources may be found with a simple online search to assist teachers in using *Minecraft* for a variety of courses, and teachers interested in using *Minecraft* should certainly consult not only the online sources but also teacher communities focused on *Minecraft* in the classroom. A simple Google search of *Minecraft* and your subject area will provide contacts with many other teachers using *Minecraft* in your subject, and many of those online communities share very useful information free of charge.

Finally, Short (2012) provides a series of descriptions of how *Minecraft* is currently being used in various science topics in the higher grade levels. Box 6.2 presents several of these teaching ideas for various science classes.

> **Box 6.2: Science Instruction Examples With Minecraft**
>
> **Biology:** *Minecraft* maps of the human body, including the vascular system, nerve cells, and an animal cell are currently in development. Students are immersed in a visual 3-D environment and are able to move in all directions. Cell functions may be demonstrated by moving and placing blocks in order to mimic cellular activity. As one example, in a map designed to represent the human body, the premise is similar to the movie *Fantastic Voyage* in that your friend is sick and you or the class has to go inside his body to cure him by solving puzzles, or killing bacteria and viruses, while exploring the human body.
>
> **Ecology:** *Minecraft* worlds can represent various biomes, including communities of plants, animals, and soil organisms. In *Minecraft*, biomes are created by the map generator and display different heights, temperatures, and foliage. Examples include forest, swampland, hills, desert, plains, oceans, or tundra. Trees and animals are included, as appropriate for the environment created. This can also be used to document how competing human populations might deplete the existing resources, leading to depopulation.
>
> **Chemistry:** In *Minecraft*, students can literally enter a chemical reaction when they represent particles of matter. Stephen Elford, an Australian primary school teacher, has developed a phase change simulation for the basic states of matter (solid, liquid, gas) using players as particles. A four-by-four area is bounded with wooden blocks, simulating the solid phase. Students enter the area and are told that they are particles of matter with limited mobility. The area is made larger by burning (simulating an increase in temperature), leading to a phase change to the state of a liquid. Students have more freedom of motion as the liquid phase but are still constrained by the boundaries, which are set a further distance away. Finally, the last boundary is removed, thus simulating the gas phase.

Other Virtual Worlds

While *Minecraft* is one of the worlds that is most frequently found in the classroom, there are other virtual worlds that teachers may use. For example, sixth-grade students at Nature Hill Intermediate School in Wisconsin recently studied history and English in a virtual world called *Quest Atlantis* (Milwaukee Journal Sentinel, 2012). In that multiuser 3-D game space, students direct avatars in various missions while interacting via chat functions with other students' avatars about the content under study. Also, the material written by students must be evaluated and accepted by the Council (who is, in reality, the teacher), so virtually all written material is checked and evaluated for accuracy.

Wheelock and Merrick (2015) identify the five most commonly used virtual worlds, and each of these is becoming more common in classes today. Box 6.3 presents a brief description of these virtual worlds.

> ### Box 6.3: Virtual Worlds Used in Classrooms Today
>
> ***World of Warcraft:*** *World of Warcraft* (http://eu.battle.net/wow/en/) is a highly popular multiplayer role-playing game, and that worldwide popularity makes this a virtual world to consider for use in the classroom. While the focus is warfare, this game engages students in learning about economies, English language arts, and history, and the game format keeps students extremely engaged. Various supports are available for teachers choosing to use this game. Wheelock and Merrick (2015) recommend that teachers explore the World of Warcraft in School project (http://wowinschool.pbworks.com/w/page/5268731/FrontPage), a brainchild of Lucas Gillespie and Peggy Sheehy, which provides an English language arts curriculum linking the study of what it means to be a hero to the reading and discussion of *Lord of the Rings*.
>
> ***OpenSim:*** Schools in a suburb of Atlanta are using the *OpenSim* virtual world platform (http://opensimulator.org/wiki/Main_Page). This software is found in many classrooms today (Wheelock & Merrick, 2015) and allows educators to create virtual worlds related to their class content (Georgia district, 2012). Educators engage students in authentic problem solving within the virtual world. Role playing is used, and students act out their lesson content in science, social studies, mathematics, or other content areas (Georgia district, 2012). Wheelock and Merrick (2015) suggest that teachers explore Kitely, Active Worlds, and Quest Atlantis Remixed. Each of these worlds is highly dynamic and will engage the most unengaged students as they build their own virtual environment. Each of these is free of charge.
>
> ***Second Life:*** *Second Life* (http://secondlife.com) is another virtual world that provides many options for teachers to engage student interest (Anderson, 2014; Wheelock & Merrick, 2015). This is designed for students ages thirteen and up, and includes tools for problem-based learning, collaboration, and small-group discussions. It can also provide a global audience for student work (Wheelock & Merrick, 2015).
>
> ***Unity:*** *Unity* (http://unity3d.com/) is a program teachers can use to create avatar-based environments and intricate scripted activities. For example, the U.S. military is using *Unity* to create simulations that pretrain soldiers for dealing with dangerous or problematic situations without putting them in actual danger. Also, the U.S. Department of Education is supporting *Unity*-based games as educational tools (Wheelock & Merrick, 2015).

Beginning Gaming in the Classroom

Start With What You Know

Several authors have presented suggestions for how to begin gaming in the classroom (Bender & Waller, 2013; Shapiro, 2014). First, teachers should begin with what they know. If you have personally never played an educational game, don't jump into the most difficult ones initially. Specifically, teachers who have never played *Minecraft*, *World of Warcraft*, or *Second Life* should not dive into them expecting to use them the next day in the classroom. Rather, those teachers should carefully select one or two websites that provide simpler stand-alone games focused on specific instructional content. Many of those games are quite engaging and can be used the next day, after an initial teacher exploration. Teachers might then assign several students to play it.

Match Games / Virtual Worlds With Your Content and Instructional Purpose

Teachers should ensure that the game content is consistent with the appropriate curricular standards. Of course, games created for educational purposes typically are developed with standards in mind, but games or virtual worlds developed for entertainment purposes are not. While gaming is a great activity that students are supposed to enjoy, teachers must select games to maximize student learning, and some games have much richer, deeper content than others. Also, teachers must consider their use of the game. Is the game to be used for initial instruction or practice of previously learned content? Different intended uses can inform which games teachers might use in the classroom.

Preview the Game

Teachers should preview any game or virtual world selected for classroom use, and for most stand-alone games, this involves playing the game at least once (Shapiro, 2014). This preview will allow the teacher to determine possible uses of the game and, in many cases, set up differentiated levels of game play for students at various academic levels.

Relate Game Themes to Non-Game Content

Games and virtual worlds in the classroom are most effective as educational tools when the relationship between game content and activities and the content in the instructional unit is highlighted. While students can learn content from games, it is ultimately the teacher's role to demonstrate for the students the relationship between the game content and the subject matter, and this can typically be done with a well-planned postgame activity that reinforces the instructional content.

Teach Digital Citizenship

Many of these games and real-time virtual worlds can be unsafe online environments, and teachers must consider student safety. This provides an excellent opportunity to teach cyber safety and appropriate use of the Internet. Because gaming is likely to be a significant part of instruction in the future, student safety should always be paramount.

Do Not Limit Game Usage

One mistake many teachers make is unintentionally limiting what students might accomplish with educational games and virtual realities. Thus, while teachers must set parameters relative to their expectations for students' use of the game, teachers must likewise take care to not let their assignments limit what students can accomplish in gaming formats. For virtual worlds in particular, teachers should make specific assignments, complete with general rubrics, without killing any opportunity for creativity in creation of the virtual world.

Play, Quiz, and Repeat

With the previous steps accomplished, teachers should assign several students to play the game and then report back to the teacher. Teachers may wish to follow most gaming sessions with a quick-check quiz to ensure that students are picking up the content as anticipated. If students don't do well, the teacher may assign them the game again, once they see the types of learning expected of them.

Research on Games and Virtual Worlds

Research shows many advantages to teaching with games and virtual worlds and demonstrates that game and virtual world instruction encourages high levels of student engagement (ISTE, 2010; Miller, 2012). Student attitudes toward learning are enhanced when games are utilized in the classroom (Sáez-López, Miller, Vázquez-Cano, & Domínguez-Garrido, 2015; Shah, 2012). Other research on gaming or virtual realities in the classroom suggests that games and educational simulations are very effective instructional tools for increasing achievement (Ash, 2011; Hattie, 2012; ISTE, 2010; Maton, 2011). Hattie's (2012) meta-analytic research, for example, showed that simulation-based instruction yielded an effect size of 0.33, suggesting that simulations were more effective than traditional instruction.

Games and simulations can teach content in exciting ways, and these tech tools have the advantage of actually putting the student into the situation or event under study (Miner, 2015; Rapp, 2008). This immersion advantage alone has already motivated many educators to explore game- and simulation-based instruction, and proponents of gaming view this as the future of schooling (Miner, 2015; Short, 2012).

Summary

Virtual worlds, games, and simulations are likely to be a definitive element of classroom instruction in the next decade, and teachers are well advised to get ahead of their personal learning curves as quickly as possible. Many teachers are only now beginning to explore this gaming/virtual-world instruction option, and the creation of virtual worlds for instructional purposes in games such as *Minecraft* involves a set of skills that many teachers do not possess presently. However, research has shown the validity of virtual world instruction, and teachers should launch themselves into exploration of what these teaching tools have to offer in the classroom.

Strategy 7

Virtual Field Trips

Another virtual option for engaging students is the virtual field trip (Anderson, 2014; Nussbaum-Beach, 2014; Singer, 2015; Smith, 2015a, 2015b; Smith, 2015, Stoddard, 2009). Whereas a virtual world exists only online, a virtual field trip is the use of distance education technologies (Internet, virtual reality, television, satellite, or recorded videos) to help students travel to and study a specific location of interest while physically remaining in their classroom. Of course, virtual field trips are not new, since television- and satellite-based field trips have been available for teachers for the last several decades from providers such as public television. However, the concept of the virtual field trip has received increased interest recently, with the development of web tools that are much easier to use in the classroom.

> A virtual field trip is the use of distance education technologies (Internet, virtual reality, television, satellite, or recorded videos) to help students travel to and study a specific location of interest while physically remaining in their classroom.

For almost every group of students across the grade levels, some virtual field trip is probably already available. Topics range from swimming with whales to studies of the Underground Railroad and virtually everything in between, and additional topics become available almost daily. Of course, teachers have long been aware that student engagement increases when students are allowed to actually see and experience the content under study, which is one reason both virtual worlds and virtual field trips are so engaging for almost all students (Nussbaum-Beach, 2014; Swett, 2015). In most cases, the richness of the virtual field trip can be enhanced by both pre– and post–field trip activities. Use of various worksheets, games, and cooperative group activities focused on the content to be studied during the virtual field trip will increase learning. Also, many teachers encourage students to complete various participatory organizers or worksheets of factual and conceptual information during the virtual field trip itself. Again, such work can enhance the learning experience during the virtual field trip (Stoddard, 2009).

In today's classroom, there are three different options for virtual field trips.

1. Predeveloped virtual field trips: These trips are developed by some company or historical site for use in schools. Some of these involve a fee for service, and others are free.
2. Teacher-developed field trips: Often individual teachers or teacher teams develop virtual field trips, which might be based on a local scientific site, historical site, or specific ecosystem.
3. Student-developed virtual field trips: With the development of various tech presentation options and the power of the web, students often develop virtual field trips by using slides and publicly available video, coupled with informational dialogue or graphics presentations.

New Tech Tools for Virtual Field Trips

While virtual field trips are not a new teaching strategy, they have received increased attention because of the recently developed technology options that allow for both teacher- and student-created virtual field trips. For example, Google recently announced the development of additional web tools for virtual field trips like Google Expeditions Pioneer Program (www.google.com/edu/expeditions; Smith, 2015a). This system, supported by Google and field-tested in 2016, will offer everything a teacher needs to undertake a virtual field trip, including smartphones, a tablet for the teacher to direct the tour, a router that allows Expeditions to run without an Internet connection, and Google Cardboard viewers or Mattel View-Masters that turn phones into virtual reality headsets (Smith, 2015a). The Google Expeditions program is based on the Google Cardboard, a simple headset that can display stereoscopic 3-D environments.

The Expeditions Pioneer Program is this company's next step toward making virtual reality easier for the teacher. Teachers will eventually be able to launch an immersive virtual field trip anywhere that has been photographed with a 360-degree camera. To date, Google has been pretesting the program, including trips to the Museum of Natural History, the Palace of Versailles, a coral reef, the surface of Mars, the Great Wall of China, Independence Hall in Philadelphia, and El Capitan, a rock formation in Yosemite National Park (Singer, 2015; Smith, 2015a). Approximately one hundred such virtual field trip locations have been filmed for use in the classroom (Singer, 2015).

However, Google is certainly not the only game in town when it comes to finding or developing virtual field trips. For example, Microsoft has developed the Skype option for educators as a virtual field trip tool (Smith, 2015b). Further, other organizations have begun the process of making virtual field trips available for students worldwide. These include fee-for-service field trips (e.g., www.virtualfieldtrips.org) and free options for virtual field trips (e.g., www.discoveryeducation.com/Events/virtual-field-trips/explore/index.cfm?campaign=flyout_students_virtual_field_trips).

Case Study: Virtual Field Trips in Science Class

Ms. Highdigger was seeking ways to make her fifth-grade earth science class more engaging, and she wanted to consider the use of virtual field trips as one way to do that. She had not used virtual field trips previously, so she decided to use prepared virtual field trips rather than develop her own. In conjunction with the implementation of virtual field trips, she decided to undertake a baseline and instructional treatment experiment with her class to demonstrate the efficacy of virtual field trips. She believed that this would be worth the time, thinking that even if the virtual field trips didn't work for her class, she could at least use the experiment to show the class how the scientific process might be used to answer questions in the real world. In this case, she decided to state a hypothesis as follows: "One virtual field trip per instructional unit will increase unit test scores for both average and below-average achievers."

She used the unit test grades from the previous two instructional units and divided the class into students who scored above eighty-four and those who scored below. This helped her identify two groups—average achievers and below-average achievers. She then averaged those unit test scores for each of those groups, and that provided a baseline from the previous two instructional units, as shown in figure 7.1 (page 78).

Next, Ms. Highdigger selected a virtual field trip for each of the next instructional units she planned to cover: volcanic activity and tectonic plates, weather, and the solar system. Each was planned as a two-week instructional unit, and she anticipated using the virtual field trip on the first day of the unit. Using a variety of sources, she was able to secure high-quality virtual field trips, complete with fairly extensive pre– and post–field trip activities. Further, the field trips seemed to be consistent with her instructional chapters in the text, indicating that these particular field trips meshed nicely with her science standards.

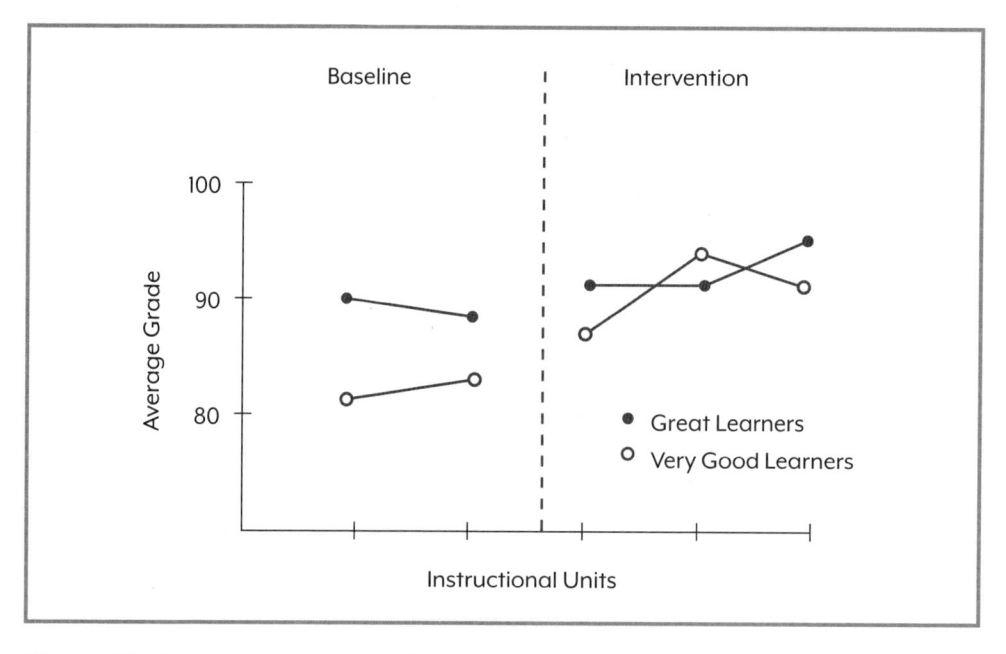

Figure 7.1: Achievement scores from science units with virtual field trips.

Ms. Highdigger then began to use the virtual field trips, and in each of the next two instructional units, she completed those on the first day of the instructional unit. During the next week, a school assembly was called during her usual science period timeslot, so she merely held a fifteen-minute discussion of the third unit topic (the solar system) and then completed the virtual field trip on the second day of that unit. Further, in each of these three instructional units, she was able to complete at least three days of instructional activities associated directly with the virtual field trip. This ensured that the virtual field trip was well integrated within the instructional unit and not merely a one-day fun-time type of experience.

The intervention data in figure 7.1 demonstrate that student achievement increased when virtual field trips were used. The grades for the average achievers increased by several points, but the largest increase was seen among the below-average achievers in the class, whose unit test scores increased an average of six points for each instructional unit in which virtual field trips were used. These data allowed Ms. Highdigger to prove her hypothesis about the effectiveness of virtual field trips. Further she was very proud of two unplanned, post-experiment occurrences. First, she was able to share a single-subject experiment with her students as an example of science at work. Next, her principal, upon hearing of this experiment on the use of virtual field trips, invited her to explain her work for a thirty-minute presentation to the entire faculty, several of whom indicated an interest in undertaking similar virtual field trip experiments in their classes.

Guidelines for Teaching With Virtual Field Trips

Guidelines for using virtual field trips in the classroom are somewhat different depending on whether the teacher is using a predeveloped virtual field trip or developing a virtual field trip, either individually or with class participation. In each case, the following guidelines will help teachers get started.

Check Multiple Sources

Finding a high-quality virtual field trip is the first step for many teachers, and initially, teachers may wish to simply google their next instructional unit topic, along with the words *virtual field trips*. Remember that while many sources exist, finding high-quality virtual field trips that parallel your instructional content standards will be critical to the efficacy of your efforts. Virtual field trips should be highly engaging, with good video, photos, and graphics. Box 7.1 provides some suggestions on places to begin.

Box 7.1: Sources of Virtual Field Trips

Virtual Field Trips (www.virtualfieldtrips.org/pricing.html) provides K–12 educators with a fee-based virtual field trip option providing high-quality educational videos for social studies, geography, and science. Selected trips are offered in English, Spanish, and French, making this useful for language classes, as well as the subjects above. Fees are very reasonable at $45 per class or $225 for a schoolwide virtual field trip.

The JASON Project (www.jason.org/) is a nonprofit, STEM-focused group that connects students to real science and exploration to inspire and motivate them to study and pursue careers in science, technology, engineering, and math. Both prerecorded events and live events are available, and live webcasts connect students with inspirational scientists. Materials include reading selections, inquiry-based labs, videos, and online games. For teachers, JASON provides lesson plans, assessments, and comprehensive professional development programs. Some of their instructional topics include Seas of Change, Monster Storms, Tectonic Fury, and Resilient Planet.

Discovery Education (www.discoveryeducation.com) is an excellent option since it provides virtual field trips in many science and social studies areas. Teachers can explore virtual field trips in science, earth and space, plants and animals, social studies, art/design, and manufacturing.

Pinterest (www.pinterest.com) should always be checked for virtual field trip ideas and suggestions from other teachers.

> **GEO Virtual Field Trips** (www.ismennt.is/vefir/earth/mhcur/netdays.htm) was developed by Hamrahlio College in Iceland. These field trips show the impact of historic volcanic eruptions and present a series of web pages and links that take students to an interactive route map from where they can visit such famous active volcanoes as Hekla, Katla, the Laki eruption site, the Vestmann Islands, and the subglacial eruption effects on southeastern Iceland. The web pages were authored during college field trips and include student comments and contributions.
>
> **NASA Virtual Field Trips** (http://quest.nasa.gov/vft/) offers a variety of virtual field trips (e.g., Moon Math), complete with interesting photos, videos, and lesson plans. These are immersive multimedia experiences focused on exploration of areas on Earth that have been identified as analog sites to regions on Mars or the moon. Students are taken from a global view directly down to a surface view of a site. They are then seamlessly placed into a 360 degree spherical virtual reality surface panorama of that location, and then they navigate around the site selecting various objects to learn more about.

View the Field Trip

If possible, the teacher should view the entire virtual field trip prior to purchase. Most virtual field trips come with a fee for service, so these will cost some money. Therefore, teachers should review and consider the quality, the student engagement value, and the actual educational richness of the field trip before purchase if at all possible.

Review the Supplemental Materials

As discussed previously, the educational value of virtual field trips is highly dependent on supplemental educational activities (Stoddard, 2009). At a minimum, the virtual field trip should include multiple options for pre– and post–field trip activities and perhaps a participatory organizer to be completed during the field trip itself. Teachers should compare the content of these materials to the learning standards and select a virtual field trip that most closely meets their students' needs.

Consider Interactive Elements

Some virtual field trips allow for student interaction in a variety of ways. This can range from simple surveys of students' opinions on questions embedded within the field trip (questions that would then be addressed in the next segment) to actual student control of robots presented on screen. As one example, the JASON Project (www.jason.org), created in 1989, allows students on real-time virtual field trips to actually control an underwater submersible in explorations of the *Titanic* and other undersea environments. Such interaction options not only provide for rich virtual field trip experiences but also may help launch educational projects in future instructional units.

Consider Cost

In education today, cost is always a factor, and virtual field trips can be expensive, particularly if purchased for a single class at a time. Schoolwide licenses will save some funds and provide the virtual field trip to a larger segment of students at the school, so teachers wishing to explore predeveloped virtual field trips should discuss the purchase options with their administrator and the curriculum development specialists in the various subject areas.

Guidelines for Creating Virtual Field Trips

While the guidelines are somewhat different for the development of virtual field trips, many of the concerns noted in the previous section likewise apply. The following suggestions are presented for teachers who are developing virtual field trips using student teams, but also apply to teachers developing virtual field trips alone (Lamb, 2016; Mongan-Rallis, 2006).

Brainstorm Content

Teachers should plan the general content for the virtual field trip well in advance and, if possible, plan this content along with their students. You might begin by considering local festivals, historic or scientific sites, natural areas, or various ecosystems in your area (Lamb, 2016). All of these can provide the basis for an effective virtual field trip. Once the location is selected, list specific pictures or video segments you want to include for the field trip (assuming you can find or create them). Remember to include many artifacts such as diagrams, drawings/paintings, maps, interviews and oral histories, digital videos, audio recordings, diaries, letters, and newspapers (Lamb, 2016; Mongan-Rallis, 2006).

Do a Teacher Visit

If possible, either the teacher or the entire class should make a trip to the location under study in the field trip and get individual videos and photos that relate to the specific content and standards to be studied. In some cases, teachers use an actual field trip one year to develop a virtual field trip for subsequent years. To prepare for the visit, teachers or students should list desired pictures and other artifacts in advance of the trip. While taking enough photos, teachers should be careful to not take too many pictures—this gives you more work to do later. Also, teachers might collect any brochures or printed information about the location.

If a visit is not possible, the teacher or a student committee might contact the site and request any printed information or video segments that are available and couple that with an Internet search of photos that can be used in the virtual field trip (Mongan-Rallis, 2006).

Collect Artifacts

Artifacts may include photos, brief videos, diagrams, charts, maps, or other informational material that should be presented in the virtual field trip. The teacher can scan any printed material such as brochures and any photos that can be useful. Each should be selected based on the importance of the concepts represented by the artifact.

Develop Supportive Information

Supportive educational materials are critical for enhancing efficacy of the virtual field trip (Stoddard, 2009), and developers of virtual field trips should consider supplemental information in two forms: information presented during the virtual field trip itself (e.g., dialogue presented when a photo or object is shown) and information intended as pre– or post–field trip activities. Development of these supportive materials provides the teacher with an excellent opportunity to relate the various aspects of the virtual field trip to the concepts and content standards.

Teachers should work with students to develop some supportive information relative to all artifacts, pictures, and video clips that are included. Television programming practices suggest a somewhat limited interest level for most students, so teachers should plan to develop a dialogue lasting from fifteen to forty-five seconds for each photo or stationary artifact.

Video segments that are included may be considerably longer, since they typically show movement through the environment under study. The student development team might also check YouTube for video examples on the chosen location. Supportive information should include specific questions for students. Further, teachers and students should develop participatory organizers to be completed by the students during the virtual field trip. As the supportive information is developed for the virtual field trip itself, teachers or student teams might develop discussion questions and activities for students to complete after the field trip (Lamb, 2016).

Select a Presentation Platform

While predeveloped virtual field trips usually present high-quality video, teachers rarely have time to develop an hour or more of professional-quality video. However, many engaging options exist today for developing virtual field trips. In addition to the options previously discussed, these may include slideshows, PowerPoint presentations, Inspiration software, or a class or school website or wiki. Regardless of the presentation option you choose, it is important that you focus on the purpose of the field trip and not become lost in the various options embedded within the chosen presentation format (Lamb, 2016). Of course, teachers should always choose an option that accurately reflects their current personal technology skills.

Storyboard the Virtual Field Trip

This is the step when teachers and students place artifacts and information in a reasonable, readily understandable order, usually based on time frame. The storyboard should allow for virtual field trips that last between thirty-five and sixty minutes and given an average of thirty seconds spent on any single photo. This may suggest a range of 70 to 120 different artifacts for a photo-based virtual field trip.

Make Content Interactive

Depending on the platform used, teachers may have the option of making the virtual field trip more interactive. For example, once a specific picture or video is presented, the presentation may ask a question and have students do a "one-minute discussion with a friend" about that question. Next, students might be instructed to click the screen to see the answer (Lamb, 2016).

Develop an Introduction

Virtual field trips are enhanced when students understand the purpose of the trip and can focus on specific content during the field trip (Lamb, 2016; Mongan-Rallis, 2006). The introduction should include engaging video content as well as a brief statement of what the virtual field trip is about. After a general purpose statement, teachers should focus on the importance of specific content. For example, teachers might include a chart of key concepts and a brief statement on each to help students focus their efforts. However, remember that the introduction should be brief, usually no more than one or two minutes.

Cite Sources

In all teacher- and student-developed content, sources are important (Mongan-Rallis, 2006). When using pictures or videos from the Internet, make sure to use items that are free and cite the sources of the photos or videos. A simple graphic at the end of the virtual field trip is also useful for fully disclosing sources.

Put It All Together!

After all the various brief segments are prepared, the storyboard becomes the outline for putting these artifacts, supportive information, video clips, and such together.

Research on Virtual Field Trips

In terms of student engagement, research has been supportive of using both field trips and virtual field trips (Cassady, Kozlowski, & Kornmann, 2008; Heuvel, 2008; Noel, 2008; Noel & Colopy, 2006; Stoddard, 2009). Research has shown that students are more engaged with the learning experience of virtual field trips than in traditional classroom instruction (Spicer & Stratford, 2001). Further, virtual field trips, when developed carefully and intentionally related to the content standards to be learned, do enhance learning (Nussbaum-Beach, 2014; Singer, 2015; Stoddard, 2009; Sweat, 2015). In particular, the efficacy research shows that well-designed virtual field trips, coupled with both participatory organizers and follow-up class activities will enhance learning (Cassady, Kozlowski, & Kornmann, 2008; Heuvel, 2008; Noel & Colopy, 2006; Stoddard, 2009).

Summary

As technology becomes increasingly available, and more and more schools move toward one-to-one computer availability (one computer for each student), use of these tech tools consistently increases. Clearly, using more virtual field trips in the class is one way to make technology work to enhance engagement and increase learning. As these studies indicate, the use of virtual field trips in the classroom is an effective way to increase student engagement, and thus more virtual field trips should be included in the curriculum for all grades in which students are capable of working alone or in small groups with the appropriate technology.

Of course, the value of virtual field trips will vary depending on how well integrated the field trip is with the content under study, so teachers should select or develop field trips with appropriate participatory organizers as well as in-depth follow-up activities that will highlight the critical aspects of the learning standards. Further, use of peer buddies or study teams during the field trip activities is likely to increase student engagement even more, and as both teachers and students become experienced in using one of the newly emerging virtual field trip platforms, the possibilities are seemingly endless. Therefore, virtual field trips can be recommended for many more than just one instructional unit during a year or semester-long course. While not every instructional unit is likely to include a virtual field trip, many should in a 21st century school. This is a learning technology to implement, both for today and in the future.

Strategy 8

Coding and Robotics

Few technological developments in recent years will engage students' attention more so than programmable robots, and that is one reason that robotics are quickly finding their way into classrooms around the world (Bloom, 2015; Dredge, 2014; Fears & Patsalides, 2012; Nyren, 2016; Powel, 2014; Schwartz, 2014; Yohana, 2014). While some teachers have experimented with coding and robotics, others have not, and to date, the use of robotics in the classroom has been very limited. Also the cost of robotics, until recently, has been a significant concern. However, teachers are quickly reaching the conclusion that coding and robotics are likely to define many science and mathematics classes in the very near future, even while robotics are redefining the modern workplace.

Coding is the first step toward using robots in the class. Coding involves teaching students computer programming using simple programming languages, many of which are specifically developed for younger students (Gardiner, 2014). Coding is basically learning to tell a computer or other machine (such as a robot) what to do. Anyone who has ever programmed a modern smartphone is familiar to some degree with the problem of coding, and in today's world, students seemingly consider this type of digital communication to be a fundamental birthright! Various games and activities are available to help teach coding (Nyren, 2016), and students know the value of these skills. Therefore, schools simply must get ahead of this curve to keep up, not only with demands of the modern workplace but also with the interests of many of our students.

It is important to note that proponents of coding instruction are not advocating such instruction in order to make everyone a computer programmer. Rather, these proponents see coding as one way to help students learn to love learning and build pathways to other critical skills such as problem solving and collaborative work (Gardiner, 2014; Nyren, 2016).

> Coding involves teaching students computer programming using simple programming languages, many of which are specifically developed for younger students. Coding is learning to tell a computer or machine what to do.

As this book was written, schools in the United States were still gearing up to teach coding, and only about 10 percent of schools were doing so (Dredge, 2014; Gardiner, 2014). However, in the same year, all students in England, beginning at the age of five, were receiving instruction in coding (Dredge, 2014). Students in Estonia were learning to program to create computer games in the first grade, and students in Singapore began coding in elementary school in 2016 (Gardiner, 2014). With this level of sophisticated training, these students represent the talented, disciplined minds that American, Australian, and Canadian students will compete against in the global marketplace of the future. Again, the importance of teaching coding and robotics seems clear. As summarized by Nyren (2016), educators "must all face the truth: coding is the new writing."

Aside from these emphases on global literacy and world economic competition, coding and robotics seem to invigorate students, increasing engagement rather dramatically. In fact, the avid use of video games, and the fluency with which students master the rather intricate instructions for such games suggests a background that is often directly transferable into the coding paradigm. Thus, it is not inaccurate to suggest that many of our students are already exploring coding, and again, many educators must now play catch-up.

While various advantages can be noted for teaching coding and robotics in the classroom, there is really only one major disadvantage: initial expense. While simple classroom bots can be purchased for between $60 and $100, these are usually intended for kindergarten and primary grades and are quite limited in function. The cost for highly programmable bots tends to be much higher. For example, the RobotLab robotics kit (described in more detail later) costs approximately $4,000, and that is typically more than many school budgets can allow for such instruction in a single classroom. Still, like most digital teaching tools, these costs are likely to drop fairly quickly (Schwartz, 2014), and educators should not be dissuaded based on this concern alone. This instruction is simply too important to postpone.

Coding in the Classroom

Many free or low-cost coding options are available in schools today (Nyren, 2016). Some codes require reading, while others are based primarily on pictures or icons, and these can help younger students or nonreaders grasp the concepts of coding. A variety of coding languages may be found online, some of which are free. Several of these are described in Box 8.1.

> **Box 8.1: Popular Coding Languages for Young Students**
>
> **RobotBASIC** (http://robotbasic.org): This is a free robot control programming language with advanced graphics and free animation. It is among the most powerful programming languages available with over eight hundred commands and functions. Intended for use by all ages, this language includes not only simple commands but also highly complex tasks (floating point math, multidimensional arrays, matrix algebra, and statistical functions). Teachers from kindergarten through high school find this language useful, and there is some advantage to selecting a coding language that doesn't change from one grade level to the next. Robots can be represented on screen and programed using this language (see the video demo: https://www.youtube.com/watch?v=27Gt3lgdcMc&feature=share&list=UUixBQVQIGJ8ja-pLLm3NSjg).
>
> **Scratch** (http://scratch.mit.edu): Many schools use a programming language called Scratch, a free programming language for students aged nine and above, which was developed by MIT. Teachers and students can easily download this tool. Scratch allows players to create (mix and match) commands to program animations, games, or stories, and is highly engaging. Also, the same group developed ScratchJr (www.scratchjr.org), a simpler version intended for students aged five through nine. In order to understand coding generally, I urge educators to review a brief tutorial on Scratch and consider the skills that are taught in the coding instructional process (https://search.yahoo.com/search?fr=mcafee&type=C211US662D20141212&p=Scratch).
>
> **Code Studio** (www.code.org): This is another option for teachers to consider for the classroom. The programming language is fairly simple, and the associated website allows students to sign up for a wide variety of tutorials on coding, to explore environments using movie characters, or to write their own computer games. Courses on coding and programming for ages four through eighteen are available, and skills such as performing real-life algorithms, solving mazes, creating stories, and debugging are taught. With an assessment component built in, this option is certainly one for teachers from kindergarten through high school to consider.
>
> **The Foos** (www.thefoos.com): This is a coding language from codeSpark for preschool students and nonreading students. This language teaches the

basics of coding, including sequencing, pattern recognition, and conditional logic (if/then statements). This language is aimed at students as young as five and has been downloaded 700,000 times by teachers in over 150 countries.

Further, there are a wide variety of games and educational activities that can assist in teaching coding to primary and elementary school students, even when an actual robot is not available in the classroom. Nyren (2016) presented a brief review of five of the most popular coding games for students, and that information is summarized in Box 8.2.

> **Box 8.2: Coding Games**
>
> **Kodable** (www.kodable.com): This game is useful for kindergarten students and others up through age seven and is available by quotes to schools. The game can be taught to students in twenty minutes and is currently in use by one in five elementary schools in the United States. Kodable also provides supplementary worksheet-based activities so students begin to understand the terms, the basics of coding, and the logic of coding even before they arrive in the computer lab (Nyren, 2016).
>
> **CodeMonkey** (www.playcodemonkey.com): This game teaches real coding languages to enable students to build their own website. Intended for students aged nine and above, the cost is $29 per child per year, or $295 for the entire class. This game also offers a competitive option.
>
> **Lightbot** (http://lightbot.com): This coding game is an app for either iOS or Android devices, and is intended for students aged eight and up. Players learn simple logic such as sequencing and if/then statements, and then create a full code sequence in an engaging challenge to complete a puzzle. Unlike most of these other tools, there is no teacher portal or progress tracking system in this app, but this can be a simple first step in teaching the logic and process of coding (Nyren, 2016).
>
> **SpaceChem** (www.zachtronics.com/spacechem): This game is for kids from age ten through adulthood and involves a multisubject space action adventure. Content includes space, chemistry, and programming, and the game stresses higher-level problems and story lines for building machines necessary for survival or self-defense from various space monsters. A free demo is available, and the game can be purchased for iOS or Android devices for $3 (Nyren, 2016).

A quick review of these coding tools will demonstrate that teaching coding involves much more than merely learning a coding language or a set of symbols (Bloom, 2015). To code, students have to identify a problem, break the problem into steps, logically order the steps, identify a solution to the problem given that sequence of steps, and then tell the robot how to proceed in terms of what to do and when (Gardiner, 2014). Thus, skills such as planning, problem solving, deconstructing a problem, identifying steps in a problem solution, sequencing those steps, finding errors in the program, and then reprogramming those steps are all stressed in the coding instructional process. The payoff comes for the students at the end of the process when a coded program works. At that point, students are rewarded by seeing their task accomplished either in the digital realm or in the real world as a robot performs the programed tasks.

It should be noted that coding instruction may be taught either in a digital environment or in the context of actually programming simple robots. For example, a code can be developed digitally to move a dot, representing a robot, around the computer screen. However, teachers have long used real-world examples in all subject areas, and while students seem equally enthusiastic about coding instruction in both the digital and real-world arena, when coding is coupled with actual hardwired, real-world robots, their enthusiasm seems to explode (Fears & Patsalides, 2012; Powel, 2014; Pressly, 2014)! Following is an example of coding instruction coupled with real-world robot programming.

A Classroom Example: First Time Coding in Grade 1

Eleanor Ivester is a veteran of twenty-eight years in the classroom in grades ranging from kindergarten through grade 4. She holds an undergraduate degree from West Georgia College and an MEd in elementary education from Clemson University. She teaches grade 1 at Liberty Elementary School in Georgia. While bots have been included in several technology classes at the middle school in her district, neither she nor her first-grade students had explored coding or robotics in the classroom.

> I decided to implement coding and robot instruction in conjunction with a thematic unit focused on the students' place in their environment. I obtained a Bee-Bot and a Mat (a grid-pattern floor map that serves as a backdrop for Bee-Bot's movements). Bee-Bot is a simple robot for preschool and primary grades. It looks like a bumble bee with seven coding buttons on the top to create different movements or actions (a forward arrow, a backward arrow, a right-turn arrow, a left-turn arrow, a pause button, a clear commands button, and a go button to tell the bot to execute the sequenced commands). Pushing a code button once either moves the Bee-Bot one space across the grid or causes the bot to turn.

I used the bot in conjunction with a book called *Me on the Map* (Sweeney, 1998). In that unit, we focused on where my students lived. The book includes pictures with captions. (For example, "This is me and my room. This is me in my house. This is me on my street. This is me in my town, me in my state, and me in my country.") In conjunction with that study, I created labels for the Mat so that different grid locations on the Mat would represent locations in the school (e.g., my classroom, library, lunchroom, and the school office). On the first day, I placed the bot on the floor with the class sitting around it, and I asked the class, "How do you think we might make Bee-Bot go?" One student suggested pushing the arrow button that means go forward, but the Bee-Bot didn't move. They tried that idea several more times and then realized that they had to push the forward arrow, and then tell the bot to go (by pushing the go button that means "execute the command").

Once the students learned that several commands could be programed at once, prior to having Bee-Bot execute the commands, they began to actually code various movement sequences. Initially, I asked what the bot needed to do to move from one area of our building to another, with the various rooms represented by blocks on the Mat. Then I began to give assignments like, "Take Bee-Bot to the lunchroom."

In response, the students might say, "Bee-Bot needs to move forward two times, turn right, and then move forward one more time." At that point, they were actually developing a coding sequence! On the first day, I wrote the code myself when the students gave the instructions, but the students watched me several times and then took over that coding task as well. In our class, code is written by listing the code or the signs for the movements vertically on a sheet of paper. Thus, the code instructions for the movement above would be:

↑

↑

→

↑

Go!

Simple coding of this nature became relatively easy for the majority of the class after only a week or so, and that really surprised me. I thought it would take more time before they learned to code, particularly for the longer coding sequences. Still, in short order, the sequenced commands grew to multiple destinations (e.g., "Today, we'll go first to the office and then to the lunchroom"). Bee-Bot can accept up to forty code commands in any one sequence, providing plenty of options to move the bot around the Mat for younger students.

One difficulty I noted with this group of students is that they could not orient themselves without some degree of practice. For example, if the Mat or Bee-Bot was turned in a different direction than the day before, or if they simply sat on a different side of the Mat than previously, the students occasionally had some difficulty understanding how to program the desired movements. They tended to program based on how they were sitting rather than where Bee-Bot was or where Bee-Bot was facing. In some cases, they executed a left turn when a right was needed or made other orientation mistakes. However, when Bee-Bot didn't get to the desired destination, the mistakes were clear, and they soon began to help each other to check and correct the code. After a few days, if I merely told them they'd be using the Bee-Bot, they got excited, grabbed a clipboard, and began to write code.

Overall, my kids loved it! They were all highly engaged whenever we were doing assignments with Bee-Bot. In fact, they enjoyed this experience so much that, after a time, I actually used the opportunity to play with Bee-Bot as a reward for work at the end of class. If the students collectively earned a smiley face for good participation and behavior, they got to use Bee-Bot late in the day. One of the brightest children in my class always gets really excited and helps all of the others with their coding, particularly when a mistake is made. He loves the challenge of coding and wants to send Bee-Bot everywhere in the school!

I like the fact that this helps students with problem solving, planning a course of action, sequencing, and correcting the code when the bot doesn't get to the assigned location. They are working cooperatively with others frequently, whenever I place them in pairs to code together. I always have students help *each other correct their code. At this point, I'll be using Bee-Bot for the rest of the year to continue their growth in coding skill. I'm planning on ordering more support materials, particularly different Mats for Bee-Bot to use! We'll be studying the continents soon, based on our social studies standards, so I might relabel the Mat to represent the continents!*

Robotics: The Next Step

An increasing emphasis in the maker movement, and engineering in general, has fostered an increase in robotics instruction in the schools. As shown previously, robotics represent the future of technology in many work environments, and that trend will only increase in the future (Fears & Patsalides, 2012; Powel, 2014; Pressly, 2014; Schwartz, 2014; Yohana, 2014). Further, robots are highly motivating for students (Nugent, Barker, & Grandgenett, 2012). Because these curricula emphases seem to most students to represent their experience of the digital world better than many hardcopy textbooks, students are much more highly engaged in coding and robotics instruction (Fears & Patsalides, 2012; Nugent, Barker, & Grandgenett, 2012; Powel, 2014; Pressly, 2014) than in traditional science or mathematics instruction, and that increased interest translates into higher levels of learning (Gardiner, 2014; Nugent, Barker, & Grandgenett, 2012; Schwartz, 2014; Yohana, 2014).

The Future Impact of Robotics

Another positive impact of coding and robotics instruction is the fact that these strategies seem to involve young girls much more in science than more traditional instruction (Gardiner, 2014; Nugent, Barker, & Grandgenett, 2012; Schwartz, 2014). In fact, coding is actually empowering for women in the future, since students who code are empowered to undertake computer and/or engineering careers, areas in which women have been underrepresented in the past. While young boys have always enjoyed computer science and simple engineering types of class assignments, coding and robotics involve young girls much more intimately, a group of students who have not been traditionally drawn to mathematics and science. Schwartz (2014), for example, indicated that robot manufacturers are beginning to understand how to design the look of their robots (e.g., fewer external wires, wheels, or motors; more curves; and a softer appearance) to make them more attractive to girls. Empowering young girls in these areas should certainly be the goal of every educator.

Also, and perhaps most important, teaching with robots demonstrates for future generations the potential for robotics. Imagine for a moment the potential of a robot controlled merely by one's thoughts! At the University of Minnesota, that robot already exists, and it is truly incredible to watch in action (www.youtube.com/watch?v=-h3kiws4I54). By developing a mind/robot interface that literally reads one's brain waves, these scientists have developed a mind-controlled flying robot that can negotiate an obstacle course of balloons scattered around the room. Their flying bot is controlled by a student wearing a skullcap with sixty-four brain-wave-reading sensors. The student simply thinks of making a fist with his right hand, and a computer reads the student's brain waves in his muscle cortex, while translating that command into the code for the robot that means "turn right." At that point, the flying bot turns right. When the student thinks of making two fists, the bot climbs straight up. Seeing this potential mind control of a robot enriches one's understanding of the future of our world.

But What Do I Teach With a Class Robot?

The answer to this question is simple: a robot will do virtually anything you tell it to do, and thus, robots can exemplify anything the teacher conceives, given certain limitations of computing power, size, strength, and the onboard sensors available. Robots can help teach almost anything! Here is a higher-level mathematics example of what a robot can demonstrate. In one RobotsLab lesson, quadratic functions are taught using a drone quadcopter robot to demonstrate what the mathematical equation means in a real-world example. The camera attached to the flying robot correlates the area viewed on camera with the mathematical algorithm and the associated graph. Specifically, when the robot is programmed with a quadratic equation, the quadcopter rises to specific, designated heights, demonstrating the visible relationship between the hovering robot and the area captured by the camera. As this example indicates, virtually anything that can be programmed into a robot (and virtually everything can) will provide content options for a lesson, not only in STEM subjects, but in many others as well.

Further, specific curricular activities and lesson plans that teachers can easily access are currently available, and more are developed daily. Most robots that have been developed for class instruction come with some type of curricular activities, so unlike Ivestor in the previous example, teachers will not need to develop these activities on their own. Box 8.3 presents several robots that are currently widely used in schools.

Box 8.3: Robots for the Classroom

WeDo (https://education.lego.com/en-us/lesi/elementary/lego-education-wedo/getting-started-with-wedo): WeDo is a LEGO-based robotics program focused specifically on STEM instruction that is intended for grades 2 through 5. The program incorporates LEGOs, digital learning, cognitive learning, and fine motor skills to help students construct simple machines in the classroom.

Using a simple icon-based coding language within the accompanying software and the LEGO bricks, students are shown how to create a variety of machines that include working motors, sensors, and a simple program to actually build movable, controllable robots. In that sense, even kindergarten students can now build simple working robots and other simple machines in the classroom.

Dash and Dot from Wonderworkshop (www.makewonder.com): These are small, blue, circular robots designed to help students as young as kindergarten begin the coding/robotics curriculum. Students use an icon-based coding language to program these robots for a variety of tasks, so nonreaders can do programming. Robots can be programmed to travel, turn, detect objects, light up, make sounds, and interact with each other. These robots range from $169, and kits and accessories range from $39 to $299. A brief video shares the opportunities these inexpensive robots provide in the kindergarten classroom: www.makewonder.com/robots/dashanddot. Also, a variety of lesson plans are available for these bots (https://teachers.makewonder.com/lessons).

Bee-Bot (www.bee-bot.us): Bee-Bot is an exciting robot that looks like a bumble bee and is designed specifically for younger children from preschool up through grade 2. This bot can teach many early learning skills, such as sequencing, simple mathematical concepts, estimation, early problem solving, and collaborative skills. Students not only learn a bit of coding (up to forty commands) while enjoying their play with the bot, but the Bee-Bot blinks and beeps as each command is completed, providing rewards for the young learners. This bot can also reinforce less tangible skills such as perseverance and collaboration (Yohana, 2014) and sells for just under $100.

EZ-Robot (www.ez-robot.com): EZ-Robot provides a variety of robots for STEM education that may be used across the grade levels. The AdventureBot is a small circular robot for beginners that sells for $149, whereas the JD Humanoid is a more complex humanoid robot listed at $429. Beginners learn logic, construction and soldering, electronics, and modular design, all while creating the robot, turning a toy shell into a personalized robot (Pressly, 2014; Yohana, 2014). This looks like a very promising product for schools, but there have been some shipping and supply problems. It seems to speak well of them that they cannot build the robots fast enough.

RobotLab (http://robotlab.com): RobotLab provides elementary and middle school teachers with a robotics kit, including a drone quadcopter, a tablet, a robotic arm, a spherical robot, a circular robot, and a set of lesson plans. Because this kit is preprogrammed, teachers do not need coding or programming skills to begin using this teaching tool in the classroom for demonstrating different STEM concepts. Nao is a small humanoid bot made by RobotLab. It is one of the more common bots in its price range found in schools. It was designed with STEM instruction in mind and has won endorsements from *EdTech Digest* and the Edison Awards. Students often

> respond better to humanoid robots, and Nao comes with many lesson options across the grade levels. Teachers might consider this when purchasing a robotics package. Nao allows for all the functions one would expect and sells for $9,500, though certain discounts are available to educators.

There is no shortage of predesigned coding/robotics lesson plans covering many content standards for all grade levels. Further, the scope of these materials will only grow in the future, so teachers are much more likely to be following curricular guidelines rather than developing activities by themselves. In fact, this content is growing so quickly that some proponents of coding/robotics instruction foresee a day when virtually all concepts classes can be represented with robotics lessons (Powel, 2014; Pressly, 2014; Schwartz, 2014; Yohana, 2014).

Steps for Teaching Coding/Robotics

As indicated previously, only about 10 percent of schools were teaching coding in 2015, and while a higher percentage was teaching robotics in one form or another, it is a safe assumption that many teachers are still new to both of these areas. Thus, the following steps will assist those who are beginning to teach coding and robotics.

Partner Up

Partner with another teacher or two in your school, and discuss how coding and robotics might fit into your teaching, with consideration on using these newly evolving tools in conjunction with your state's curricular standards. Investigate schools that your students might attend later. If you are in the elementary grades, find out what coding/robotics instruction might be taking place in the middle school, and consider using the same coding and robotics options they are using. Also, by partnering up, you might find that you can afford a more sophisticated effort, and this will help when you request school funds to purchase a robot.

Try Coding

For preschool and primary grades, codes are typically supplied with the robots. For elementary and higher grade teachers, I suggest that teachers download Scratch (or another free coding language) and just play with it. A variety of interesting tutorials are available free for Scratch on YouTube, and with a free coding language and good tutorials, virtually every teacher across the grade levels can gear up for this instructional strategy.

Seek School and District Support

As teachers begin to explore new instructional methods, I suggest that they approach both their school principal and the science and mathematics coordinators at the central office for support. While school budgets always seem to be limited, perhaps funds can be found for a small bot or for attendance at a conference on teaching coding and robotics, particularly if pairs of teachers show an interest together.

Pick up a Bot

At some point, teachers should purchase a simple, lower-end robot and explore its use in their classes. Even in higher grades, these inexpensive robots can capture students' attention and motivate them to explore coding and robotics. I urge teachers to explore the bots described here as well as others, since many options are available. Again, find out if others in the district are using specific coding languages and/or bots, and seek their advice.

Explore the Curriculum

Most bots come with some curricular lessons, and these should provide a good first step for teachers in considering how to use coding and robotics in class. Further, the Internet is loaded with lesson plans teachers should explore. These websites can provide a place to start: http://robotics.usc.edu/~agents/k-12/curricular.php, www.raspberrypi.org, and www.pinterest.com/weareteachers/stemsteam-lessons-activities-and-ideas.

Dive In

Teachers should not wait to become experts in coding and robotics prior to trying both in the classroom. Rather, after three or four hours of initial exploration to complete the steps above, teachers should dive in, using the simple coding languages and coding games presented here. You will have found plenty of lesson plan options for use in your subject and grade level, and the novelty of coding and robotics instruction will so engage the students that you will wonder why you didn't try this sooner.

Research on Coding and Robotics

As the discussion thus far has indicated, only limited scientific evidence is currently available on the efficacy of coding and robotics instruction, but this limited scientific evidence is supportive of coding/robotics instruction (Nugent, Barker, & Grandgenett, 2012; Schwartz, 2014; Yohana, 2014). Also, a great deal of additional anecdotal evidence is available that is supportive of these innovations for increasing student engagement (Bloom, 2015; Dredge, 2014; Fears & Patsalides, 2012; Powel, 2014; Pressly, 2014; Schwartz, 2014; Yohana, 2014). Of course, it is often the case that experimental evidence on efficacy lags behind anecdotal and testimonial evidence with new educational innovations, and when the anecdotal evidence is strong, teachers should not hesitate to explore the new instructional options. Schwartz (2014), for example, indicates that "students universally enjoy the robotic lessons, and respond very positively, often wishing to continue the lesson long after the lesson time has run out." Further, the extant literature presents no real downside (other than expense) to coding and robotics in the classroom (Bloom, 2015; Dredge, 2014; Fears & Patsalides, 2012; Powel, 2014; Pressly, 2014; Schwartz, 2014; Yohana, 2014).

Jerry Moldenhauer's positive teaching experiences with bots is typical (Schwartz, 2014). Moldenhauer has been using robots in his engineering classes at Eastside Memorial High School in Austin, Texas, for several years and reports that the bots boost engagement and help students grasp challenging concepts: "Kids are calculating the velocity of the robot without realizing they're using algebra. It really makes the connection better for them." Moldenhauer also suggests that the robot is especially useful for explaining the math behind more advanced engineering topics (Schwartz, 2014).

Summary

As this discussion makes clear, the twin instructional strategies of coding and robotics are soon coming to a class in your school, if they are not already there, and all teachers should begin their explorations of how these tools may help in their subject area and grade level. The only real limitations seem to be expense and teachers' imaginative use of these tools, and the field suggests a positive outlook on both. As bots become more ingrained in the school, prices will come down (as they did for computers), and with many millions of teachers joining the coding movement, there is no shortage of brainpower exploring how to move forward with robotics in the classroom in the foreseeable future.

Strategy 9

Individualized Computer-Driven Instruction: Khan Academy

Few teaching strategies will engage today's students more than completely individualized, computer-driven instruction (McDowell, 2016; Sparks, 2011). Of course, computers, apps, and modern software are merely tools that must be carefully integrated into effective instructional practices in the classroom, but when technology and individualized, computer-driven instruction are well integrated and tied intimately to ongoing class content, they become powerful instructional tools. Further, the use of these tools is not only expected by today's students, such use is virtually demanded.

For several decades now, in addition to thousands of simple educational apps (many of which are free!), various high-quality, self-directed, computer-based instructional programs have been available. Programs such as Successmaker, Khan Academy, Academy of READING, Academy of MATH, and Fast ForWord are designed as individualized curricular programs in reading, science, mathematics, or other subjects (Bender, 2017, 2013a). In these self-instructional programs, a student's academic skills are initially diagnosed, and the student is placed in a specific spot within the curriculum. Then the computer program delivers the instruction and monitors the student's progress, under teacher direction (McDowell, 2016).

In various workshops around the country, I have, jokingly, referred to individualized, computer-driven curricula as the "fire and forget missiles" of the modern classroom. Once a student is placed, the software leads the instruction and the teacher has the freedom to move on to other instruction with other students in the class. Of course, I would never suggest that teachers leave any student completely unmonitored during his or her work, even work that is computer driven. However, I use that *fire and forget* phrase to point out a subtle yet critical advantage to using individualized, computer-driven curricula in every classroom. With these curricula available on several computers within each class, the teachers in those classes can much more easily address the needs of students who are not functioning on grade level and, at the same time, address the needs of students who may be functioning way beyond grade level.

Many of these computer-driven curricula include diagnostic assessments that will place a student at his or her appropriate instructional level, such that a sixth grader in a sixth-grade mathematics class can receive both his core mathematics instruction at the sixth-grade level delivered by the teacher and some individualized, computer-driven instruction targeted at certain fourth- or fifth-grade skills that have not been mastered (Bender, 2013a). Further, students in the classroom who have already mastered a concept can spend time on the computer-driven program doing skills at a higher grade level, leaving the teacher free to address the needs of others.

Most of these individualized programs can be done daily by the students in a fifteen- to twenty-minute session, giving the teacher freedom to assign students to these programs as needed. I recommend use of one of these self-directed curricula in virtually all reading and mathematics classes, as well as other classes as the programs become available.

Of course, no teacher can possibly use all the computer-based technological innovations today. The sheer number of educational apps and individualized computer instructional programs make this virtually impossible. My general recommendation for teachers is to select one computer-driven curricula, or perhaps one new educational app every few months, and experiment with it multiple times in the classroom. This is one way for teachers to keep current with tech-based teaching and not become overwhelmed with the massive innovation in this area. While no teacher will use all of these tools, all teachers should use a number of them and continually experiment with others.

In this chapter, we will focus on only one frequently used, completely individualized instructional program: Khan Academy (www.khanacademy.org). I've selected this program for several reasons. It is free to use, and cost is a very important consideration for many teachers. Also, the content presented, while not including all subject areas, is very extensive in certain subjects, most notably mathematics—an area that Khan Academy covers thoroughly.

With that noted, there are many commercially available individualized instruction programs and several others that are free for teachers to access. Of course, many simple educational apps are freely available also, and while not all apps can be listed in this context, Box 9.1 does present some additional computer-driven individualized curricula that many teachers are using, and if you are not familiar with these, you should investigate those of interest in your teaching situation.

> **Box 9.1: Individualized Computer Instructional Curricula**
>
> **Fast ForWord** (www.scilearn.com): Fast ForWord is a very intensive, web-based, individualized reading intervention program that begins with diagnostic work involving discrimination among phonemes and moves on to higher-level reading skills. Targeted skills include phoneme discrimination and recognition, letter sounds, language, memory, attention, and processing skills. Founded in the most recent research on how brains function, this program requires significant time each day, but research results have documented efficacy of this program for improving reading skills.
>
> **SuccessMaker Math and SuccessMaker Reading** (www.pearsonschool.com/SuccessMaker): These are two of a number of commercially available instructional programs (K–8) that have received widespread research support. This is a comprehensive standards-based program that is partnered with online curricula in science and foreign language. Delivered online, SuccessMaker uses adaptive software to adjust the difficulty level automatically in response to the student's answers, thereby providing a series of questions at exactly the correct level. Reporting and assessment components ensure that the student is placed in the correct level and helps monitor progress.
>
> **ORIGO Stepping Stones** (http://resources.origoslate.com): Another program recommended by teachers (McDowell, 2016) is ORIGO Stepping Stones. This program provides a complete K–5, web-based, Common Core–aligned math curriculum, with an online teacher's edition. The program provides instruction and offers many ways to differentiate instruction. In addition to being aligned with the Common Core, the website suggests that this program is also modified and related to the curricula of several states, including Georgia, Texas, Florida, and Virginia. McDowell (2016) recommends this as a good way to move toward one-to-one instruction.
>
> **Academy of MATH and Academy of READING** (http://eps.schoolspecialty.com/products/online-programs): These are well-designed, well-researched, commercially available curricula (grades 2–12) that deliver significant academic progress. These web-based intervention programs include assessment and progress-monitoring components and provide a self-paced, personalized curriculum for each student depending on his or her exact needs. They have helped many students struggling in mathematics and

> reading, via various scaffolded, intensive, well-sequenced lessons targeted to the individual student's deficits.
>
> **SAS Curriculum Pathways** (sascurriculumpathways.com): This site provides extensive free online curricula with materials and instructional activities in English language arts, science, social studies, mathematics, and Spanish. While this is not a self-directed curricula, it is a high-quality supportive curricula that will enhance any classroom. These materials were developed by content experts in various subject areas and include high-quality graphic designs in 3-D presentations. The lesson activities herein are designed around the Common Core State Standards and are appropriate for grades 6 through 12. The curriculum is free and teachers need only log in to access the material. A brief tutorial video is available on the website. This is a free option that all teachers in these curricular areas and grades should consider.

Khan Academy

Khan Academy (www.khanacademy.org) is a free set of online curricular materials and videos for self-directed learning, including a full range of work in mathematics, chemistry, and physics, with some content in other subject areas such as astronomy, earth sciences, history, and health. This program is housed on the cloud, so students can access this anywhere (McDowell, 2016; Sparks, 2011; Toppo, 2011). As of 2016, the Khan Academy instructional videos had been viewed 365 million times worldwide, suggesting the widespread use of this program.

> Khan Academy is a free set of online curricular materials and videos for self-directed learning, including a full range of work in mathematics, chemistry, and physics, with some content in other subject areas such as astronomy, earth sciences, history, and health.

Khan Academy includes a nearly comprehensive mathematics curriculum, stressing all types of mathematical problems up through algebra. The program was developed by Sal Khan and is currently structured as a nonprofit organization, receiving funding from a variety of foundations. Organizations such as the Bank of America, the Bill and Melinda Gates Foundation, and Google have provided support in order to ramp up the service capabilities and make Khan Academy available at no cost to students and teachers worldwide (Sparks, 2011).

Three Components of Khan Academy

Khan Academy includes three major components: game-based online exercises, video demonstrations of specific content, and an individualized knowledge map to follow each student's progress over time. First, there are thousands of online learning exercises and game-based activities in mathematics, physics, and chemistry as well as academic content in other areas, and these provide the basis of Khan Academy. In mathematics, each exercise focuses on one specific type of mathematics problem (e.g., level-one linear equations: $4x + 5 = 29$). Students are presented with a number of examples of this one type of problem, and they are expected to solve them successfully. Rewards, in the form of digital merit badges, are presented for successful problem solution.

Second, the website presents video demonstrations that are partnered with each type of math problem. The videos show an interactive whiteboard where the various steps of the problem appear, as a disembodied voice guides the students through the problem while explaining the necessary steps. As the steps in the problem are discussed, the narrator explains the reasons for various steps and mathematics operations. When the online exercises are coupled with the support video demonstrations, this curriculum can function, for many students, as initial instruction on that type of mathematics problem. Over 3,700 videos are included in Khan Academy, presenting demonstrations of particular problems or other content on which students might need help, and more are added each month. Each video is a single chunk of topical information, and these range from seven to ten minutes each.

If a student attempts two or more examples of the problems without success, he or she can then review the accompanying video and learn how to solve that type of problem. Thus, the videos support the exercises. However, many teachers today utilize these videos as demo videos in their classes, and while that, in and of itself, is not a problem, some of those teachers may believe they are using Khan Academy to the fullest. While there is certainly nothing wrong with such usage, Khan Academy is primarily intended as a self-instruction online exercise curriculum. Therefore, the exercises and other aspects of Khan Academy should be employed to realize the maximum benefit from this tool (Bender, 2017).

Perhaps the most important aspect of Khan Academy is the third component: the knowledge map, which allows teachers or parents to capture a long-term picture of progress for each individual student. The knowledge map for an individual student presents something resembling a star chart that monitors each individual student's progress and suggests the next skills the student should attempt. When a student earns a digital merit badge, the badge appears on the knowledge map, documenting that the student has mastered that skill. Generally, students are highly motivated by the gaming and reward aspects of the online exercises. They seem to love the opportunity to add badges to their knowledge map. The more students challenge themselves, the more they achieve, and the more badges they earn. While some badges can be earned by successful completion of one or two exercises, other badges take many months or even years to earn.

Teacher Tools in Khan Academy

While Khan Academy is intended as a self-study curriculum, it does include certain tools for students' coaches. Parents, teachers, or others can serve as coaches and follow groups of students. In fact, many teachers around the world are using Khan Academy for their entire class (SRI, 2014). For example, teachers can place their entire class on a class profile and begin a knowledge map for every student. Because the individual student work and map is housed on the cloud, teachers can access each student's knowledge map as long as the teacher has that student's individual password. Teachers can then ensure that students are following a logical order in their online work, because the knowledge map itself suggests a logical progression of work.

Also, students' performance data are presented as an X/Y axis chart showing individual student growth over time. Using these teaching tools within Khan Academy, teachers will know immediately if a particular student is having difficulty and can assign other remedial work on that content or work directly with the student. Further, all of these data are saved so that teachers can review students' progress and make determinations about students' rates of progress relative to stated goals.

Steps in Implementing Khan Academy

Familiarize Yourself With Khan Academy

The first step in using Khan Academy is to become familiar with it. A teacher should play around on the website for thirty minutes or so and look at the resources for teachers. Carefully consider the fit between Khan Academy coverage of content and terminology and the content and terminology used in your math or science curriculum. Also consider the knowledge map and possible use of that in your class. The website presents many tools for coaches to use as they guide students through Khan Academy learning experiences.

Sign Your Students In

Khan Academy is most effective when teachers and students use it in a comprehensive fashion. Ultimately, teachers should register their entire class, including students who have no computer or Internet access at home, and encourage students to use all the main components. Working at home, students can then use the gaming online exercises to study and practice any particular type of problem, while referring to the support videos as necessary. Also, each problem in the game-based practice sessions is broken down into simple step-by-step instructions, and feedback is immediate, should students experience difficulty with a particular type of problem. Once they demonstrate their ability to do that type of problem on several specific problems, a merit badge appears on their knowledge map.

Use Khan Academy in Class

While Khan Academy is structured as a stand-alone teaching tool, having students access and use it in the classroom two or three times initially is recommended, because in those in-class sessions, teachers can troubleshoot any issues that arise. Teachers should place students at the level of material they need to master, even if it is several years below grade level. This usually results in a fairly wide range of skills, but it does address individual student's needs. I usually recommend that teachers use Khan Academy in class two or three times for twenty minutes or so, to ensure students are comfortable with it. During those initial sessions, teachers should point out how the components, online exercises, videos, and the knowledge map all fit together.

As an alternative in-class implementation idea, teachers can refer students to a Khan Academy video when they ask a question in class. This will help get students in the habit of seeking answers for themselves in this resource. Viewing these videos is also a great partner activity in class.

Share Khan Academy With Parents

Khan Academy is a great tool to help parents work with their children in mathematics. Some parents may fear math, since they may not have done well in mathematics themselves, and in those situations, Khan Academy can help parents feel more comfortable helping with homework. I have often recommended it to parents in that regard.

Consider Class Time for Khan Academy

Some teachers provide 20 percent of their class time for Khan Academy individual work, while others do this for thirty minutes twice a week. Of course, the more time kids spend with Khan Academy, the more useful it will be. However, I often recommend an alternative that takes no class time, after the initial two or three in-class sessions. In that scenario, teachers can choose to introduce it in two or three sessions, and then stop using class time for Khan Academy. Research has documented that for many students, Khan Academy is rewarding enough that they will continue to use it outside of class, and teachers who don't spend class time using this tool can still offer daily reinforcement for outside use of Khan Academy.

For example, teachers might ask, "Who earned a merit badge in Khan Academy this past weekend? Great! Let's give Jonathan, Jamel, and Alison a round of applause! Now, did anyone earn more than one merit badge?" Another option is the use of more structured reinforcement. Teachers might say, "OK. Every Monday you guys earn ten minutes of computer game time if the class as a whole has earned at least twenty merit badges! Let's count off and see how we've done!" Many teachers have stated that this will keep many students quite motivated to earn merit badges on their own. Thus, a little verbal reinforcement or class applause can help keep students moving through Khan Academy, even when no class time is devoted to it.

Continually Check Knowledge Maps

The individual students' knowledge maps are the key to student achievement in Khan Academy. Because all of the students' work is cloud based, both teachers and students can access the knowledge maps and track progress. Further, anecdotal testimonies indicate that perhaps 5 percent to 10 percent of the class will begin to work on skills that are beyond their grade level (Bender, 2017; SRI, 2014), and while these will typically be the highly skilled students, one can only imagine what this would do to the average achievement scores in mathematics for the class or the school. It is the knowledge map within Khan Academy that will make this possible (Toppo, 2011). Clearly, earning these badges and seeing them appear on their individual knowledge map is quite motivating for most students. For students who do excel, additional classroom or schoolwide recognition is always recommended.

Use Khan for a Flipped Lesson

Using Khan Academy, teachers might wish to try flipping a class or two. Simply pick a topic and assign the appropriate Khan Academy video. Teachers can then have students engage in a class project or knowledge application type of activity for the entire class period. Coupling the flipped class idea with Khan Academy has proven to be a winning strategy in many mathematics classes and more than a few science classes.

Ultimately, each teacher's goals in using Khan Academy should be both increasing engagement and academic achievement, as well as instilling in all students the belief that they can seek out, find, and master difficult academic content on their own. In fact, those are excellent goals for all educational endeavors in the 21st century.

Research on Khan Academy

Early evidence suggests that Khan Academy is an effective self-instructional curriculum that students can use as a self-directed learning tool, and both students and teachers responded very positively to Khan Academy (Sparks, 2011; SRI, 2014; Toppo, 2011). In fact, students are highly motivated to work on Khan Academy, and research documents that many students even begin to complete this work at home, when no assignment has been made (SRI, 2014). While research is ongoing, the website (www.khanacademy.org) presents a number of research results and several testimonials as anecdotal evidence of efficacy, including examples from Spain, Ireland, Poland, and the United States.

In a more detailed study, SRI International (2014) investigated the use of Khan Academy in a number of different schools across the grade levels. Their results demonstrated that when Khan Academy was used to supplement in-class instruction, the students showed improved attitudes toward mathematics and increased math achievement. Further, the SRI (2014) research demonstrated high levels of student engagement in all of the test classrooms using Khan Academy. In student surveys, students reported that they enjoyed their "Khan time" more than traditional mathematics classes. Further, the majority of teachers were happy with their Khan Academy experience and believed this program helped them support students of varying abilities more effectively (SRI, 2014). Mathematics self-concept also improved while math anxiety decreased when Khan Academy was implemented.

We should also note one subtle lesson resulting from Khan Academy, a personal commitment to lifelong learning. A self-directed curriculum such as Khan Academy sends a message to students: "It is your job to learn!" While schools have historically presented curriculum to groups of students of the same age, covering content at the same time for all, the self-directed instruction in Khan Academy offers an alternative opportunity—student-driven learning. I would love to believe that all students graduating next year from high school would graduate knowing that, if they needed to know something, they could find that information on the web and learn it themselves! That is a potent message—that your learning is your responsibility—and this provides a compelling reason for implementing Khan Academy or another self-directed learning curriculum. In this fashion, the systematic use of Khan Academy for all students will foster that insight, and thus such use of Khan Academy holds many positive implications for lifelong learning for the 21st century.

With these advantages noted in the research, several concerns have arisen with the use of Khan Academy. First, the video demonstrations within this program are not well developed. The videos are not interactive in any fashion and present merely a math problem on a whiteboard and a teacher voice explaining the problem. This type of noninteractive instruction is quite dated and represents work done on chalkboards since the early 1900s.

Next, content coverage in Khan Academy is quite spotty in many subject areas, including some of the sciences, though the area of mathematics is developed enough to be considered comprehensive. While all teachers should explore using Khan Academy, mathematics teachers will find it more useful, simply because of content coverage.

Finally, in an era in which deep conceptual understanding is being stressed in most state curricula, Khan Academy is almost exclusively procedural in nature. The curriculum emphasizes step-by-step problem solution, with only one solution strategy presented. Also, each type of problem is presented in isolation with little emphasis on when students might use that specific mathematics skill in real-world scenarios. In contrast, modern math instruction stresses finding alternative correct ways to solve the problem, in an effort to develop deeper mathematical understandings.

Summary

Many individualized, computer-based instructional software programs are available, and many are effective in developing both student engagement and student learning. Of those available, Khan Academy has received much of the recent attention because it is free for all users. While schools are still struggling to become completely Wi-Fi friendly and to obtain computers for all students, neither is a requirement for using Khan Academy. As long as students can get online somewhere in the school, they can use Khan Academy, and such individualized supplemental instruction will foster impressive student engagement and academic growth.

I strongly recommend that all teachers consider implementing Khan Academy or one of the other self-directed, individualized computer-based instructional programs. Making students independent, self-directed learners through constant use of a self-directed curriculum is perhaps one of the most important lessons that educators can impart, so this is certainly worth the time.

Strategy 10

Storyboarding for Comprehension: Comic Life

Teachers have long used the storyboarding strategy to teach comprehension of content and, specifically, sequencing of related content. Decades ago, teachers learned to cut up the comic stories from the newspaper to assist students with understanding the critical nature of sequencing, cause and effect, and the components of a story (introduction, characters, plot explanation or story problem, sequence of events, climax of the story, and story ending). Recently, students' interest in comics has grown, as has teachers' use of comic strips for classroom instruction (Lyga, 2006).

Storyboarding activities that utilize comic strips involve the student in the creative process of detecting or creating a story line focused on the content under study, and this typically enhances student engagement and understanding of that content (Lyga, 2006; Stillwell, 2011). Even in subject areas such as history or science, development of a story line can greatly enhance students' engagement with the content and ultimately each student's understanding.

> Storyboarding involves the student in the creative process of detecting or creating a story line involving the content under study, and this typically enhances student engagement and understanding.

For example, following the time line of the development of atomic energy (beginning with Einstein's development of the theory of relativity through the development of Fermi's atomic reactor in Chicago to the development of the atomic bombs in Los Alamos, New Mexico, during World War II and ultimately the use of nuclear power to generate electricity) will engage students and facilitate a deeper understanding of the science of the atom. As students develop a comic story following this scientific development, they will learn the sequence described above and how one development built on the previous accomplishments.

Of course, comic strips have been popular with students for many decades, but more recently, graphic novels have captured students' imaginations. Graphic novels are rather long stories told in a comic-book-like set of cartoon images that are often presented as a small book that is usually between 50 and 150 pages. They present a short novel using both text and cartoon pictures. Introducing written comics or graphic novels into the classroom, along with the option of student creation of these comics, will increase engagement with the content under study, improve writing skills, and focus many students more readily on the content at hand (Stillwell, 2011).

Comics and graphic novels can be used to help students in both reading and writing. For example, comics can serve as a bridge to help students practice complex reading skills before transferring those reading skills to larger texts or literature assignments (National Council of Teachers of English, 2005). Allowing students to use comics in the classroom provides them with an opportunity to visualize what they are reading, and this format for reading instruction will help many reluctant and struggling readers succeed (National Council of Teachers of English, 2005). Following the format of a comic also helps students understand the plotline. In this format, students are able to see the basic story elements and follow the story or even create their own work (National Council of Teachers of English, 2005).

Today, teachers are using various relatively inexpensive software programs to facilitate their instruction with comic strips. A variety of software programs are available via a simple Google search, but one program that has captured wide teacher interest is the software tool called Comic Life (http://comiclife.com).

Comic Life

Comic Life is an inexpensive, user-friendly software tool that will help teachers and students create their own comic strips using the academic content from a variety of subjects. Students can use virtually any content when developing their storyboard comic strips, while allowing students to plan the story and customize the characters and background. With Comic Life, students become intricately involved in every step of the creation process from planning to completion of the storyboard (Lyga,

2006). Comic Life is compatible with Windows, Mac, and iPad software and hardware, making this usable in almost any classroom.

> Comic Life is a user-friendly software program that helps teachers and students create their own comic strips using the class content.

Creation options with Comic Life are nearly endless. Students can drag and drop pictures from digital cameras, cartoons, computer web cameras, scanned photos, hand-drawn images that can be photographed, or any other digital images into their comic strip. They then add dialogue to create their story. All of this work can be either individual or partner/team based. Students then add text boxes, thought balloons, speech boxes, or annotations to hold the written content, and they can even use various filters to customize their uploaded pictures, thus making those digital images appear to be hand drawn. Allowing students to work through the visual components of the creation process on a team is likely to help them practice visualizing stories, verbalize their visions, and in turn, strengthen their understanding of the content (Lyga, 2006).

The options for integrating Comic Life software into subject areas are virtually endless. Teachers can find a plethora of these ideas at www.comiclife.com/education. Box 10.1 lists several examples.

> **Box 10.1: Using Comic Life for Storyboarding in Subject Areas**
>
> English teachers can have students write an original story or play in comic book form. Alternatively, they may assume the role of a character from a story they read in class and use Comic Life to help explain that character to others, emphasizing the character's thoughts, feelings, and actions.
>
> Health teachers can use Comic Life to tell the story of various systems in the body, such as how blood circulates through the heart, lungs, and the rest of the body, or how air is taken in via the respiratory system.
>
> Geography teachers may require students to use geography content for the travels of trash in gyres in the oceans. Also, teachers may have students develop a Comic Life travel guide to explore various regions in the United States or other countries.
>
> Science teachers might have students plan and create a comic strip to explain the experimental process they followed in a recent lab class and discuss what would have happened if a particular step had been left out.
>
> History teachers can have students create a comic strip detailing a time line of events for a specific historical period.

A Classroom Example: Using Comic Life

Mr. Sanders taught students in the fifth grade and wanted to increase student engagement in his science class. While his text and curriculum supplemental materials were mildly interesting, he believed that he could better engage his students if he could present the chapter content as stories of individual scientists seeking to solve specific problems. He mentioned this to a co-worker, who then told him about Comic Life. Mr. Sanders began to explore the option of using this strategy once or twice during each two-week unit of study.

As an initial assignment, he created three-person teams and provided each team with ten to fifteen content statements as the basis for the comic strip. For a given unit of study, he decided that two comic strips could be developed, covering different content, so several of the teams were developing comic strips on the same content during a given unit. The students then had to storyboard that content, research and select appropriate digital images for the content, and then develop a finished comic strip for use by the class.

Like all assignments, some of the teams did an excellent job, while others seemed to struggle with the assignment. Mr. Sanders quickly determined, within the first assignment, which students grasped the concept of telling a story to present scientific content. He realized that it was important to focus on how a scientist or group of scientists developed a theory, tested it, and then moved on to the next step in development of knowledge. Also, Mr. Sanders noted that the students enjoyed this type of assignment and seemed much more engaged in the science content when Comic Life was used within the unit.

Steps in Using Comic Life

Choose a Purchase Plan

The Comic Life website offers a variety of purchase plans, most of which are reasonably priced. Using Comic Life in your individual classroom may be as little as $20 to $25, and a free exploration option is available.

Practice With Comic Life

You should spend some time learning the features of the software prior to introducing this to your students. You might wish to develop a comic strip to use in class as a part of your next lesson. You should also review the tutorials available. To engage students at a high level, put digital photos of local scenes that students many recognize into the first comic strip they see, as long as those images relate to the content under study. This will heighten student interest and make them focus on the content to see what else they may recognize as a local scene.

As you practice with Comic Life, you should determine what level of creativity you are aiming for on the part of the students. For students new to this creative experience or for younger students, the teacher may identify most of the components of the comic strip and provide those to the students when giving the assignment, whereas older students, or students with more experience with this software, may be expected to do much more of that work themselves. Also, consider whether Comic Life should be an individual assignment or a small-group project.

Choose a Template

To make this software user friendly, it offers over 2,000 templates that may be used for the initial comic strips. The first task is choosing a template and background for your creation. These templates are categorized to make your selection easier, and there is even a category devoted to education where you can find templates for comic strips about science projects, time lines, and historical events.

Identify and Upload Photos

Photos and images provide the backdrop for the comic strip and should present the action involved in the story line. Depending on the age of your students, you have the option of either uploading a selection of digital images (which may be advisable in lower grades) or having students search and retrieve them as part of their assignment. Millions of images are available from the Internet, but searching for exactly the right image can be a creative and instructional act in and of itself. Remind older students to go beyond Google and to search collections that may be found in the Library of Congress and topical museums. Older students can easily upload photos from the hard drive of the computer or any other digital source. Depending on the age of the students, some teachers might wish to include a brief lesson on using copyrighted material. Once the photos are identified and uploaded, students can move to the next step of actually planning the comic strip.

Developing Text and a Plotline

In addition to images, students will have the option of including text in the comic strips, and text components provide the best opportunity for presenting new content information to be mastered. Some assignments in various topical areas such as history or science may require that the content be presented within a story or plotline, whereas other topics may necessitate a comic strip that is more informational or tutorial in nature. Some content can be developed as sequenced, cause-and-effect stories.

Like the previous digital components, teachers may wish to suggest a plotline or, for informational comics, a list of content concepts or ideas that should be covered in the comic strip. In some comic strips, sequencing is critical, whereas in others, subjects may be included based on topical similarity, and again, arranging the content information in a way that makes sense is both a creative process and an excellent instructional assignment.

Storyboarding the Comic Strip

A storyboard serves the same purpose in developing a video or comic strip that an outline serves in writing a theme. Again, depending on the age of the students, teachers may either plan the storyboard or outline for the comic strip or have the students develop those components within the assignment. The storyboard will be based on the components identified above: the text describing the overall message or story theme to be included and an array of digital photos or drawings that can be used to communicate that theme. Once the pictures are uploaded, all that is required is a simple drag and drop to place them into the appropriate locations on the comic strip, as suggested in the storyboard.

Enter Text Content

Text content associated with the digital images is typically included within a text balloon on the various pictures. Developing the text will, of course, follow the story line or topical content and should be specifically related to each image. When text content seems to be too long for a specific image, the creators may wish to add a second, similar picture, and place some of the text there. In Comic Life, students can stretch and modify the text containers to fit appropriately within their comic strip. This freedom for customization gives students a sense of independence and promotes creativity within each assignment.

Publish the Comic Strip

Each comic strip represents a student creation and should be published widely. For example, printing these comic strips in hard copy and placing them on display in the class will increase student engagement with the content. These comic strips may also be placed on the class or school website or a class wiki for sharing with parents and other students. In some cases, comics that were developed by previous students may provide the teacher with content for use today. It is important to remember that publication indicates an intentional valuing of student work, and therefore, publication will increase student engagement throughout the year.

Research on Storyboarding With Comic Life

Research has shown the efficacy of storyboarding using Comic Life in various academic areas (Artigliere, 2016; Thacker, 2016; Lyga, 2006). Comic Life has been used successfully individually, in small groups, or as a whole-class activity (Thacker, 2016; National Council of Teachers of English, 2005). This tool has been used across all grade levels, even in college instruction. While Comic Life has been used more in language arts and literacy areas, the research does support its use in all areas. Also several of these articles specifically indicate that students' engagement is higher when Comic Life is used within the subject content (Thacker, 2016; Lyga, 2006).

Summary

Storyboarding is a teaching strategy that will enhance understanding, and Comic Life is an excellent software tool to facilitate storyboarding that can increase student engagement in any subject area at any grade. By using Comic Life, the teacher will invigorate the class and provide content instruction coupled with student creativity. Many tools can be found on the Comic Life website that are specific to various subject areas, and teachers should certainly explore these options as they implement this storyboarding tool across several instructional units. Also, I suggest that teachers explore multiple options for implementation ranging from individual usage to group projects.

Strategy 11

Animation

Animation is another tool that can be used in almost any classroom to engage the attention of students (Barak, Ashkar, & Dori, 2016; Zimmerman, 2014). Animation involves the creation of one or a series of attention-grabbing cartoon characters that make academic content come alive in virtually any subject and enrich the visual representations associated with subject content. Thus, this strategy can enhance long-term memory (Stansbury, 2013; Moreno, 2009; Zimmerman, 2014).

Of course, teachers have long recognized that learning involves not only focused attention but also concentration on the specifics of the content and ultimately transfer of that content into long-term memory. Animations enhance each of these aspects of learning (Kuchimanchi, 2013). In short, animation offers an exciting way to present topical information and make otherwise dull subject matter come to life, by adding movement, illustrating processes over time, and showing relationships (Stansbury, 2013; Moreno, 2009; Zimmerman, 2014).

> Animation is the creation of one or a set of attention-grabbing cartoon characters that make content come alive in virtually any subject and enrich the visual representations associated with subject content.

In today's classrooms, tools are available that allow both teachers and students across the grade levels to animate the content under study, providing a powerful technology for learning (Hatten, 2014; Kuchimanchi, 2013; Moreno, 2009; Stansbury, 2013). Stansbury (2013) describes animation as a universal language that reaches virtually all students, including lower-achieving students or others with varying backgrounds, languages, or academic strengths. In addition, allowing students to learn through animation lowers the intimidation aspect of the content in difficult areas like science or mathematics, thus providing a less threatening learning environment. Finally, many teachers have reported that students are more engaged and retain more content material when they are able to creatively express themselves through animation (Detroit Schools, 2011; Stansbury, 2013; Zimmerman, 2014).

Animation in the Classroom

Animation can provide the teacher with an interesting way to present information, but when animation is used by the students themselves, student creativity explodes! Student animations may involve a one-time cartoon creation or the development of an avatar, an animated digital character that represents the teacher, the student, or even a scientist or historical figure in multiple animations. When appropriate content-oriented text is developed for the avatar, the digital character comes to life and presents that text or dialogue, making this a highly effective instructional tool.

> An avatar is an animated digital character that represents oneself or another figure and can be made to engage in prerecorded dialogue in multiple animations.

The use of avatars and animation is limited only by the imagination of the teacher and students and can be used in a variety of classroom instructional activities (Hatten, 2014; Moreno, 2009; Stansbury, 2013). Following are several options for animation in the classroom.

- **Present material:** Students can use their avatar to present their oral reports, book reviews, or theme papers. This is an excellent tool for student engagement, particularly for shy and reluctant students, who can be encouraged to present in a much more entertaining fashion. Student or teacher animations can be added to PowerPoint presentations, and animations can be developed by students at virtually every grade level. Even debates and persuasive arguments can be done via animation.

- **Study with animations:** Animations, like all digital files, can be saved, such that reports from students' avatars might be uploaded to class wikis or blogs for use or reference by other students. Teachers and students might create a portfolio of avatar presentations and share that with parents or other teachers. Students can also access their peers' avatars to review content material throughout the year.

- **Make assignments and grade with animations:** Within some animation websites, teachers are presented with various instructional options. For example, as a part of the Voki Classroom (www.voki.com), teachers can outline an assignment on the website for students to complete. Once they have completed their assignment with their avatar, the teacher can go online, access the animation, and evaluate the work.

- **Teach patterns and processes in mathematics and science:** Various mathematics and scientific processes are best illustrated with movement. Therefore, animations can be critical in understanding processes such as planet rotation, life cycles, steps in solving a linear equation, moon phases, erosion, or even genetics across multiple generations (Hatten, 2014). Various math concepts can be illustrated with moving animations, including skip counting, the relationship between addition and multiplication, or creation of algorithms. In this sense, animation lends itself to the effort to teach the deeper relationships that are emphasized in modern mathematics instruction.

- **Use student avatars for proofreading:** Students can check their papers and reports by listening to their avatar read it. As students hear their avatar speaking, they can read along, and this partner reading process makes errors more obvious. Students can then make corrections based on the avatar's speaking, by adding a period or rewriting the text a bit, for example (Bender & Waller, 2013).

- **Use avatars for recitation:** Some students are shy about reading in front of the class or reciting their own written assignments such as poems or stories. Avatars can be used to do that type of assignment and alleviate that problem. It will also help struggling readers, who can practice recording their voice for the avatar several times to get it exactly right (Bender & Waller, 2013). When avatars read, students and teachers can then jointly analyze the reading fluency rates. The avatars can also be used for repeated readings of the same text.

- **Use animations to develop automaticity with math facts:** Teachers might encourage students to recite math facts using their avatar. These animations can be uploaded to a class wiki so that there is a bank of facts for the entire class to use as a memory task. Students can also use their avatars to explain any tips and tricks for remembering such math facts (Bender & Waller, 2013).

- **Use avatars to represent scientists or historical figures:** Have students choose a historical figure and produce an avatar to represent that figure and explain why that historical figure acted in a certain fashion.

For example, an animated John Adams might explain his theory of governance for other members of the Continental Congress.

Animation can be used in a limitless number of ways in the classroom. Creative teachers and students together are likely to find additional uses for animations. As these instructional avenues are explored more fully, students get excited about animation and become much more engaged with the subject content.

A wide variety of animation apps and software programs are available for classroom use, as presented in Box 11.1. Some of these offer free use options for teachers, while others offer both free and fee-for-service options. Teachers might explore any of these as all options are currently used in schools, and fifteen to twenty minutes on the various websites will give a teacher a sense of what might be involved in learning the software. Further, if a teacher is already using a particular animation tool, teachers should consider using the same option, since that would essentially ensure the novice teacher of some in-school support.

> **Box 11.1: Animation Tools for Teachers**
>
> Many software options are available for animation, and the related websites offer information for teachers (TEEContributor, 2011).
>
> **Toontastic** (https://toontastic.withgoogle.com): This is a widely used animation site, with over 7 million cartoons created in over 200 countries. Using drag-and-drop options, kids create and animate virtually anything in a small amount of time. This is a great place to begin with simple animations for beginning teachers and younger students.
>
> **ABCya.com:** ABCya.com is a free gaming website for young children that provides games and apps for use under the guidance of parents and teachers. No personal information is collected at this site. Here, students can draw pictures in frames and present them in sequence.
>
> **Animation Desk:** This app for Apple and Android allows students to begin animation immediately, using a tablet. The screens of the app resemble professional animator tools and allow for work in each frame of an animation individually, making this very useful for older, more experienced students.
>
> **DoInk.com:** This website allows students of various ages to create an animation and then clone it to place it in a sequence of scenes. Thus, this is a great site for creation of larger project-based learning assignments focused on specific content.
>
> **GoAnimate.com:** This website is appropriate for middle and high school learners, and many teachers use this to create animated videos for teaching purposes. The site provides various lesson plans that can be explored. This tool also provides the option of comic strip creation, and the site is relatively easy to use.

A Case Study: Animation to Increase Student Engagement

Mrs. Fields taught eighth-grade students in an earth science class in middle school, and she wanted to find a way to increase students' engagement with the topic. After discussions with other teachers, she decided to try two strategies and see which increased engagement more. She further decided to do an action research project within her classroom and compare the impact of animation on student attitudes toward the various instructional units. In order to measure student engagement, she devised a two-question student survey using a Likert scale (see figure 11.1), which she administered once toward the end of several instructional units during the fall of the year.

	Strongly Agree				Strongly Disagree
I enjoyed the way this instructional unit was presented!	5	4	3	2	1
I was more excited about this unit than some others!	5	4	3	2	1

Figure 11.1: Survey using Likert scale.

In order to score this survey, Mrs. Fields added the raw score of the two questions for each student (creating a student score ranging from 2 to 10), and then averaged those totals for the entire class. Higher scores represented higher student satisfaction with the instruction in a given unit and thus (presumably) increased student engagement. Because she taught three separate periods of earth science, she chose to collect those data for each of those three classes individually.

She began using the survey during the first two instructional units in the fall, which she considered a baseline score. Then she began a video-viewing instructional strategy wherein at least two content videos were viewed in each instructional unit. Finally, she began using student animation in each class for at least two days in each unit. This offered her the option for a multiple baseline type of action research design. She then charted those data for eight weeks. The final data are presented in figure 11.2 (page 124).

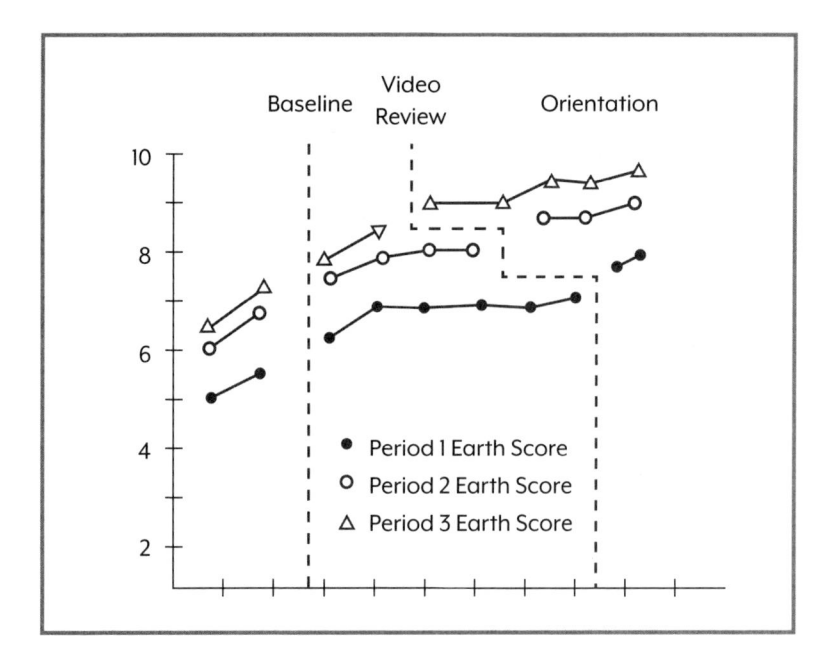

Figure 11.2: Student engagement data.

As these data show, both video-viewing assignments and animation assignments tended to increase students' positive attitudes toward the instructional units. All of the class averages for instructional units that included video viewing are higher than the baseline instructional units. However, the data also reveal that student attitudes toward the subject content was highest when an animation assignment was provided within an instructional unit. Thus, this action research suggests that Mrs. Fields did increase student engagement, as measured by student attitudes, by using animation in the classroom.

Creating an Avatar Animation

Here I present more detailed guidelines on using one animation option called Voki, but these guidelines will generally be appropriate for whatever animation option you choose. A Voki is an individual avatar created by the student or teacher and subsequently used for animation throughout a given school year. The Voki website (www.voki.com) provides excellent support for teachers, and there is a YouTube video (www.youtube.com/embed/304rQXcBrp4) that presents this teaching option for second grade through high school students. Teachers may wish to view the video to get additional ideas on using animation.

Learn the Animation Software

At the Voki website, a wide variety of tutorials is available to help you get started. Some of these were created by teachers using Voki. Whatever animation option you choose, you should plan to spend thirty to forty-five minutes using one or more of the available tutorials and then create an animation yourself. This will help you understand the process and how these student avatars may be used in the classroom.

Select Your Level of Service

Some animation apps are free, but in most of the more involved animation software programs, teachers are offered various levels of service, some of which are fee options. For example, the Voki Classroom is a fee-based service, which is $29.95 per year (or $2.50 monthly) for one class. Of course, you may wish to experiment with the free service for a while prior to jumping into the subscription service. Follow the steps on the website to sign up—you will need to give your name and email and create a password. You can opt to sign up for two years and receive a pricing that lowers the cost to $1.87 a month.

Create an Animation

In some animation software, the creation of the first animation by the teacher is one component of the early tutorials, but if it isn't in the software you choose, I do recommend that the teacher create an initial animation. In Voki, you should create an avatar. Of course, for these software programs, creation is very user friendly. For example, students as young as kindergarten and first grade have successfully created their own avatars. When you are ready to create a new Voki avatar, you will need to decide on four basic things including the avatar's style, look (customization), voice, and background, and while different terms may be used in other animation programs, the concepts are the same.

Tweak the Look of the Animation or Avatar

Animations and avatars tend to be continually used, so tweaking the look of the animation or avatar is critical—you want a look that you will be happy with all year. Students have options when creating avatars to make their character an animal, an edgy oddball, a VIP, a historical figure they admire, or anything else. Once they have chosen an avatar character, they can change the character's clothing, hair, and mouth style, and even add accessories. Students can change (or tweak) the color of the character's eyes, hair, skin, and mouth to create the final look of their avatar. Teachers should set a time limit for this part of the students' avatar creation assignment, in order to get to the academic components of the assignment.

Select a Background

Selecting a background for the animation involves more than merely tweaking the look, since backgrounds help tell the story of the animation and thus should represent the content accurately. For example, in the John Adams example, one should select a room background without electric lighting, since such lighting didn't exist in that time period. Teachers should discuss theme and content to be learned using the animation. If students are creating an avatar for an oral report in science, they may wish to choose a scientist in a lab. If they study a foreign culture, they may wish to choose a background representing the chosen culture. Thinking about and using appropriate background customization will give students that much more comprehensive coverage of the content material in context.

Select a Voice Option

Many animations provide different voice options, and many let students record their own voice. In Voki, students can record their voice or upload an audio file, call in to the website and record their voice through the phone, or simply type in content text, and the software will turn the text into speech. While typing in the content is usually much faster, having students use their actual voices can be quite motivating.

Create Content for the Avatar

By inputting text or voice, the teacher and students are creating the dialogue content for the avatar or animation. This is where teachers and students can determine the level of content to be presented. Thus, after a voice option is selected, students will need to create and input the content for the animation. Students can create a dialogue that is focused on deep learning content and upload that dialogue, or they may merely create a brief, introductory type of content, depending on the intended use of the animation.

Publish the Avatar

Publication of student animated creations is the motivating force that increases student engagement, so publication of animations is a must. When a student has finished an animation or avatar presentation, and the product has been graded and approved by the teacher, he or she should publish it for the widest audience possible. In Voki, the student simply clicks "Publish" and the website will provide the teacher and student with a code that can be emailed or uploaded to a class blog, wiki, or school website for parents to see. Once the avatar has been reviewed by the teacher, uploading the avatars to other websites is an easy process. These student-created avatars an also be set to private, such that only the student and teacher can see them.

Research on Animation

Research on the use of animation has been ongoing for a number of years and is almost universally positive. Use of animations in various academic subjects results in increased comprehension of the subject content as well as increased student engagement (Barak, Ashkar, & Dori, 2016; Hatten, 2014; Moreno, 2009; Rosen, 2009; Zhang, 2012). Further, student attitudes toward their learning are enhanced and engagement is increased when animations are used routinely within the curriculum (Ruffini, 2009; Zhang, 2012; Zimmerman, 2014). Moreover, most teachers indicate that animation is relatively easy to master and that once they expose their students to student-developed animations, the students will move forward on their own (Barak, Ashkar, & Dori, 2016; Moreno, 2009).

Summary

As noted previously, research on the use of animation is universally supportive of this teaching strategy, showing that students love using animation for learning. Animation will increase student engagement and understanding of the content, so teachers should certainly explore the use of animation in the classroom. Moreover, for shy and withdrawn students, this may be the most powerful tool teachers have to help integrate those socially reluctant students with the rest of the class. Clearly, animation is a teaching strategy that all teachers should explore.

SECTION III

Collaborative Instruction to Increase Engagement

Educators have long realized that few instructional strategies will increase student engagement as well as students working collaboratively. In joint work assignments, all human beings tend to either become more focused on the task at hand or engage in some form of social play. If teachers can help students maintain focus in joint activities, the engagement level will tend to go up and this will increase learning. This section discusses a variety of instructional approaches based on collaborative work that will increase student engagement in virtually any subject area. These include blogging, using Twitter or other social media in the classroom, using wikis, peer tutoring, and role-playing in the classroom.

Strategy 12

Blogging

Teachers have used journaling as an instructional strategy for many years. A blog is an online journal where posted information from both teachers and students is arranged and archived in reverse chronological order (Blog Basics, 2012; Ferriter & Garry, 2010). Using a blog, teachers and students can work individually or together to create self-published content on the topic under study and create links to other documents and videos online (Richtel, 2012). Blogs provide the opportunity for collaborative work in that the students are usually required to leave comments on each other's work. Also, when teachers create classroom blogs focused on the academic content, students are able to interact with that content long after the school day has ended. Finally, given the desire of most students for online interaction with their friends, most students enjoy blogging as a classroom strategy (Lampinen, 2013; Richtel, 2012).

> A blog is an online journal where posted information from both teachers and students is arranged and archived in reverse chronological order.

In terms of student engagement, few strategies are more effective for increasing engagement than blogging. Richtel (2012) points out that students are much more motivated to complete homework, classwork, or student projects when those assignments are posted to a class blog, because they realize that many people are likely to see and review that work. Further, students are demonstrating by their out-of-class behavior that they enjoy social interactions online, and teachers should certainly tap into that student behavior by using blogging in the classroom. The general popularity of social networking sites demonstrates students' desires to be connected, and class blogs meet that desire for socially mediated learning by offering high levels of student-to-student interaction (Bender & Waller, 2013; Richtel, 2012).

To use a blog in the classroom, teachers simply create a blog for the class, write a post about a particular topic, and have students respond to that posted entry on the blog itself. This can be a simple assignment for all students or as a group task for small groups of students. Students should be required to post responses to both the teacher's post and the entries of other students, and in that fashion, assignments on the blog tend to be quite collaborative in nature. This assignment also goes well beyond the class, since students can log onto blogs and make blog entries via personal computers, mobile devices, or any other Wi-Fi capable device. Students also have the option to follow blogs so that the students would be notified via email whenever there is a change on the blog itself.

Using a Classroom Blog

There are many other uses for a class blog, and these uses fall into three general categories: blogs used for class communications, blogs used for instruction, and blogs that do both (Bender & Waller, 2013). For communication purposes, blogs can be used to keep students and parents informed of all that is going on in the classroom. Instead of the usual note to parents (a written note that frequently doesn't make it home!), the blog will provide timely information for the parents and is always accessible online. Teachers can post homework assignments, announcements, class requirements, and handouts for specific content. Students and parents can use the blog as a board for questions and answers with the teacher.

Blogs also provide an excellent opportunity for ongoing class discussion outside of the classroom. This can be a great way to increasingly involve students who might be somewhat hesitant to participate in discussions in class. In fact, survey research has shown that students prefer writing in class blogs to other types of writing assignments (Richtel, 2012), and that fact alone makes blogging an excellent classroom strategy. Also, since students can post their work in their own time frame, there is no pressure for anyone to react to any assignment quickly, thus providing more time for students to reflect on their answer before posting.

Students can also use the class blog to collaborate on class assignments by posting documents for peer review and teacher comment. As students upload more individual work, the blog serves as an ongoing digital portfolio where progress can be analyzed over time in the archives (Blog Basics, 2012).

As this discussion shows, there seem to be as many potential uses for blogging in the classroom as there are for pencil and paper work, within each of the three general areas noted (Blog Basics, 2012; Wallagher, 2015). The types of uses of a class blog are limited only by Wi-Fi access and the teachers' and students' imaginations. However, in consideration of the fact that students today desire more authentic lessons that result in a much wider audience (Lampinen, 2013), increased access to the blog is desirable, since wide publication will enhance student engagement with blog assignments. Students will tend to go the extra mile when they know that classmates, parents, and others outside the class might review their blog entry (Lampinen, 2013). Box 12.1 presents a sampling of potential uses for a blog in the classroom.

> **Box 12.1: Classroom Uses for Blogs**
>
> Ask a thought question and require students to work in pairs and respond with a three-paragraph response.
>
> Create an organizer blog about class happenings so parents and students can review class announcements from anywhere.
>
> Store online lessons or supplemental materials for student access at home.
>
> Organize collaborative assignments and post them for review.
>
> Create online quizzes (either as optional or required assignments).
>
> Post work on the instructional unit topic from previous years, which students can use in their research.
>
> Invite comments from parents and community members.
>
> Create discussions among students in various sections of the same course.
>
> Emphasize writing skills, since the blog may be seen by many more people than merely a teacher.
>
> Create an online publishing opportunity for student term papers.
>
> Teach Internet safety and etiquette.

A Classroom Example: Using Blogs for Differentiated Instruction

Ms. Guzzo is teaching a fourth-grade class in science, and the standards state that students must be able to "understand the composition and uses of rocks and minerals." Ms. Guzzo has several students with mild disabilities who generally require extra time and help in science, as well as a few students who need an extra challenge. In order to provide a differentiated lesson on this educational standard, Ms. Guzzo teaches the characteristics and properties of three basic minerals in the following differentiated lesson.

First, after an initial introduction of ten minutes or so, Ms. Guzzo has the average students log onto the class blog, where she had previously posted a link to a video about minerals, along with three questions. Those students are required to watch the brief video and then post individual answers to the questions about the minerals and their uses.

At the same time, those students needing extra help find a link on the blog to another video about the same three minerals that presents a simpler discussion of their composition and uses. These students are asked to work in pairs to address those questions after they watch the video, and in that way, the student pairs can assist each other with the work. Thus, the blog-based assignments actually assist Ms. Guzzo in differentiating the content without embarrassing any students in a class setting.

For students who excel in class, blog entries are required that are much more complex. Those students are required to watch a video presenting highly complex uses of the minerals under study and then answer a few questions on the content. However, in addition, those students are required to create an assignment on those minerals for later in the class. Such creation might involve identification of additional websites, audio clips, videos, graphics, and extra links to documents for the class on that topic. The advanced students then post these, along with appropriate follow-up questions, to the class blog. In this fashion, use of a class blog can assist the teacher in providing differentiated assignments for the students in a large science class.

Guidelines for Beginning a Blog

For a veteran blogger, beginning a classroom blog may be as easy as starting with a blog platform and naming the classroom blog. However, for others, some consideration should be given to a variety of issues. Evans (2016) provides a twenty-minute tutorial on how a novice teacher might set up a blog for the classroom, and for teachers considering this strategy, I do suggest they watch that tutorial. Also, a variety of other sources provide additional guidance on how to set up a class blog (Bender & Waller, 2013; Blog Basics, 2012). Following is a synopsis of those recommended steps.

Select a Blog Hosting Site

A blog is housed on the Internet on a web-hosting website, and usually the teacher pays a small fee for that hosting service. Thus, the first step is for teachers to select a blog hosting website for their blog (Blog Basics, 2012). There are numerous choices, and some are available at no cost. Teachers new to blogging should consider several factors such as cost, built-in support, and student security when selecting a blog hosting site.

By selecting one of the more commonly used web hosts, teachers are likely to find that their host site provides more tutorial assistance for them (Evans, 2016). Edublogs (edublogs.org), as one example, has created a YouTube channel on which a variety of tutorials are available for teachers to review, and tutorials such as these are usually very helpful for the novice teacher in setting up a blog.

I suggest that teachers use a secure blog that is protected by passwords so that only class members, the teacher, and the parents can see the entries. This provides the maximum protection for students. These blogs will typically require login information to ensure higher levels of security for students (Bender & Waller, 2013). Passwords and login information can be shared with parents and administrators so those individuals can review the blog as well as the teacher and the students. Also, making blogs available to the school and parent community engages the students more with their work, since they realize many people might read their entries. In turn, this fosters student excitement about using the blog (Richtel, 2012). Instead of merely writing a research paper or doing a class presentation that only the teacher will see, students using blogs are able to create work that is shared with a much larger audience, and ultimately, this increases their motivation and commitment to the assignment.

Wallagher (2015) reports on a survey of teachers on classroom use of blogs. In that survey, five different blog hosting sites were identified. Of these WordPress was the most commonly used blog hosting site in the classroom, so unless a teacher has a rationale for using another web host, he or she may wish to begin with WordPress as the hosting site (Wallagher, 2015). Following are possible blog hosting sites.

- Edublogs (https://edublogs.org) is one of the most popular blog hosting sites for teachers.
- Blogger (www.blogger.com) is a blog hosting site now owned by Google.
- WordPress (https://wordpress.com) offers free and fee-based options.
- Weebly (www.weebly.com) offers free and fee-based options and has 40 million users.
- Tumblr (www.tumblr.com) is a host site owned by Yahoo, with over 555 million monthly viewers.
- KidBlog (https://kidblog.org) offers a free trial month and one of the lowest fee-based services at about $44 per year for teachers.

Follow Blog Host Instructions

Each blog hosting site offers step-by-step instructions on how to set up a classroom blog, and these differ from site to site. We recommend that teachers look at one or two of these blog hosts and review one of the tutorial videos on each. Most blog sites encourage teachers to enter basic account information including name, address, and email address and then set up a trial blog. Also, most blogs offer a template so that anyone can point, click, and post to the blog, which is what you want in an educational setting. When creating a post, the blogger will choose a post title and then simply enter the content. Links to outside documents, websites, videos, pictures, and audio clips can also be included in the blog.

Post Your First Blog Entry as a Simple Assignment to Engage Students

Once you have experimented with an initial blog post, you should write a second blog entry to share with the class that requires some student participation. However, you should carefully consider the type of assignment you wish to present to the class initially. Many class members may be new to blogging, so assignments requiring briefer student entries are probably best as students learn how to blog. Perhaps students might be required to read a text selection and then answer one of three simple questions on that content. Then they might be required to respond to another student's answer to a different question. In that way, students will get used to both doing an initial post and doing a response post.

Consider the Appropriate Length of Assignments on the Blog

After your blog is established and students are used to blog participation based on short student entries, you might consider requiring a longer blog assignment from the students or perhaps even requiring a peer-partner or small-group type of blog entry assignment. However, the length of assignment is always a concern in blog assignments. Richtel (2012) points out that blog entries are, typically, much shorter than are themes or term papers, since blogs share quick thoughts in a couple of sentences or a paragraph or two. In contrast, term papers are typically much longer and require students to organize their written arguments in a much more complex and systematic fashion. For this reason, while blogging is encouraged in virtually every classroom, the use of blogs in the classroom should not result in the elimination of longer, more complex writing assignments (Richtel, 2012). In the 21st century, students are required to do both types of writing, so both should be emphasized in our classes.

Unlock Student Creativity

As with most classroom technology options, blogging can provide a wonderful showcase for student creativity. With most blogs, any type of digital media can be posted to the blog, so student presentations, projects, or one-act plays can be developed, videotaped, and then posted. In fact, projects from former years can be saved on the blog (or reposted next year), and these will provide academic content that greatly enriches the text. In this fashion, class blogs will help unlock student creativity, and again, knowing that projects might be viewed over a series of years tends to engage the students more so than traditional assignments.

Research on Classroom Blogging

While research on classroom blogs is not extensive (Wallagher, 2015), both teacher testimonies and research has shown that blogging works in the classroom (Lampinen, 2013; Richtel, 2012; Wallagher, 2015). For example, Lampinen (2013) notes that student writing improved after she introduced a class blog in her high school literature class. Also, student engagement with the content increased as they discussed via the blog the topics under study with other students. Noting that students value authentic writing experiences, she found that students would put more effort into their blog entries than in a paper assignment that was merely destined to be read and graded by the teacher.

Wallagher (2015) reports on a 2014 survey among public school teachers and college teachers about their use of blogging. The survey was conducted by Edublog, one of the blog hosting services that is most frequently used in the classroom. The data showed that blogging use was increasing in both public school and college classes and that students' writing skills and communication skills improved as a result of blogging regularly with their peers. Also, teachers across the grade levels frequently used blogs as digital portfolios to showcase student work.

Summary

In today's classroom, students are looking for increased use of modern communication tools that were not available ten or fifteen years ago. From that perspective, use of a class blog seems to be virtually a requirement for modern instruction, and the good news is blogging in the classroom is relatively easy, particularly with all the tutorial assistance available from the blogging websites. Students' engagement will increase, as students realize their work is being reviewed by a larger audience, and a blog presents that reality for every student posting. Thus, teachers should consider using a class blog in virtually all classrooms today.

Strategy 13

Social Networking for Learning: Twitter

Students and adults worldwide are routinely using tools such as Facebook, Twitter, Google+, Snapchat, Ning, and many other social networking sites to share information about themselves, and most find these activities highly enjoyable. Of course, this presents another collaborative option for engaging students more actively with the educational content (Bender & Waller, 2013; Ferriter, 2011; Richardson & Mancabelli, 2011). Today, many teachers are tapping into that social networking excitement and using these tools as instructional, interactive teaching networks rather than social networks. Because different social network websites allow for different uses in the class, a number of teachers are exploring different networks. Several of these are discussed in Box 13.1.

> **Box 13.1: Social Networking Sites Used in Education**
>
> **Facebook** (www.facebook.com): Facebook is one of the first social networking sites and currently has over a billion users worldwide. Almost all students over the age of thirteen are already using Facebook, and this can be a powerful tool to use in education to increase students' engagement. In this networking site, participants present themselves by creating a profile, and for educational purposes, teachers might create a Facebook page for their specific class and then invite students to follow them. Using Facebook or other social networking tools allows teachers to catch students where they already are!

> **Google+** (https://plus.google.com): Google+ is a social networking site operated by Google. Using either circles (small groups of people such as your students) or hangouts (a chat feature), teachers can create learning-based social networks for their students. A teacher might start a hangout prior to a unit text, for example, as a study assist option, and a message will go out to everyone in that teacher's circle (the class) to join. As teachers become more familiar with this platform, they can identify the instructional networking strategies that work best for them.
>
> **Celly** (https://cel.ly/): Celly is less well known than other social networking options. It is an app that teachers and students can use for the usual networking functions. This app can be customized with various themes and avatars, as desired, making it a user-friendly option for younger students in the schools.
>
> **Ning** (www.ning.com): Ning is a social networking site that was originally intended for use by business and industry, but recently teachers have begun to use it as a more protected option than Facebook or Twitter. As teachers began to use this, Pearson Education worked with Ning to create free options for individual teachers to establish a class-only social networking site similar to Facebook (Bender & Waller, 2013). If your district has restrictions on the use of social networking sites such as Facebook for instruction, use of Ning as a more protected option may be warranted.
>
> **Edmodo** (www.edmodo.com): Edmodo offers a controlled social networking option, developed specifically with teachers in mind. It is available on a fee-for-service basis and may be used as a class networking option but may also be used as a teacher-based, idea-sharing website. This program has found wide uses in schools to date and is one of the better known systems.

In the context of student engagement, we'll discuss the use of Twitter in the classroom. Twitter (www.twitter.com) is a free social networking site. In addition to the typical social networking function, Twitter can also be used by teachers in a variety of ways. In fact, many teachers are already exploring the use of Twitter in the classroom (TEEContributor, 2011a, 2011b; Ferriter, 2011). Since 2008, Twitter has been one of the fastest-growing social networks (Richardson & Mancabelli, 2011), and there seems to be more use of Twitter in the classroom than other social networking sites.

Using Twitter in the Classroom

Twitter is essentially a microblogging service in which each Twitter posting (called a "tweet") is specifically limited to 140 characters. Because of that limitation, Twitter is intended to present brief instructions, reminders, initial thoughts, or opinions. Once a Twitter account is established for a particular class, other Twitter users can follow the postings in that account. In most cases, teachers who use Twitter for instruction will try to limit the followers of the class Twitter feed to class members and perhaps their parents, which is a good idea since the intended purpose for using Twitter in the classroom is instructional in nature rather than social networking in the traditional sense (Grisham, 2014).

> Twitter is a microblogging service in which each tweet is limited to 140 characters and is intended to present brief thoughts or opinions on the topic under discussion.

Twitter During Lectures

When used as a teaching tool, Twitter can greatly enhance student engagement, particularly for specific types of instructional activities. Here is an example. While most teachers have long realized that a lecture represents one of the least effective forms of teaching (specifically because most students are likely to be less engaged with the content during a lecture), many teachers still feel the use of lecture instruction will assist them in covering all the required content. As a result, many classes, particularly in the higher grades, still include extensive time in lecture-based instructional activities. However, a tool such as Twitter can change the narrative of uninvolved learners simply staring at the teacher during lecture (Ferriter, 2011; Richardson & Mancabelli, 2011).

Imagine a teacher establishing a Twitter account specifically for the class to use during lecture and discussions. During a lecture, each student is expected to tweet two or more times. The teacher sets up the class Twitter feed on a computer to present those tweets during the lecture on the class whiteboard, such that during the lecture the class tweets are shown directly to the class. In that context, students will be actively, collaboratively participating in the lecture, rather than merely listening passively. Also, in their efforts to impress their classmates, students are likely to share more well-developed thoughts or questions during the lecture. The teacher can read and address those during the activity and respond to them as he or she deems appropriate, or merely continue the lecture. Further, the teacher could also note who was and who was not tweeting during the lecture and could then prompt all students to participate more actively. In this example, Twitter can turn a lecture activity into a highly engaging learning activity.

Other Class Uses of Twitter

Because Twitter limits the length of each tweet, this is not a tool for posting lengthy assignments, content discussions, or long lists of readings. However, brief messages and suggestions for study can be posted to the class Twitter feed. Also, both brief videos and photos can be embedded within tweets, as can a web address for news articles or research articles that the teacher may wish to highlight for the students. When students click on the web address, they are immediately routed to the news or research article the teacher wished to share. Teachers can also use Twitter to remind students of specific class activities ("Remember the readings tonight! Quiz tomorrow on mammals!"). Teachers can also encourage parents to sign up to follow them on Twitter, and when some parents get a reminder like the one above about a class quiz, they might then remind their kids to study for that quiz.

In fact, the uses of Twitter for individual or collaborative instruction are nearly endless, and many educators have provided specific examples that can be used in either fashion (Ferriter, 2011; List & Bryant, 2009; TEEContributor, 2011a, 2011b; Walsh, 2011). Here are several creative examples of the use of Twitter in the class.

- Requesting tweets in character can be the basis of online role play! Teachers can require that students pretend to be a character from history or science and tweet as their character might have. Teachers can then have students explain to the class why they tweeted in a particular way (TEEContributor, 2011a, 2011b). For a variation of this, teachers may require that the characters do their tweets within specific time frames (e.g., FDR tweeting about WWII just after the Pearl Harbor attack, as compared to just after the Normandy invasion).

- As another variation of this idea, students can reenact historical events as if they were participating by using Twitter to communicate their thoughts as the events unfold on TwHistory (http://blog.twhistory.org). In this approach, students should be encouraged to tweet in specific time frames during various events. To prepare for this type of assignment using Twitter, students should examine primary historic sources to get into their character.

- Twitter can be used as a backchannel for brainstorming. Because tweets can be either open to all followers or sent as private messages to a particular student or teacher, Twitter is often used as a one-to-one communication between teachers and students. Students are more engaged and feel freer to ask questions in this private message format, and teachers can then determine whether or not to share a specific tweet (Ferriter, 2011). Ferriter (2011) indicates that Twitter has a more casual feel than Facebook or other social networking sites, and this casual feel and the private message function seem to encourage a more open exchange of ideas.

- Teachers may encourage their students to watch a candidate debate on TV and tweet with the class during the debate. This can be both educational and entertaining. Tweeting during a presidential election in former years can also be quite educational within a history class, as well as very interesting.

- Students should be encouraged to follow various scientists, mathematicians, or other professionals on Twitter. Having students follow scientists who may be involved in cutting-edge research on the topic under study can add an element of excitement to the instructional unit.

- Foreign language teachers may require students to communicate in a foreign language in a variety of ways (TEEContributor, 2011a, 2011b). Teachers may also tweet a sentence in a foreign language each day for students to interpret.

- Some teachers use Twitter to conduct quick classroom polls and then report on majority/minority opinions in the class, and this tends to encourage student interest in the topic under study (TEEContributor, 2011b). In fact, this idea could easily be expanded to schoolwide polling on local or national issues.

- Having students assist each other during research can be highly engaging, so teachers should encourage students to tweet information on sources and other resources that might help with assignments (TEEContributor, 2011a).

As these examples indicate, there are many instances in which classwork and homework can be enriched by using Twitter, and teachers report seeing increased student engagement with their subject as their students are invited to participate in their studies using this exciting tech tool (Ferriter, 2011; TEEContributor, 2011a, 2011b).

Guidelines for Using Twitter

Set Up a Twitter Account for Personal Professional Development

Many educators are using Twitter to take control of their own professional development. By following other teachers in your subject area or experts and authors in your field, you can create a professional learning network (sometimes called a PLN) to share teaching ideas. When using the Twitter platform, users can form topical groups on virtually any topic imaginable. These may be identified using hashtags (i.e., the symbol #, as in #mathchat or #socialstudies). A hashtag will group tweets on the same topic together and will help in your use of Twitter. Also, using Twitter initially for personal professional development gives the teacher who might be new to Twitter some experience with the platform prior to trying this with the class.

Investigate School Policies on Social Networking

On some occasions, teachers have found their students posting inappropriate tweets or using social networks in an inappropriate fashion. As a result, some school districts have policies that govern the use of social media between teachers and students, while others prevent any use of social networks at all on school property. Teachers should investigate such restrictions by asking their principal if such policies exist. I suggest that teachers also invite the administrator to follow the class account, as an additional safeguard against inappropriate usage.

Set Up a Separate Twitter Account for the Class

For instructional purposes, I recommend that teachers set up a separate Twitter account specifically for class instruction, and then invite students, parents, and school administrators to follow that account. Once that account is established, the teacher should determine what instructional activities he or she wishes to try on the account. The list is nearly endless as shown in the examples previously, and those ideas will help you get started.

Try Twitter for Outside-of-Class Communications First

Once a class Twitter account is established, teachers should use it for some of the outside-of-class uses discussed previously, such as reminding students of assignments or calling student attention to specific news stories that may relate to class. I also suggest that teachers send at least one private message to each student on a specific class topic to ensure students know about that function within Twitter. Only after the teacher and students are comfortable in that form of communication should teachers try using Twitter during a lecture or other lesson assignment, since by that point, students will be more familiar with using Twitter. Also from the teacher's point of view, it can be quite daunting to deliver a lecture or lead a class discussion while also trying to keep up with class tweets that may show up on the whiteboard! Some fluency with the Twitter platform is desirable before a teacher launches a lecture using a Twitter feed.

Research on Social Networking in the Classroom

With so many teachers using various social networking platforms in the class, it is no surprise that researchers are beginning to investigate the efficacy of this practice. There is considerable anecdotal evidence supporting the use of social networking in teaching, as well as several case studies that show the efficacy of this strategy (Curtis, 2015; Ferriter & Garry, 2010; Junco, 2011; Madge, Meek, Wellens, & Hooley, 2009; Prescott, 2014; Walsh, 2011), though much of this has been conducted in college classes rather than public schools. For example, Junco (2011) shows that use of Twitter increased student engagement and resulted in a 0.5 standard deviation increase in semester grades. That author also notes that Twitter use seemed to promote increased student/teacher engagement. Prescott (2014) reports that professors' use of Facebook in the class enhanced communication between the teacher and students, and that shy students, in particular, preferred this type of interaction. Also, Curtis (2015) presents several case studies on the use of Facebook in college classes, and in each case, student excitement about the content under study increased. While research is ongoing, and more will need to be done in the context of public school classes, use of social networking for instructional purposes is certainly supported by existing research.

Summary

Given the desire most students have for connecting via social networking, teachers should certainly begin to use this strategy to increase student engagement and academic performance. Of course, Wi-Fi and computer availability may not yet allow for this instructional strategy in your teaching situation, but most schools are quickly gearing up for this type of instruction. If at all possible, I encourage teachers to explore the use of Twitter or another social networking tool as an instructional strategy to increase student engagement.

Strategy 14

Wikis to Enhance Student Engagement

Teachers have long realized that students will put more time into assignments that will be shared with others, whether that sharing is posting a paper on a class bulletin board or uploading a digital presentation to a school website. Because student engagement increases with published work, many teachers are seeking ways to publish collaborative or individual work more broadly, and a class wiki provides that opportunity. Using this simple strategy, teachers can immediately create endless collaborative instructional options for any instructional unit.

Using any of the free wiki sites, teachers can establish a private website for their class (Tomaszewski, 2012; Pappas, 2013; Richardson, 2010). They can choose to create a wiki for each instructional unit or one for the entire year. On that wiki, teachers and students can post collaborative or individual work of virtually any length, share web links, post videos, or compile group presentations.

Because wikis can be edited by everyone who is signed on to the wiki, students can collaborate on joint written assignments and edit each other's work. Teachers can evaluate that work, when finished, and then invite parents, grandparents, or other teachers to review the work done on the wiki. Teachers might even have experts in the field comment directly on students' work using a wiki!

What Is a Wiki?

A wiki is an editable webpage or set of pages that selected persons can edit, which allows students to collaboratively write, create presentations, or post any digital files, such as digital photos, audio, or video files (Pappas, 2013). Certainly, the best-known wiki is Wikipedia, a very popular encyclopedia set up in wiki format to enable any users to edit the content. Even if someone posts incorrect content on Wikipedia, there are so many users that incorrect content is likely to be edited quite quickly to return the topic to a presentation of more accurate information.

> A wiki is an editable webpage or set of pages that selected persons can edit, which allows students to collaboratively create and post written work or digital files, such as digital photos or digital videos.

Of course, for classroom use, wiki participation should be limited to teachers and students only, though parents may be invited to review work from time to time. Using wikis, there is virtually limitless collaborative flexibility because any student can edit, add to, or reflect on every other student's work. Most education wiki sites allow teachers to follow every entry to see who has posted which edits and also to identify students who are not participating. This facilitates immediate, individual feedback within the wiki from both teachers and other students.

Using a Class Wiki

Wiki usage has become more prevalent in schools recently, though wikis have been used in some classrooms since about 1995 (Richardson, 2010). Teachers not familiar with wikis might wish to think of a wiki as an online syllabus for an instructional unit, coupled with daily instructional activities that students complete online. Should a teacher choose, any student or student team can edit any work done by others, making this one of the most collaborative of the recent technology options available for teachers.

When a student group is working together on a class presentation, video, or science experiment, any student who wishes to contribute a thought or idea merely gets into the wiki and makes a comment (Pappas, 2013). The student's new idea is embedded directly in the original work. This interactive and collaborative functionality makes the wiki an excellent tool for increasing the types of highly engaged collaboration and social learning that students expect and enjoy.

Prior to using a wiki in the classroom, I suggest that teachers view one or more YouTube videos and look over one or more of the following wikis:

- www.youtube.com/watch?v=-3MTJ5rz8Cc—a YouTube video on using wikis
- http://maggilit.wikispaces.com/home—a teacher-created wiki for literature
- http://dino.wikia.com/wiki/Main_Page—a wiki about dinosaurs that anyone can use
- https://grade7wiki.wikispaces.com—a nice teacher-created wiki about math, science, and other topics, including PowerPoint presentations that can be used in your class

Because wikis are used in many ways in the classroom, a list of advantages is quite long. Students respond well to wikis, since they see wiki contributions as collaborative creations that will be seen by more than merely a teacher. Teachers may make assignments on a class wiki or direct groups of students to create their own wiki on a specific topic under study. Both teacher- and student-created wikis encourage students to publish their own work and critique others' content. Over time, wiki usage leads to an online, collaborative community of information providers that is highly engaging for students.

Developing content for wiki pages can also be collaborative in nature. In developing written or video content for the wiki, students learn how to work together, sort through information, evaluate information using other sources, create newly synthesized information, and make contributions to the content already available on the wiki (Richardson, 2010).

Wikis are powerful tools that teach students to evaluate information from others. With students inundated with information today, each teacher must teach students how to interpret, evaluate, and sift through information. This is the essence of online research, and wikis provide an excellent medium for teaching those skills.

Finally, wikis are a great tool for teaching subject-area vocabulary and will save time in the process! Within a wiki for a particular instructional unit, teachers might list the vocabulary terms and make an assignment that students provide definitions and examples. In many cases, students will pick up the definitions for each term as they work through the wiki for that unit, and teachers will not have to spend initial instruction time teaching those terms.

A Classroom Example: Using a Wiki

Ms. Jessica Shoup, the teacher who provided an example of a flipped classroom, also uses wikis in her classroom in Charlotte, North Carolina.

Teaching STEM classes comes with a challenging task of motivating students and keeping them engaged in rigorous activities that allow for high levels of success. When used properly, technology in the classroom will achieve this task. While technology should never be used as a substitute for the teacher, technology tools, such as wikis, can be used to enhance lessons and provide learning opportunities that a teacher may not be able to provide.

While teaching middle school science, I used Wikispaces (www.wikispaces.com) in my classroom. Our district required every teacher to have a wiki page. When I first created mine, it had my course syllabus, a calendar that listed activities we had done in class, links to important class documents, and links to videos and websites that related to the content. I was proud of what I had done until I learned how much more wiki pages had to offer and how my website could be a learning tool for students. Wikis can not only provide information, but when structured appropriately, they can help students interact with one another, collaborate to arrive at joint answers or complete an activity.

At the beginning of each unit, I typically added an essential question to the wiki page. My students knew that it was their job to find the answer to the question during the unit of study. As they found facts or pieces of evidence to answer the question, they posted it to the class wiki. Students were expected to not only add facts, but to respond to those posted by other students. We discussed etiquette for responding politely and for offering constructive criticism if necessary. All students, especially the introverts, were included in the conversation and were learning from one another. While reading those student posts, I added comments to clear up misconceptions or asked questions to guide them in the right direction.

For a few years, I made detailed reading the focus of my wiki. To encourage my students to read closely, the wiki page was used as a debate platform. Articles were chosen on a topic that clearly had two sides, such as genetically modified foods. As the students read the articles, they gathered evidence to build a strong case either for or against genetically modified foods. The evidence was used to build a powerful opening statement that would make everyone agree with their perspective. Comments were then added by other students to either agree or politely disagree. After a certain period of time, a vote was cast and a team was chosen as the wiki debate winner!

Virtual labs and virtual field trips were also added to my wiki page. As students explored the field trip location, data tables were completed, observations were noted, and student questions were answered. Students were able to discuss their findings with one another while working, using the wiki, and each student was able to work on his or her own device while collaborating with others in the room. With each lab/field trip, students were to post their gem—i.e., the biggest takeaway that they had from the experience. They were also asked to comment on the gems of others.

My favorite part of using wikis was the immediate feedback that students received from their peers. Many students were more comfortable sharing on a computer than in an open class discussion. We had a no-judgment rule for our wiki work, and that made everyone feel that what they had to say was important and that it was valued by the other readers. Students often posted work to the wiki page, and peer evaluations were completed on the page as well. The evaluations came in different forms such as rubrics or posting one wow and one wonder. I noticed an increase of pride among the students for the work completed on the wiki.

So many educators use wiki pages today, and like me, they may not realize that these pages may not be meeting the full interactive-teaching potential. I would encourage all STEM teachers to look at these ideas, and others, for interactive wiki work. I strongly feel that students' STEM discussions should not end with the class bell. Instead, wiki pages will keep the STEM discussion alive outside of school, and students will love it!

Setting Up a Class Wiki

For novice teachers, setting up a wiki takes thirty minutes to an hour, and several websites provide the option of free wiki development for teachers, along with their more functional fee-per-service options. Teachers should select a free wiki option for their initial wiki experience. The following sites provide instructions for teachers, and set-up procedures are very similar across the sites.

- www.wikispaces.com
- www.wikisineducation.wetpaint.com/
- www.wikia.com/Wikia
- www.plans.pbworks.com/signup/edubasic20

Select a Wiki Option

Personally, I prefer Wikispaces, a site used currently by millions of educators. To use this wiki, teachers should begin with a review of videos from the Wikispaces homepage (www.wikispaces.com/content/wiki-tour). While many demonstration videos are found there, the first two are titled *Introduction* and *Creating Educational Wikis*. These are very brief and will help in the creation of your wiki.

Create the Wiki

Next, teachers should build their first wiki at the Wikispaces website for teachers (www.wikispaces.com/site/for/teachers). Teachers will be asked to select a username, a password, and a wiki name. Then teachers should click on the option on the lower right to create a free wiki. Next, teachers should select the "Private" wiki option. This is a free option, and allows only class members or others that you specifically allow to have access to participate. As teachers begin to get comfortable with their wiki, they can choose a more public wiki option later. Within the private option, teachers should add an administrator's name (perhaps the principal or assistant principal) as a "child" in the class. That will allow the administrator to carefully monitor the wiki content.

Create a Wiki Homepage

I use the term *homepage* to mean the first page of a wiki. If a teacher is creating a wiki to use during a two- to three-week instructional unit, the homepage provides the basic information on that content. This page introduces the instructional unit and should include a unit title and a general paragraph about the topic under study. When writing that title and paragraph content, you should remember that the goal for the homepage is to hook the interest of the students, so high-interest information, some video content, and a few questions is usually the best option.

To create the title, type in an appropriate, descriptive title and highlight it in the text box. Next, click on the "Heading" function at the top of the page, and select "Level One Heading." That will place the title in bold and increase the font size. Then, in the text section, write a general introduction paragraph that will generate interest. Perhaps you can highlight controversial areas within the topic or challenge the students to find answers to various unanswered questions.

Add Videos or Digital Photos

Pictures and videos enrich the homepage and will help generate interest. Teachers should add a picture or two and perhaps a link to a brief introductory video about the topic. If there are several videos, teachers may wish to create a second heading a bit lower on the homepage (using the same procedure as creating the title above) and call that "Recommended Videos." Below that heading list two or three websites that present brief introductory videos on the topic. Teachers can find interesting, content-rich videos anywhere, and should begin with sites they currently use such as YouTube, Nova Channel, the History Channel, TeacherTube, PBS.org, Discovery Channel, or NASA, depending on your subject area.

Teachers should remember that the homepage is designed to heighten interest and not teach content in depth, so shorter videos are recommended for this page. Later pages may involve the presentation of a longer, content-rich video on one aspect of the unit under study, along with questions or some other type of activity for students to complete based on that video. Those video links should be placed on subsequent pages rather than the homepage. Of course, teachers should always review any video they list. Finally, for each video, I recommend that teachers add a brief study guide (three to four questions or points to consider). Of course, that could be done as an assignment for a group of students the first time a wiki is used in class (e.g., "Your assignment is to write a paragraph synopsis of this video and develop a ten-question quiz on that content").

For longer instructional units, teachers might add a schedule of activities that includes dates and specific assignments students should undertake that day on the homepage. This will help students navigate the wiki, and should a teacher be absent, a substitute can get into the wiki (the students can help with that) and continue the planned activities for any particular day.

Create a Navigation Option

Students will need a way to navigate from page to page within the wiki. While only one page (the homepage) has been discussed up to this point, other wiki pages should be created, and each page will need a navigation tool that moves the student to those pages. Thus, teachers will need to add a navigation tool to each page of the wiki.

To create a navigation option, click the button in the edit bar at the top of the page titled "Widgets." A list of options will open, one of which is "Add the Navigation Tool." When you click that, a navigation button will be added at the bottom of the page you are on that will allow you and the students to navigate to other wiki pages.

Lock the Homepage Content

The power of using wikis is the collaboration stemming from the fact that anyone can edit the wiki content, so many pages in the wiki will be open for editing by all class members. However, some content, such as the homepage, should not allow an editing option. Thus, that page should be locked, which means the content cannot be edited or changed by anyone other than the creator of the wiki. To lock a page, move the cursor to the top right of the edit bar, and click on the series of dots. That will open some options, one of which is "Lock." Click that once, and you are completely done with your homepage. For other pages that you want students to edit, you simply don't perform this step.

Create Other Wiki Pages

Next, you should create additional wiki content pages, including activity pages for each day of the instructional unit. Most wikis for two-week instructional units have from eight to fifteen pages, with activities listed on each. As students add reports and other content to the wiki, it will grow tremendously, and teachers should help students in making those additions at the appropriate place. These extra wiki pages will, for the most part, be unlocked pages, and thus will allow students to make contributions to the wiki.

We discussed a vocabulary page previously. Another page might be a content study page that presents a link to a longer video or a PowerPoint presentation on one aspect of the unit, along with an extensive study guide for students to complete. Having students watch that video and do the study guide with a partner is one way to increase engagement and foster some discussion of the content. This can provide an excellent initial instruction assignment on new content.

Another page option involves the creation of a collaborative writing project. Teachers can create a wiki page that includes the beginning text for one or more story starters that students, working in teams, are required to complete. In many cases, having thematic writing that presents opposing views and giving students a choice between them increases student engagement and excitement about the task.

A webquest assignment can easily be housed on a wiki page, and this makes a great partner-type assignment. Of course, teachers should develop a webquest that is more complex and involved than merely a Google search on a topic. Students should be required to research factual material up front in the webquest and more conceptual content later in the webquest. Toward the end of the webquest, students could be required to do something such as create a paragraph reflection on the new content or take an online classwide survey on students' positions or opinions of the content.

The webquest could be created as a digital word file and then pasted into another wiki page for further study later.

Tomaszewski (2012) identifies a number of additional ideas for wiki-based exercises, including an online debate page, a role reversal page (e.g., have Newton argue for a sun-centered solar system), or a newsroom page on which teachers post daily news items on the topic under study and ask for student comments. A schedule for the instructional unit page can help students understand how the unit assignments fit together. The collaborative instructional possibilities are nearly limitless, and here are several more examples of things that might be on wiki pages:

- Daily written work assignments for the unit
- Study guide questions or graphics
- Descriptions of unit-length class projects
- Scanned digital reading assignments
- List of sample questions for the unit test
- List of subject content links

As this indicates, the wiki should become not only a set of lesson plans but an organizational outline for an entire instructional unit, complete with online work pages for students to complete. Using wikis in that fashion makes this information available for students at home via the Internet, so the distinction between classwork and homework becomes less meaningful, leading to increased student engagement. In short, most teachers, once they become wiki fluent, begin to do most of the instructional planning and development within a class wiki, because students enjoy this type of instruction and are more highly engaged with the content.

Input the Students

When the wiki is ready for use, the teacher must invite students and perhaps parents to join the wiki (using the "User Creator" button) or import the class list. Teachers then need to help students walk through wiki navigation, but that can also be done with an instructional video from the wiki website. Generally, this is not terribly time consuming, and students pick up these skills quickly. At that point, the teacher merely assigns students to read through the homepage and begin their work on the vocabulary page or elsewhere.

After using a wiki for one or two instructional units, you will be experienced and, at that point, might consider inviting parents to join the wiki as observers. This helps involve parents in the class, and generally improves the parents' perception of the class. Some teachers choose to do this, while others don't, so I suggest you make that determination after some experience in teaching with wikis.

Adapt the Wiki

The look of the wiki can help in engaging students, and once teachers become comfortable in wiki creation, they can find nearly unlimited options to create any look and feel for the class wiki they desire. Using the "Edit This Page" tab in the tool bar at the top of the page, you can manipulate text, change fonts, set colors, and set the spacing for each page. Of course, there are standard default options that can be used, so you might not wish to adjust the look of the wiki at first. However, as you become more fluent in using wikis, you will probably begin to experiment with these features to enrich the wikis. Have your students explore these wiki creation options also.

Research on Wikis in the Classroom

Research on the efficacy of wikis is universally positive. Wiki usage will increase student engagement and lead to increased student collaboration (Benson, Brack, & Samarwickrema, 2012; De Pedro, Rieradevall, Lopez, Sant, Pinol, Nunez, & Llobera, 2006; Deters, Cuthrell, & Stapleton, 2010). For example, Mak and Coniam (2008) show that wiki usage does enhance collaborative writing skills among high school students, and other research has likewise documented increased collaborative work when wikis are used (Bruns & Humphreys, 2007; Churchill, 2007; Trentin, 2009).

Other research has investigated student response to the use of wikis. For example, De Pedro and his co-workers (2006) show that wikis improved students' collaborative writing projects in a higher education course. Deters, Cuthrell, and Stapleton (2010) conducted research on students' responses to the use of wikis in college classes and results indicated an initial hesitation on the use of wikis by the students. Overall, however, students did report a positive experience in wiki usage. Thus, these results show that wikis increase student engagement and achievement and that students prefer using this collaborative, online instructional tool.

Summary

Given the emphasis in most state curricular standards for increased collaboration and cooperative learning, all teachers are well advised to begin to set up their instructional units in a digital format using a wiki. This online presence for a class is a hallmark of 21st century teaching, and using a separate wiki for each instructional unit means that students are creating content for use by other students next year and that the lesson plans for the following year are already done! The many other advantages noted previously provide a compelling rationale for setting up one's entire instructional day using wikis.

Strategy 15

Peer Tutoring to Enhance Student Engagement

There are few strategies that will increase student engagement with the content more than having students work collaboratively, which is why this entire chapter highlights collaborative instructional strategies. Of course, the most fundamental and perhaps most traditional of these collaborative strategies is peer tutoring. Research has shown that peer tutoring increases student engagement fairly dramatically because the tutor tends to keep the tutee focused on the task, making peer tutoring one of the most effective teaching strategies available in the classroom today (Arreage-Meyer, 1998; Bowman-Perrot, 2009; Ginsburg-Block, Rohrbeck, & Fantuzzo, 2006; Greenwood, Tapia, Abbott, & Walton, 2003). Also, as a result of this increased engagement, peer tutoring increases student achievement (Greenwood et al., 2003; Hattie, 2012; NEA, 2015). For these reasons, peer tutoring in some form should be frequently employed in all classrooms across the grade levels.

There are many variations of peer tutoring, and these range in complexity. Some require training for tutors whereas less formal tutoring does not. Following are a few of the more common versions.

- **Informal tutoring:** using students who understand the class content to tutor others, with little or no training for tutors
- **Cross-age tutoring:** using older students to tutor younger students with little tutor training

- **Classwide peer tutoring:** a more involved reciprocal tutoring in which students working in pairs serve as both tutors and tutees for each other, usually requiring some tutor training
- **Peer assisted learning (PAL):** a form of classwide tutoring combined with cognitive strategy instruction; this requires more training

A Case Study: Classwide Peer Tutoring in Health Class

In Mr. Ballard's sixth-grade health class, he structured his instructional units in a fairly standard pattern. In each unit, he initially emphasized factual information and definitions of body systems such as the respiratory system or the circulatory system for several days at the first of each two-week instructional unit. These could typically be summarized into a set of factual statements, definitions, or simple concepts, which he often presented on a study guide and during a whole-class discussion on the first several days of the unit. On the third day in each unit, Mr. Ballard gave a quiz on that factual material and moved into more complex concepts later in the instructional unit (e.g., how those bodily systems functioned together, the blood carrying oxygen to the body, etc.). Finally, he ended each instructional unit with a unit test.

Mr. Ballard had noticed on several of the quizzes that students often had not mastered the basic factual material that had been covered via lecture, discussion, and study guides during the first days of each unit. In fact, this seemed to be more of a problem than the more complex material on the broader unit tests, so Mr. Ballard sought a way to increase student engagement during those first several days of each instructional unit, when he covered the basic definitions and factual material.

Upon reading about classwide peer tutoring, Mr. Ballard realized that his fact-based study guide activities, including the quiz during each unit, provided an excellent opportunity for using classwide peer tutoring to increase student engagement during those critical first few days of the unit. He decided to teach his class the classwide peer tutoring procedure described previously. The procedural teaching took about thirty minutes daily on each of the next two days.

To get a sense of the efficacy of this strategy in his class, Mr. Ballard decided to conduct an action research project. To get baseline data, Mr. Ballard averaged the scores for his students on the factual quizzes for the previous two instructional units. Then Mr. Ballard prepared his study guide on factual material, as he always did, by developing two versions of the same study guide. On the third day, when the students arrived, Mr. Ballard handed every student his or her study guide and an answer sheet. While both versions of the study guide covered the same basic content, Mr.

Ballard created a simpler version for students who had reading difficulties. Those study guides covered the same content but emphasized fewer definitions.

On the third day, Mr. Ballard began the classwide peer tutoring. He divided the class into two heterogeneous teams and then had students partner up with a member of their team. After getting the tutoring partners formed, Mr. Ballard handed out the appropriate study guide and answer sheets and had the students number off as either one or two. He then told the students, "Ones will tutor first," and instructed them to begin the tutoring session.

The reciprocal tutoring then proceeded for twenty minutes. At the end of the second ten-minute tutoring session, all points earned by each team were tallied, and the winning team was recognized as the leaders of Mr. Ballard's health class. They were rewarded by lining up first when the class went to lunch. Mr. Ballard conducted this peer tutoring for two days, rather than lecturing and presenting the factual material, and he then gave a quiz on that material on day three of the unit. He averaged those scores as his first intervention unit score. He did the same type of classwide peer tutoring on the factual material for each of the next two instructional units.

The baseline data and intervention data are presented in figure 15.1. As these data show, Mr. Ballard's health class responded very positively to the classwide peer tutoring procedure. Each class average score on the factual quizzes was higher when Mr. Ballard conducted his factual material instruction using peer tutoring rather than the traditional lecture and discussion method he had previously used, thus showing the efficacy of this procedure in his health class.

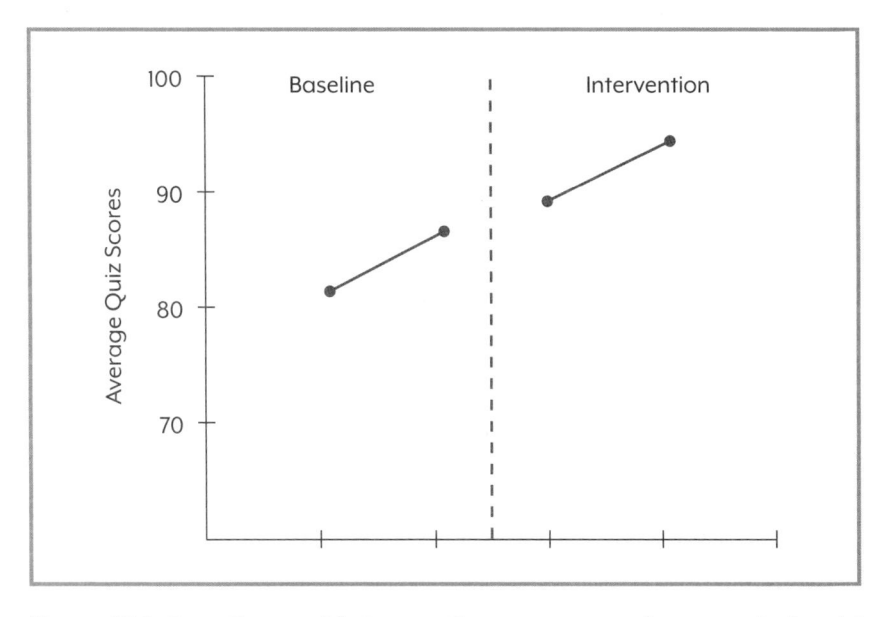

Figure 15.1: Baseline and intervention average quiz scores in health.

Mr. Ballard then decided to share his charted data with his health class and use that as an example of an application of the scientific procedure. Next, he shared his action research results with his principal, as a component of his personal professional learning growth plan. Finally, because of these data, Mr. Ballard determined to use classwide peer tutoring in each instructional unit.

Classwide Peer Tutoring

All of the previous tutoring options have proven to be effective in various subjects and grade levels (Fuchs, Fuchs, & Burnish, 2000; NEA, 2015; Greenwood et al., 2003). With that noted, the emphasis in this strategy section will be classwide peer tutoring because that tutoring approach has been researched more thoroughly and applied more broadly than some of the other options (Greenwood et al., 2003; Kamps et al., 2008). This strategy has also been widely employed across all grade levels in nearly all subjects (Greenwood et al., 2003).

In classwide peer tutoring, students form reciprocal tutoring pairs, with each student serving as both tutor and tutee during a given twenty- to thirty-minute tutoring session (Greenwood et al., 2003; Kamps et al., 2008). Students in the pair may study the same content or different content. Initially, each tutee is provided a study guide consisting of a set of factual questions, definitions, or simple concepts that he or she needs to study. The tutor is presented with the same study guide sheet and an answer sheet. When the teacher begins the session, the tutor calls out the questions or definition terms to the tutee, while checking the tutee's answers using the answer sheet.

If the tutee provides the right answer, the tutor is trained to say, "Correct! Good job! You earned two points for your team." The tutor makes a note of these points and asks the next question. If the tutee responds incorrectly, the tutor is trained to say, "Incorrect. Let me share this answer, and we'll talk about it." The correct answer is shared and briefly discussed (usually in ten to thirty seconds). If time allows, the teacher might join a pair of students when they discuss an incorrect answer. Then the tutor presents the same question again, which the tutee typically answers correctly. The tutor says, "Good job. You've earned one point for your team." After making a record of that point, the tutor moves on to the next question (Greenwood et al., 2003; Kamps et al., 2008).

After ten minutes of such tutoring, the teacher calls time, and the two students reverse roles, with the tutor becoming the tutee for the next ten minutes. After making sure that each tutor/tutee pair has the correct study guide sheet for the next tutee in each pair, the teacher begins a second ten-minute tutoring session. This reciprocal nature of classwide peer tutoring allows each student to both serve as a tutor and receive tutoring on content that he or she needs in a twenty- to twenty-five-minute session (Greenwood et al., 2003).

Steps in Classwide Peer Tutoring

As shown, this classwide peer tutoring procedure is a procedure that requires some tutoring training for students in the class. The following steps will guide you in that training, as you implement this procedure (Arreage-Meyer, 1998; Bowman-Perrot, 2009; Ginsburg-Block et al., 2006). Of course, once you train the class members, you can use this procedure in various units of instruction and in other subject areas throughout the year with no new training.

Prepare Study Guides

Classwide peer tutoring is most effective when used for learning factual material early during an instructional unit. The type of complex conceptual ideas that are most frequently presented later in instructional units can be the content for this tutoring but should be avoided until both the teacher and the class are familiar with the tutoring process. Teachers should prepare several versions of a worksheet or study guide at slightly different challenge levels for a given unit of study. These can typically be easily developed by using the questions at the end of a chapter in almost any subject. For each leveled study guide, teachers should also prepare an answer sheet. Prior to beginning the tutoring session, teachers must ensure that each pair of students has the appropriate study guides and answer sheets for each student in the pair.

Explain the Reciprocal Tutoring Procedure

When the training begins, the teacher should first describe the tutoring procedure, the specific language for tutors to use to be both clear and supportive during the process, and the scoring procedure. Note that when a tutee gets an answer wrong, he or she is supported with a brief explanation and a chance to earn at least one point for his or her team. Teachers should stress the use of correct, supportive language, as presented previously. Also, teachers can increase student engagement by letting the students know that their tutoring skills are valuable and that they are serving an important role when they tutor each other.

Model the Tutoring Procedure

On the first training day, the teacher should work with a student and model the classwide tutoring procedure, including the use of language for both correct and incorrect responses. It will not be necessary to tutor for ten full minutes during this modeling; a two- or three-minute tutoring session will usually suffice. Next, teachers should demonstrate how the tutor keeps a record of correct and incorrect responses and points awarded for each question. Finally, this modeling should include one shift during which the tutor and tutee change roles, as they will be expected to do in classwide peer tutoring.

Have Students Model the Procedure

After the teacher has modeled the procedure, two other students from the class should be called forward to model the procedure a second time. During this modeling, the teacher should emphasize that those students are working with different versions of the same study guide and stress the importance of having the right study guide and answer sheet for each student involved. While this may sound like a challenge, the research has demonstrated that students in various student pairs, even in the primary grades, soon get used to using different study guides, under teacher supervision (Greenwood et al., 2003). Again, for this modeling, only two to three minutes of tutoring needs to take place, but students should also be required to model switching roles.

Have Everyone Practice Tutoring

Finally, on the first day of training, every student should partner up and complete a tutoring session. This example should use a ten-minute time frame for each tutor before the teacher calls, "Switch roles." The teacher should carefully monitor students' supportive language when incorrect answers are given.

Subsequent Modeling

Some teachers have chosen to model the procedure on a second day, whereas others choose not to do so. This may depend on the grade level of the class or academic abilities in the class as a whole. However, research shows that even students with mild disabilities can perform very well in classwide peer tutoring if effective training is provided over several days (Bowman-Perrot, 2009; Ginsburg-Block et al., 2006).

Research on Classwide Peer Tutoring

Research has been strongly supportive of peer tutoring in terms of increased student engagement and increased achievement (Bowman-Perrot, 2009; Fuchs, Fuchs, & Burnish, 2000; Greenwood et al., 2003; Ginsburg-Block, Rohrbeck, & Fantuzzo, 2006; Hattie, 2012; Kamps et al., 2008; Kunsch, Jitendra, & Sood, 2007; NEA, 2015; Topping, 2008). Hattie's (2012) meta-analyses demonstrate that peer tutoring generates an effect size of 0.56, and in that study, peer tutoring was number 34 on his list of 150 of the most effective instructional strategies available! Also, peer tutoring will increase the time on task for both the tutors and the tutees across the grade levels (NEA, 2015).

The research has also demonstrated the effectiveness of classwide peer tutoring in more challenging academic subjects such as mathematics and science (Kamps et al., 2008; Greenwood et al., 2003). Efficacy of this instructional strategy has even been demonstrated for students with learning disabilities and other disabilities in general education classes (Arreage-Meyer, 1998; Bowman-Perrot, 2009; Ginsburg-Block et al., 2006; Greenwood et al., 2003). Clearly these research results are strongly supportive of the use of peer tutoring in practically any subject area across the grade levels.

Summary

Few strategies are as effective at increasing student engagement and achievement as peer tutoring, and teachers who are not already employing some version of peer tutoring should certainly add this strategy to their teaching practice. For the extensive factual material, definitions, and simple concepts that characterize much of the curriculum, classwide peer tutoring can easily replace lecture as the option of choice, and students will be more engaged with the content when tutoring is regularly used. In turn, teachers will see grades improve, so this is a strategy that all teachers should implement.

Strategy 16

The Role-Play Instructional Strategy

One general theme of this entire book is the idea that engaging students with the content in a more focused manner will require more than the traditional instructional methods of lecture, video support, discussions, and quizzes. In fact, new and different instructional activities are simply required by modern learners who have been raised in a digital learning environment of highly engaging content that places the student directly into the action and provides nearly instant gratification. In that sense, role-play is certainly a strategy every teacher should consider.

In fact, by having students actually act out the content under study, teachers can dramatically increase student engagement because of the immediacy of the students' experience with the academic content in a role-play situation (Graves, 2008; Sadeghi & Sharifi, 2013). Of course, many teachers have used role-play types of activities for decades, but occasional use of simple role-play examples is not likely to have the same result as systematic application of the strategy as an integral component of the instructional unit. Still, when implemented systematically, role-play is a strategy that will drastically enhance student engagement (Alabsi, 2016; Cruz & Murthy, 2006; Graves, 2008).

Role-play is the acting out of the learning content in simulations or situations where students take on the role or persona of the persons who actually lived through the events under study. In history or science, for example, students may take on the roles of historic characters in a discussion of the events of the day or of the scientific breakthroughs undertaken by one or more of the actors. In most role-play situations, students are given a character and a description of the character's role or perspective and are then placed in a situation wherein that character interacts with other characters who take on a different role (McDaniel, 2000; Morris, 2003; Starting Point, 2016). Thus, the role-play consists of (1) roles and perspectives for specific characters and (2) a situation, real or imaginary, in which they interact. While some students are actually playing the roles assigned, the rest of the class should be watching the interaction and critiquing it, based on their study of the academic content or the perspectives of the characters. This classwide responsibility will involve all of the students in the role-play.

> Role-play is the acting out of the learning content, in simulations or situations where students take on the role or persona of the persons who actually lived through the events under study.

While role-play is more effective when students are somewhat older and can understand more complex perspectives and differences in various perspectives, it is a strategy that can be used at almost any grade level. Even first graders can understand the perspective of a turtle hiding in its shell for safety reasons. With older students, the perspectives, roles, and representations can be much more complex and complete, and students themselves are able to assist in developing the role play activity.

A Classroom Example: Using Role-Play

Allison Scrivner-Limbaugh earned her BS in human development and her master's and PhD in cognitive psychology, all from the University of Alabama. She is now faculty at the University of Alabama and uses role-play to discuss Piagetian stage development in her introductory courses.

> When discussing Piaget and the cognitive development of infants and children, I have my college students act out the four stages of Piagetian development. Of course, there are many videos of babies failing or passing certain Piagetian tests on the Internet that indicate their stage of development, but I wanted a role-play type of demonstration to get students involved. Once, years ago while creating a job talk on developmental psychology, I was searching for a way to incorporate student interaction in that presentation, and I came across the idea of the "Piaget Dating Game" that other teachers had developed. Cognitive psychology lessons often consist of deep, highly detailed information, and I needed the students engaged, so I decided to use this role-play idea. I decided

to have some students role-play the Dating Game, as if they were in different Piagetian stages of development.

I used a "Whose Line Is It Anyway?" approach and wrote down a description of how a bachelor/bachelorette in each Piagetian stage of development might respond to various dating game questions. For instance, in the sensorimotor stage, one of the main cognitive limitations is object permanence. Young babies in the sensorimotor stage have difficulty understanding that an object continues to exist once that object is out of sight. That's why peek-a-boo is so much fun with babies at a certain age.

Therefore, one of my role-play actors was asked, "What do you do at the end of the date?" My sensorimotor contestant might respond by saying, "I'll cry at first when you try to leave, but once you are gone, I may forget you even exist." That response usually gets an emotional reaction from the class due to the harshness, but the response is correct given that Piagetian developmental state. While the Dating Show unfolds in front of them, the rest of the class has to decide which bachelorette/bachelor represents which Piagetian stage of development and that encourages them to pay attention and really think through the stages of development.

Something that seems so simple, a game-show approach with funny answers, actually motivates students to incorporate information in their own lives and further motivates them to be excited about the material. Of course, it is critical in the modern classroom to keep the lesson entertaining and engaging. These role-play stories, demonstrations, and skits keep material interesting, and therefore, these strategies increase students' interest in learning the material in my classes.

Steps for Implementing Role-Play

Role-play activities are not difficult to create, but they do take some time and planning. For young children, the teacher will have to do most of this development, but older students who are experienced in role-play can undertake many of these development steps. Also, a variety of authors have provided guidelines for the creation of role-play activities (Kodotchigova, 2001; McDaniel, 2000; Morris, 2003; Starting Point, 2016). A synopsis of these are presented here.

Define Content

When beginning a role-play activity, the teacher should identify the specific content that should be included in the activity. Some notes on, or lists of, anticipated topics or concepts should be prepared and provided to the students in the role-play prior to beginning the activity (Kodotchigova, 2001; Starting Point, 2016). Of course, only some of the instructional content for any given unit of study can be included in a role-play, but teachers often find that students go much further with the content than may have been intended, as they research their perspective roles.

For example, in preparation for a history unit on the Civil War, the teacher might prepare a list of causes to be discussed. Such a list might suggest that students prepare for some debate or discussion of slavery, the 10th Amendment and states' rights, and economic factors such as agricultural- versus manufacturing-based regional economies. All could be anticipated as areas for the characters to discuss in a role-play on this topic.

Develop Roles

The teacher must identify specific roles or characters for students to portray in the role-play and begin to develop their positions, based on the role. For example, in a history class, having students portray actual historical characters is always advisable. Students realize that they will need to study those characters and determine what perspectives those characters might have taken on any given topic. For example, because Robert E. Lee led the Confederate Army during the later years of the war, one might expect him to have a certain view that was pro-slavery. Ulysses S. Grant, who led the Union Army, might be expected to have held a differing view. However, students may dig up other interesting facts such as the fact that Grant's father and extended family actually owned slaves or that Lee was offered command of the Union Army by President Lincoln just prior to the Civil War.

It is essential that students be provided with some initial concrete information and clear role descriptions (Kodotchigova, 2001; Starting Point, 2016). While students should be expected to conduct additional research on the characters in the assigned role-play, having some initial perspectives, coupled with the list of topics, will help focus the students' research efforts. Kodotchigova (2001) recommends the use of cue cards as an initial presentation of the roles and characters, using the format shown in Box 16.1.

> **Box 16.1: Cue Cards for Role-Play on the Civil War**
>
> **Cue Card A:** You are General Robert E. Lee, serving in the United States Army in 1860.
>
> Greet someone you knew in the Mexican–American War who would soon become a Union general.
>
> Your perspectives on Bloody Kansas is that outside influences should not invade the state simply to vote against the slavery issue.
>
> You believe that John Brown was wrong to conduct John Brown's Raid and that he should have been hung for treason (as indeed he was).
>
> Ask your friend's perspective and what he feels might come next.
>
> **Cue Card B:** You are a veteran of the 1848 Mexican–American War and are currently a businessman named Ulysses S. Grant.
>
> Greet your former commanding officer from the Mexican–American War.
>
> You think slavery is the curse of the nation, and you hope the voters in Kansas defeat the issue so it doesn't spread to additional states beyond the South.
>
> You don't condone John Brown's treasonous raid, but you desire mercy in his sentencing.
>
> You then inquire about your friend's loyalty to the federal government.

Create a Situation and Setting

In the example in Box 16.1, one might imagine that Grant (a businessman immediately prior to the war) and General Lee might meet in a restaurant in Washington, DC, just before the outbreak of war in early 1861 to have dinner. At that dinner, they would probably discuss the issues of the day, as noted in their respective roles. Both had a military background and both were veterans of the Mexican–American War, so a dinner discussion of the nation's ongoing conflict would not have been unimaginable. Of course, no such discussion took place, but role-play activities are not bounded by reality or time—only by the character's roles and perspectives.

Note that in the cues, the characters differ in their perspectives somewhat and that such differences are likely to create differences of opinion. It is such conflict that makes role-play an interesting way to teach the content under study, so differences of opinion, even on controversial subjects, should generally be encouraged.

As the situation is envisioned by the teacher, he or she may wish to identify some setting elements that could be easily devised or created in the classroom. While most role-play activities in schools do not involve extensive setting elements, the fact is role-play activities are theater in some fundamental sense, so some setting elements might be desirable. For example, if the role-play is to be videotaped for later website publication, some minor setting elements could broaden the appeal, as well as emphasize the content. Of course, the teacher's role would be to merely suggest the types of setting elements that might be constructed fairly quickly and then let the students actually create them.

Introduce the Role-Play Activity to the Class

In most cases, the first three steps should be completed by the teacher prior to the introduction of the role-play activity to the class. By having these components in hand, the teacher can facilitate a better understanding by the students of what the role-play is designed to cover. In most cases, with these three steps completed prior to the beginning of an instructional unit, the teacher can use perhaps fifteen to twenty minutes of the first day of the unit to introduce the role-play and identify teams of students to develop the character roles further.

Some teachers have found it advisable to assign teams of students to a particular role, while not telling them which individual student may ultimately play that role. In a class of twenty-five students, if the role-play activity includes three characters, the class might be divided into teams of eight or nine students, and each team researches one role together. If any member of that team might ultimately be identified to play the role, each team member is likely to be more highly engaged in the research and development of that role.

Conduct Research

Depending on the age of the students, they should be encouraged to take the basics of the role-play (list of anticipated topics, roles, and setting) and conduct further research on what subtle perspectives their character might take. This research step ensures that the students will access additional knowledge of the content under study, and they should be expected to go well beyond the brief perspectives presented in the cue cards previously (Morris, 2003; Starting Point, 2016). Of course, the more time students spend in this step, the richer the learning experience will be, and two class periods, or perhaps three, is recommended for older students. If teams are used to explore the roles, the teacher must ensure that sufficient time is built into this step for both individual student research and sharing of information with the team members.

Write the Role-Play

Role-play activities differ a great deal in terms of how involved and developed they are. Some teachers initiate a role-play event based solely on the types of cue cards shown in Box 16.1, while others require students to actually develop an extensive script, or at least a more extensive one-act play. Of course, the more time spent in development of the role-play, the more complex and complete the learning will be.

Develop Concurrent and Follow-Up Activities

Nearly every advocate of role-play argues that the quality of the concurrent and follow-up activities will help determine not only the level of student engagement but also the achievement gains from the role-play activity (Alabsi, 2016; Cruz & Murthy, 2006; Kodotchigova, 2001; Morris, 2003; Starting Point, 2016). Thus, teachers are well advised to plan robust concurrent activities and follow-up activities for the role-play. Concurrent activities are activities that class members who are not playing a role would complete during the role-play. For example, a participatory organizer consisting of eight or ten factual questions for the audience to complete during the role-play event will help keep non-acting students involved in the role play (Morris, 2003; Starting Point, 2016).

Also, role-play events are enriched by intensive follow-up activities, which may consist of practically any type of class activities that continues the themes that were presented in the role-play. Certainly a class discussion, perhaps supported with some video or online exercises, will extend and codify the learning resulting from the role-play. Through these follow-up activities, the teacher can help ensure that extensive content is covered, including much content that was not directly included in the role-play event itself.

Finally, using students to plan and develop some of these follow-up activities can greatly enrich the student buy-in relative to the role-play event itself. In conjunction with students doing research to understand the roles and characters, they might also help develop various follow-up activities for the class to undertake after the role-play event.

Assign the Roles and Do the Role-Play

Depending on the extensiveness of the role-play activity, there may be several roles in the role-play event, and some thought should be given to who can best portray the characters in the activity. In some cases, teachers might assign specific students to play the several roles, while in others, particularly in team-based role-play development, the teams may be invited to decide who plays the various roles (Kodotchigova, 2001). If the class is quite experienced in role-play activities, they may need little direction or training for the role-play activity, while in other cases, the teacher may play a role himself or herself as a way to model role-play. The teacher should consider all these factors when planning the role-play event.

Follow Up

As noted previously, the follow-up activities should be determined in advance of the role-play event itself, but they will be completed in one or several days after the role-play. At the very least, all students should be invited to add their perspective on the role-play during the follow-up discussion and activities, since student engagement will be enhanced if all students, including the non-acting students, are expected to provide their view of the role-play.

Evaluate

Evaluation of the role-play activity ranges from no specific evaluation at all to highly developed, numeric-based, survey-type evaluations completed by the class. In a basic sense, the subsequent unit test will determine the efficacy of all activities in an instructional unit, so some teachers don't conduct an evaluation of the role-play event itself. Other teachers have students do some type of opinion survey to let students express themselves about how effective they thought the role-play event was, while others actually quiz students on the academic content covered in the role-play, as one of the follow-up activities. If teachers choose to implement this strategy in all or most of their instructional units, varying the type of evaluation follow-up is recommended.

As can be seen from this description of role-play activities, an effective role-play is an activity that takes time. The role-play might take some portion of the instructional period over six to eight days during a two-week instructional unit. Figure 16.1 is an example of a role-play event that was designed to be a very significant component of the overall instructional unit, undertaken in hour-long periods.

Day 1 of instructional unit (20 minutes)	Present content, roles, and situation to the class and set up teams for each role. Then do other activities not involved with the role-play.
Days 2 and 3 (40 minutes each day)	Conduct role-play research.
Days 4 and 5 (40 minutes)	Write role-play script and follow-up activities.
Day 6 (30 minutes)	Do the role-play and follow-up activities.
Day 7 (all period)	Conduct non-role-play instructional activities.
Day 8 (30 minutes)	Complete role-play follow-up activities.
Day 9 (all period)	Conduct non-role-play activities on the unit topic.
Day 10	Give unit assessment.

Figure 16.1: Example of a role-play event.

Research on Role-Play

Research on the use of role-play in the class has been conducted for many decades and is universally positive: role-play will increase both student engagement and academic achievement (Alabsi, 2016; Cruz & Murthy, 2006; Graves, 2008; Sadeghi & Sharifi, 2013). For example, Morris (2003) used a role-play activity in a seventh-grade history class and found that his students loved the activity. They also made more of a connection with the characters presented in this role-play activity. Morris (2003) notes that his students were more highly engaged and became more skilled at taking varying perspectives after role-play was introduced into his class.

As another example, Alabsi (2016) used role-play to teach vocabulary in a girl's secondary school during their English as a foreign language class. In an experimental class, role-play was used in two instructional units to help students practice the vocabulary in the context of a role. In the comparison class, the same units were taught using traditional methods, and the achievement results in learning new vocabulary favored the students who learned the vocabulary using role-play.

In addition to these, many other studies over the years have shown similar positive results of role-play in the class (Cruz & Murthy, 2006; Graves, 2008; Sadeghi & Sharifi, 2013). Again, these results demonstrate both higher engagement and a deeper understanding of the academic content as a result of role-play.

Summary

Due to these research results, teachers should consider conducting some instruction using role-play activities to address the needs of modern learners. In fact, deep, rich, and broad understanding should be a primary emphasis in all instruction, and this is the very depth of understanding that a role-play instructional strategy provides. Thus, teachers should undertake this role-play strategy in many, if not most, of their instructional units.

SECTION IV

Personal Responsibility and Student Engagement

It has become an axiom among coaches in practically every sport that attitude is everything, and the same axiom could be extended to student engagement and academic performance. If a student is not ready to learn, or does not believe he or she can perform well, he or she is not likely to engage with the subject matter or learn it. Thus, the strategies in this section focus on preparing students for high engagement and learning, and I'm referring to these strategies as "personal responsibility strategies to increase engagement." These strategies include increasing mindfulness, utilizing reward and response cost, practicing a growth mindset, and goal setting and self-monitoring performance.

Strategy 17

Mindfulness to Increase Engagement

Regardless of the instruction strategy implemented in the classroom, student engagement and academic performance are, to some degree, determined by personal habits associated with success in learning. These include persistence when faced with a challenging task, the habit of reflective thinking, and the personal belief that one can actually accomplish a difficult assignment, as well as an ability to focus the mind, or concentrate (Davis, L., 2015; Dweck, 2006; Symonds Elementary School, 2015). Of course, these habits do not represent academic skills in the traditional sense of the word, yet teachers have long realized that without these habits, students will not succeed academically.

One emphasis of these abilities is the mindfulness movement, a movement designed to help students reduce stress and find inner peace of mind in order to make themselves focused and more readily available for learning (Albrecht, Albrecht, & Cohen, 2012). The mindfulness strategy involves providing students with a meditative time period, during which the student reflects on his or her emotional state and level of relaxation, in an effort to boost student engagement and productivity (Klatta, Harpsterb, Brownea, White, & Case-Smith, 2013). Using mindfulness exercises, educators can teach students to assess their own emotional state, calm themselves down, concentrate on one thing at a time, and reflect more deeply on their work (Albrecht, Albrecht, & Cohen, 2012; Harris, 2015). All of this will increase the meaningful engagement the student has with the academic content. With roots in both yoga and certain Buddhists' meditation practices, mindfulness has become both an engagement and an academic enhancement strategy that is now used in schools around the world (Campbell, 2013; Cox, 2015; Davis, L., 2015; Deegan, 2015; Harris, 2015; Oaklander, 2015; Thomas, 2016).

> The mindfulness strategy involves providing students with a meditative time period, during which the student reflects on his or her emotional state and level of relaxation, in an effort to boost student engagement and productivity.

Mindfulness practices evolved from yoga in the 1970s as a way to boost energy and productivity (Davis, L., 2015). The practice has since been employed by many organizations including Google, the United States Army, and the Seattle Seahawks football team (Davis, L., 2015). Today, many educators are practicing mindfulness with their students (Greenberg & Harris, 2011; Oaklander, 2014). At Symonds Elementary (2015), for example, mindfulness is part of a broader social/emotional learning effort that includes activities to help students focus attention and learn to take stock of their emotions and to determine how those emotions might be playing out in their relationships with teachers and other students.

A Classroom Example: Mindfulness in High School

Here's an example from a high school in one of the poorest inner-city districts in New York City (Davis, L., 2015). Argos Gonzalez taught an English class with a mix of black and Hispanic students in the Bronx. When class began, Gonzalez rang a bell and said, "Today we're going to talk about mindfulness. You guys remember what mindfulness is?" When no one spoke, Gonzalez gestured to one of the posters pasted at the back of the classroom that summarized an earlier lesson on mindfulness. In the earlier lesson, the students had brainstormed the meaning of *mindfulness* and listed some phrases such as *being focused, being aware of our surroundings*, and *being aware of our feelings and emotions.*

Gonzalez continued with the following instructions: "I'm going to say a couple of words to you. You're not literally going to feel that emotion, but the word is going to trigger something; it's going to make you think of something or feel something. Try to explore it. First, sit up straight, put your feet flat on the ground. Let your eyes close."

Gonzalez then tapped the bell again, and the class became quiet. Then he said, "Take a deep breath into your belly. As you breathe in and breathe out, notice that your breath is going to be stronger in a certain part of your body. Maybe it's your belly, your chest, or your nose. We'll begin with trying to silently count to ten breaths. If you get lost in thought, it's okay. Just come back and count again. Whether you get up to ten or not doesn't really matter. It's just a way to focus your mind." Then the students practiced that mindfulness activity for several minutes (Davis, L., 2015).

Teachers like Gonzalez would not be spending the ten to fifteen minutes of precious class time on this type of procedure unless the benefits were clearly evident in their class (Davis, L., 2015). Teachers often report increased productivity among the students and a better class climate when they practice mindfulness with the students (Albrecht, Albrecht, & Cohen, 2012; Greenberg & Harris, 2012; Harris, 2015). Today, schools all across the United States and the United Kingdom are beginning to practice mindfulness daily in the classroom (Davis, L., 2015).

To get a sense of what mindfulness looks like in the classroom, readers should review the following six-minute video, promoted by actress Goldie Hawn, who is a committed proponent of mindfulness in schools: www.youtube.com/watch?v=tAo_ZSmjLJ4. Also, several mindfulness curricula, and appropriate training, are available, as described in Box 17.1. However, teachers should bear in mind that they can undertake implementation of mindfulness without using these curricula, by reviewing free materials from YouTube, this book, and other such sources. Also, the previous classroom example provides the step-by-step assistance teachers should use for initial implementation.

Box 17.1: Mindfulness Curricula Used in Schools

MindUP (https://mindup.org): The MindUP curricula is promoted by Goldie Hawn and the Hawn Foundation. It is one of the most frequently used mindfulness curricula in schools and is founded on four pillars: neuroscience, mindful awareness, positive psychology, and social-emotional learning. Students learn to quiet their minds in three-minute brain breaks three times daily—first thing in the morning, after lunch, and before leaving school. Teachers can download a guide at the website.

Mindful Schools (www.mindfulschools.org): The Mindful Schools program is another program frequently used by teachers. This program can be purchased online, along with mindfulness training for teachers. The six-week online course costs $125 and provides the basics of mindfulness meditations, techniques for navigating intense emotions, and a series of role-plays on mindfulness and communications.

Implementing Mindfulness

In addition to the published curricula, there are many individually developed approaches to teaching mindfulness in medical, therapeutic, and classroom settings, and various approaches stress different things. These range from intentional breathing to self-awareness to walking meditations (Cox, 2015; Nhat Hanh, 2010; Welham, 2014). Some approaches suggest that teaching mindfulness requires more than merely reading about the technique, and some of the existing training programs for educators take a year or more to complete.

With that noted, the compilation of suggested procedures below come from a variety of sources (Caprino, 2014; Davis, L., 2015; Nhat Hanh, 2010; Welham, 2014). While these are presented in no particular order, these activities do represent the types of mindfulness exercises that are being done in the classroom, and teachers should feel free to implement mindfulness training based on the information in this book and the examples one might find on YouTube. The description in the previous classroom example will also be of help.

Breathing Exercises

This was discussed in the previous classroom example, when Mr. Gonzalez had students count their breaths in a calm, soothing setting. Like Mr. Gonzalez, many teachers teach breathing exercises to focus students' attention and help them relax (Davis, L., 2015). Such relaxation will foster higher student engagement when academic tasks are presented later in the class.

Moods and Emotions Awareness Activities

Some teachers teach students a bit about the human brain and regions of the brain associated with different types of moods and emotions (e.g., the amygdala as the emotional brain and the frontal cortex as the planning brain). Students then refer to those brain regions while they explore their own moods and behavior or the moods and behavior of others (Welham, 2014). Some teachers have students keep a mood diary to discuss their feelings and moods daily. These activities allow students to assess their own moods and emotions and gain control over them, resulting in improved class behavior and more time on the lesson.

Senses and Sensory Experience Awareness Activities

Some mindfulness trainers have the students practice focused awareness by stressing sensory stimuli. Students might be asked to chew a raisin (only one raisin) for an entire minute—chewing slowly and focusing their attention only on the sensation of chewing or how the raisin tastes. Alternatively, students might touch different textured cloth while they concentrate on the sensations with their eyes closed. Focused sensory awareness helps students with attention deficit problems.

Focused Awareness Activities

This involves having students focus on doing only one thing at a time (e.g., walking, looking at nature, or completing a morning reading with no distractions or outside thoughts allowed). This will help students develop task persistence and focused attention.

Walking Meditation

By having students walk around the classroom or the school for a time, teachers can have students continually focus on exactly what they witness at each turn in the hallway, without latching on to something that they passed previously (Nhat Hanh, 2010; Welham, 2014).

Stress-Reduction Activities

Many parents might object to mindfulness instruction if mindfulness is approached as yoga or religious instruction. However, by approaching mindfulness with a focus on stress reduction and student well-being, teachers can usually forestall that potential parental concern. Of course, parents should be fully informed of this instructional focus and assured that no religious training is taking place (Welham, 2014).

Research on Mindfulness Training

Mindfulness has received research support in a variety of areas in both the classroom and clinical settings (Albrecht, Albrecht, & Cohen, 2012; Campbell, 2013; Deegan, 2015; Greenberg & Harris, 2011; Klatta et al., 2013; Thomas, 2016; Schwartz, 2016a), and several of these studies report improvements in attention skills after implementation. While some of the research is ambiguous (Greenberg & Harris, 2011), the majority of both anecdotal testimony studies and research studies have shown that mindfulness is an effective treatment for improving behavior and attention skills of general education students as well as students with ADHD, anxiety, and aggressive tendencies (Albrecht, Albrecht, & Cohen, 2012; Campbell, 2013; Davis, L., 2014; Greenberg & Harris, 2011; Harris, 2015; Schwartz, 2016a).

Klatta and her colleagues (2013) implemented a mindfulness curriculum called Move Into Learning in two third-grade classes for eight weeks. These classes were in a low-income urban school. Results of the pretest/posttest design showed that this intervention resulted in improved behavior on a teacher rating of behavior and improved attention skills overall. This study shows that mindfulness programs positively impact student engagement.

In another action research study, Schwartz (2016a) reports evidence that after implementation of a mindfulness program at a K–8 school in Portland, Oregon, both teachers and students demonstrate benefits from mindfulness training. In that school, office disciplinary referrals are way down, and teachers and students both report a drastically improved school climate overall, as a result of the mindfulness program. Other evidence shows that mindfulness improves attention, reduces stress, and improves emotional regulation for many students with and without disabilities (Albrecht, Albrecht, & Cohen, 2012; Greenberg & Harris, 2011).

Most of the research to date has investigated the impact of mindfulness on increasing social-emotional health and/or decreasing behavioral problems, and while the term *student engagement* has not been a specific outcome measure, increased attention skills are often reported as a result of mindfulness interventions (Albrecht, Albrecht, & Cohen, 2012; Greenberg & Harris, 2011; Klatta et al., 2013). Also, at least one study reports increased academic performance in terms of improved scores in mathematics resulting from mindfulness training (Albrecht, Albrecht, & Cohen, 2012; Oaklander, 2015). In short, research supports mindfulness as an effective strategy to improve class behavior, reduce stress, and improve attention, and these are likely to enhance student engagement over time. Teachers should watch for more research specifically on the question of efficacy of mindfulness programs directly on student engagement.

Summary

The extant research suggests that mindfulness should be considered for implementation in practically all grade levels. In particular, teachers might explore using mindfulness in the subjects that tend to produce increased stress among students such as science or mathematics. If mathematics anxiety, or other types of anxiety, and student stress can be alleviated by a series of three- to five-minute mindfulness breathing exercises, teachers would be well advised to make time for those exercises during the instructional period.

Strategy 18

Reward and Response Cost: ClassDojo

Class management approaches based in behavioral theory have long stipulated that teachers can enhance student engagement by using group contingency rewards, individual rewards, or mild punishments such as response cost procedures to increase on-task or decrease off-task behavior (see Bender, 2016 for a review). Response cost is a mild punishment in which students are provided certain rewards at the outset of class, and then those are removed for off-task or other inappropriate behavior. Like other options based in behavioral theory, which has been around for many decades, teachers are well aware of these options and frequently use them, so we need not spend limited time and space on these traditional strategies.

> Response cost is a mild punishment in which students are provided certain rewards at the outset of class, and then those are removed for off-task or other inappropriate behavior.

However, in the last decade or so, many simple phone-based apps and several more highly developed software programs have provided a new twist on this older reward/response cost theme (Mims, 2013; Schwartz, 2016b). Today, many apps and tech-based behavioral management systems can be used to provide these rewards or response cost options, and teachers should be aware of the tech-based options that are currently available.

The tech-based apps and programs that can be used to enhance student engagement range from simple phone-based apps to complex, commercially available class management systems (Bender, 2016; Mims, 2013). The apps for behavioral management in the classroom seem to be nearly endless, and more are developed daily. As one example, this book presented the recently developed LSI Tracker by Learning Sciences International. The LSI Tracker is a useful tool in tracking student understanding of concepts or any classroom behavior, and given the flexibility available in that software, teachers could certainly utilize that option for tracking on-task behavior to provide appropriate rewards. Further, a simple Google search using terms such as *apps for class behavior* will provide an extensive list of available apps. Box 18.1 provides a few options.

> **Box 18.1: Apps or Software Programs to Enhance Student Engagement**
>
> **Discipline Tracker** (manskersoftware.com/DT_New.htm): Discipline Tracker is an app that captures the discipline activity for every student in the school. The school district must enable the app, but once it is available, it allows educators to track off-task behavior, enter rule infractions, synthesize and analyze group discipline trends, develop intervention plans, and send emails to other teachers or parents. Also, it allows teachers to see what on-task and off-task behaviors a student may have demonstrated previously. Such information will typically result in a more unified disciplinary effort from one year to the next.
>
> **Rich Kids 1.10:** This is a free disciplinary reward system for use with students between three and fifteen years old by either parents or teachers (Zero2Six Technology Co., Ltd.: http://appcrawlr.com/ios/rich-kids-behavior-reward-contr). This app is founded on motivating students toward good behavior and high levels of student engagement and includes a variety of tasks for students to perform. For each task students complete, students receive pay in the form of gold coins that can be redeemed for a variety of prize coupons. The app helps mark daily success on classroom tasks with a check mark in each student's box.
>
> **Review360** (www.pearsonclinical.com/feature/R360/index.html): Review360 is a commercially available behavior management platform by Pearson Education. It is designed to increase positive behaviors, reduce suspensions, implement anti-bullying systems, implement RTI interventions, and improve school climate. Program functions range from data aggregation and analysis capabilities based primarily on office referrals to intervention and progress monitoring for individual students with behavioral issues, including on- and off-task behaviors. Web-based professional development is built into the system for both teachers and administrators. Teachers make behavioral reports online, saving much paperwork. The app also includes a parent contact system that sends emails to parents about behavioral issues.

In addition to simple apps, there are more developed software programs for behavioral management that can assist teachers in enhancing student engagement. There are broadly based programs that emphasize general social skills, conflict resolution skills, or improved behavior overall, and some of these may address student engagement only marginally. Others, in contrast, offer teachers the opportunity to directly provide rewards or mild punishments based on students' level of engagement, and one of the most extensive and most popular such programs is ClassDojo.

ClassDojo to Increase Student Engagement

ClassDojo (www.classdojo.com) is a behavioral and class management program that offers teachers a reward system that can be used for increasing student engagement. ClassDojo is free for teachers and works with both iPad and Android devices, allowing the teacher to award points while walking around the classroom. This program is useful for teachers across the grade levels, and the software also interacts with other classroom technology such as the teacher's desktop or interactive whiteboards (Mims, 2013; Schwartz, 2016b). The program allows students to create avatars (digital representations of themselves), and those avatars can then be rewarded for on-task behavior. Students can even access the program after school to keep track of their rewards for their behavior in class (Mims, 2013). Some teachers have allowed students to award their own points during in-class work, making this a great self-monitoring tool.

The software itself presents a list of positive and negative behaviors for the typical classroom, but it also allows teachers to create their own targeted behaviors for individual students, as necessary (Mims, 2013; Schwartz, 2016b). The program allows teachers to reward students for on-task work immediately, but also includes a response cost system called "negative points" that involves taking away reward points. For both positive points and negative points, the software will produce a distinctive sound—a pleasing sound for positive points and a less pleasing sound for negative points. These sounds become a cue, motivating the students toward more positive behaviors. Specifically, when off-task behavior occurs in class, the teacher can merely click on a student's avatar during the class and the negative points sound will cue all the students to check their avatar such that the non-attentive student is cued to return to task. Other uses of ClassDojo include:

- Improving class behavior
- Counting/tracking student behavior
- Identifying behavioral trends
- Awarding points for positive behavior

- Generating reports on student behavior
- Communicating with parents and other teachers

A Classroom Example: ClassDojo for Positive and Negative Behavior

This is one teacher's reflection on using ClassDojo to increase student engagement and other positive behaviors in the class. Ms. Rebecca Rodrigo teaches at Summit View School, a high school in Hollywood, California, that specializes in teaching students with learning disabilities and other learning differences. She regularly uses ClassDojo in her teaching practice.

> The school that I work in is a non-public school, which caters to students who have learning disabilities. For this reason, our students have issues ranging from focus on the task at hand to comprehension and retention. However, other behavioral issues sometimes surface due to the various backgrounds of our students. These might include ADHD or autism spectrum disorder.
>
> Before ClassDojo was used, our elementary classroom teachers used various strategies for maintaining order in our classes. Teachers of younger students used individual student index cards to note behavioral problems, while teachers of older students had student check-off charts or teacher-monitored lists of individual target behaviors. The ClassDojo program was discovered at a professional development workshop by one of our teachers, who was looking for an easier way to monitor and reinforce positive behavior and respond to negative behaviors that students manifested in the classroom.
>
> Initially, when I began ClassDojo, points were only given for positive things that the students did, such as participating and being on task. However, over time, the need to respond to negative behaviors became obvious, due to some students' impulsive actions in class. A negative point system based on response cost principles was then implemented at our school, wherein teachers were empowered to take away points for negative behaviors such as not bringing materials needed to class (e.g., pencils, papers, books, erasers), disrupting class, or talking to peers.

At first, the students were delighted to receive positive points. Additional reward categories were added so that the students could receive a significant number of points by the end of the week contingent on good behavior. Students could use their classroom credit points (their ClassDojo positive points) to buy treats such as Japanese erasers, bendy pencils, or even a homework pass or classroom movie time.

Though the use of positive points was a success, certain negative actions or behaviors continued to plague our classrooms. Off-task behaviors such as speaking over the teacher with another student during class discussion or not completing homework were just some of the actions that were an everyday occurrence in the classroom. The cost response system, using negative points in ClassDojo, was set up for that reason.

Though not as successful as the positive points during the first few weeks, students began noticing the effects of having points taken away every Friday, as they saw the decrease of credits they were getting. The impact of the negative points was greater when the treats were items that they liked. Over time, students became more aware of their actions, more conscious of their behaviors. The sound of a point being taken away helped our students center their focus on the task at hand in the classroom, and in that fashion, use of ClassDojo helped increase motivation and student engagement over time. I've enjoyed using this system and plan to continue using it in my class.

Research on ClassDojo

In one sense, any discussion of the research on the efficacy of ClassDojo might begin with the large body of behavioral research on the efficacy of rewards and response cost practices in the classroom in general. However, space limitations will not permit that discussion here. I will only state that reward / response cost systems are very effective in changing student behavior, and that efficacy has been repeatedly demonstrated in the classroom over recent decades (see Bender, 2016 for more on this).

A limited body of recent research has demonstrated the efficacy specifically of ClassDojo for improving student engagement (Halleck, 2012; Maclean-Blevins & Muilenburg, 2013; Mims, 2013; Schwartz, 2016b). For example, Maclean-Blevins and Muilenburg (2013) studied twenty-three third-grade students over a four-week period including a three-week intervention period. They targeted six specific behaviors: raising a hand, working quietly, focusing on work, using resources, interacting with directions, and double-checking work. Results showed an increase in these positive behaviors, including an increase in students' focus on their work. Also, eighteen of the twenty-three students reported that ClassDojo made the classroom exciting and helped them understand what behaviors were appropriate in the class, while three students did not enjoy using the system. Like the classroom example from Ms. Rodrigo, this research suggests that teachers can use ClassDojo to increase student engagement.

Summary

A large number of teachers are currently using ClassDojo or other class behavioral management systems to increase positive behavior and specifically students' engagement in the class. Certainly, teachers should not overlook the tried-and-true behavioral principles of reward and response cost in changing students' behavior, and using a tech-based system only demonstrates teachers' savvy in using modern tools for these proven practices. We might well find that ClassDojo or similar systems dominate classes in the near future, and I recommend this system to all teachers.

Strategy 19

A Growth Mindset Strategy

From time to time, an instructional idea emerges in the literature that seems to codify and maybe even define the efforts of educators for the next decade. One could argue that the concept of a growth mindset, originally suggested by Carol Dweck (2006), has made such an impact. Dweck was teaching courses on motivation and personality at Stanford University when she published her book *Growth Mindset: The New Psychology of Success* in 2006. In that book, she posited that one's sense of how one succeeds—either through one's work, effort, and persistence, or through one's innate talent or ability—plays a large role in defining one's level of success. Dweck discussed a fixed mindset as the belief that one's success is limited by one's talents and abilities and that such abilities are fixed and highly stable. In that sense, a fixed mindset often tends to limit one's overall efficacy, since the role of effort and hard work tends to be de-emphasized when one believes that all success is a result of innate, fixed ability.

> Fixed mindset is the belief that one's success is limited by one's talents and abilities and that such abilities are fixed and highly stable.

In contrast, a growth mindset—a belief that hard work and persistence make a difference—tends to lead to higher levels of success. When students believe that they can accomplish success with hard work and persistence in the face of challenges, they are generally more willing to make the effort required to master difficult material. Dweck (2006, 2015) then identified strategies for teachers to undertake to foster among their students the belief that effort and hard work pay off. In short, a growth mindset can be defined as the belief that qualities can change and that someone can develop their own intelligence and abilities (Mindset Works, 2016; Dweck, 2006; Schwartz, 2015b).

> Growth mindset is the belief that someone can, through persistence and hard work, develop their own intelligence and abilities.

Understanding the Concept of Growth Mindset

Soon after this concept emerged, research began to show that a growth mindset among students did, in fact, lead to increased motivation, student engagement, and achievement (Blackwell, Trzesniewski, & Dweck, 2007; Good, Aronson, & Inzlicht, 2003). At that point, other educators began to identify strategies teachers can use in the classroom to help foster a growth mindset on the part of the students (Mindset Works, 2016; Finley, 2014; Waller, 2016). By 2016, growth mindset had become one of the most discussed topics in education, and research continues to show benefits of growth mindset among various groups of students.

Malleability of the Human Brain

Dweck's concept of growth mindset was also based, in part, on recent advances in neurology, or the study of the brain (Doidge, 2007; Sousa, 2010). Research on the human brain, using recently developed neuroimaging techniques, has exploded within the last two decades, and we now know much more about how brains develop and function during the learning process (Doidge, 2007). For example, we now know that emotions and attitudes about learning have a great impact on learning for individual students (Sousa, 2010). Further, negative beliefs about one's own potential—referred to as negative stereotyping—can be quite detrimental to learning (Blackwell, Trzesniewski, & Dweck, 2007). Examples of such negative stereotyping might include young girls who believe "I'm no good in math" or some inner-city, minority youth who might believe "I can't read as well as other kids." Research has now shown that teaching students to avoid such negative stereotyping can reverse these negative outlooks, foster a growth mindset, and actually improve academic performance (Blackwell, Trzesniewski, & Dweck, 2007).

One of the more exciting recent findings from the neurological sciences is the malleability of the human brain, or the brain's ability to change over time, by making new neural connections between brain cells or even growing new neurons (Doidge,

2007). It has now been documented that learning can be measured in increased neurons in the brain as well as increased neural connections between brain cells (Sousa, 2010). Further, this means that brains are malleable and can, through hard work, grow in capacity. Also, the ability to develop new neurons and new neural connections persists throughout life (Doidge, 2007). In short, brains are much more malleable than was previously thought, and students who understand that will typically be more engaged, and thus more empowered, with the belief that "I can learn anything if I work hard enough!" That is a growth mindset.

Such growth has now been shown in a large body of psychoneurological research (see Doidge, 2007 for an extensive review). In one study, for example, researchers followed students' brain development during their teenage years and documented substantial changes in performance on IQ tests associated with hard work on challenging subjects (Ramsden, Richardson, Josse, Thomas, Ellis, Shakeshart, Seguier, & Price, 2011). Further, using neuroimaging, they found corresponding changes in the density of neurons in the relevant brain areas. In that study, an increase in neuronal connections in the brain accompanied an increase in IQ, while a decrease in neuronal connections in the brain accompanied an IQ decrease. In other words, hard work and persistent study not only led to increased academic skill—it led to actual changes in brain structure and neural functioning. This can be a powerful incentive for students and will help motivate students to study harder.

Attribution Theory and Growth Mindset

Another basis for the current concepts of growth mindset stems from earlier research on students' motivation and, more specifically, on attribution theory (Blackwell, Trzesniewski, & Dweck, 2007; Good, Aronson, & Inzlicht, 2003). Attribution theory focuses on the question "To what do I attribute my own successes or failures?" If someone attributes a positive event or outcome in his or her life to just plain luck or events not under their own control, then that person may be described as having an external locus of control. However, if that person attributes the same event to his or her own hard work, that person may be described as having an internal locus of control.

Several decades ago, proponents of attribution theory postulated that an internal locus of control was empowering for students and more likely to lead to academic success, and research over the years has proven that hypothesis (Dweck, 2006; Good, Aronson, & Inzlicht, 2003). For that reason, attribution of one's successes or failures is critical in one's overall success. Building upon that work, Dweck's work (2006, 2015) has resulted in increased discussions on how teachers can foster an internal locus of control, and thus a growth mindset, in their students. Further, some of the early research has actually taught students the basics of attribution theory as one approach to building a growth mindset (Good, Aronson, & Inzlicht, 2003).

Growth Mindset Curricula

As these varied lines of research came together to formulate the current thinking on growth mindset, educators wanted specific strategies to foster a growth mindset among students. This led to the development, or refocusing, of several commercially available curricula. First, Dweck developed a curriculum to help teachers foster a growth mindset in their students. Brainology (www.mindsetworks.com) is an online commercially available interactive program in which middle school students (grades 4 through 9) learn about how the brain works and how to strengthen their own brains. The program can be implemented by either teachers or parents, and the website offers a free fourteen-day preview of the program. Basically, the Brainology program is designed to improve motivation and achievement through building a growth mindset among students. Interactive animations, coupled with classroom activities, help students discover how brains function, how brain cells communicate with each other, and how new neural connections can be constructed with hard work and effort. This helps students boost their own confidence in their learning ability.

As another example, the ClassDojo (www.classdojo.com) class management system described previously has recently been supplemented with a series of five interactive animation videos designed to foster growth mindset (Schwartz, 2016b). Those titles include:

- Video 1: *A Secret About the Brain*
- Video 2: *The Magic of Mistakes*
- Video 3: *The Power of "Yet"*
- Video 4: *The Mysterious World of Neurons*
- Video 5: *Little by Little*

To date, there is no research on this new modification of ClassDojo to document the efficacy of this curriculum in fostering a growth mindset. However, research on that question is surely forthcoming, and teachers who are already using ClassDojo should certainly explore the use of these growth mindset lessons.

For teachers with a limited budget for such curricula, the available research does provide specific guidelines on teaching strategies to foster a growth mindset without having to purchase a new program (Dweck, 2006; Findley, 2014; Good, Aronson, & Inzlicht, 2003; Waller, 2016). The following lessons present these instructional suggestions.

Lessons to Foster a Growth Mindset

A number of theorists have provided strategies for fostering a growth mindset among students (Dweck, 2006; Findley, 2014; Good, Aronson, & Inzlicht, 2003; Waller, 2016). Further, several research articles have documented that a training period of only several days is enough to foster a change to a stronger growth mindset (Aronson, Fried, & Good, 2002; Blackwell, Trzesniewski, & Dweck, 2007; Good, Aronson, & Inzlicht, 2003). The eight daily lessons described in this section are a synthesis of the guidelines from these sources.

I suggest that teachers implement these eight lessons based on thirty minutes per lesson over a period of eight days. However, this training may be spread over several weeks, with two or three lessons done per week, if that fits better into a teacher's schedule.

Teach Students About Brain Function (Days 1, 2, and 3)

Teachers should teach students about their brains and brain function for three days, using approximately thirty minutes per day. Specifically, students should be taught about the physiological result of hard work, effort, and concentration—that hard work and persistence in challenging tasks actually helps grow brain cells! I'd suggest the use of one or two age-appropriate brief videos, coupled with various graphics on brain functioning; both videos and graphics can easily be found online. For example, many videos are available with merely a search of YouTube (use indicators *neurogenesis*, *dendrites and dendrite connections*, *brain plasticity*, or *malleability*). Most of these emphasize brain plasticity and show the positive results of hard work and persistence. Again, students should be taught that hard work on difficult subjects really does change their brains and make them smarter. Here are some suggested videos from YouTube.

- *Neurons and What They Do—An Animated Guide* (www.youtube.com/watch?v=vyNkAuX29OU)
- *Structure of a Neuron* (suggested for younger students) (www.youtube.com/watch?v=Ta_vWUsrjho)
- *How a Neuron Fires* (www.youtube.com/watch?v=C4Gt322-XxI)

As one example of this training, Good and her colleagues (2003) taught middle school students about neurons and dendrites and how brain cells use dendrites to communicate with each other, using various diagrams of brain cells. Students were taught that hard work, effort, and concentration will actually cause more brain cells to develop dendritic connections with other brain cells, resulting in increased IQ and actual changes in the brain throughout life (Good, Aronson, & Inzlicht, 2003).

Teachers should create participatory organizers to accompany the videos they choose to use, while creating lessons for three days. Students should complete these lessons and be absolutely convinced that they can grow their own brain potential.

Teach Students About Appropriate Praise (Day 4)

Successful teachers have long used praise in the classroom. However, the new focus on growth mindset suggests that our use of praise can be more focused with the ultimate goal of helping students develop a growth mindset (Finley, 2014; Waller, 2016). After students understand that hard work, persistence, and focus on challenging problems will change their brains and increase their ability, they should be taught to praise themselves for these work-habit attributes. Using one or two lessons, teachers should teach students about the impact of praise by focusing on two types of praise—praise from the teacher and self-praise.

First, for five minutes at the beginning of this lesson, the teacher should talk with the students about how and why praise is used in the class. They should be taught that you don't praise them only for a good grade (e.g., "Rebecca earned the highest score in the class on this math test!") but rather for the work that went into earning that grade ("Rebecca's hard work and study really paid off for her. I know she studied hard for this quiz, because she earned the highest grade in the class!").

In the first example, the focus of the praise is the grade, but in the second instance, the emphasis of the praise is on the hard work Rebecca put in. Teachers must develop the habit of praising for hard work, effort, and persistence, rather than for grades themselves, in order to increase those traits among their students.

Of course, once the students are taught about brain functioning, that topic can also be woven into the praise as follows: "After this test, I can tell that Rebecca surely grew a number of brain cells and new brain cell connections! She studied very hard and earned the highest grade in the class." Of course, the teacher should also praise others for their hard work and persistence, even if they didn't get the highest grade: "I know who else studied hard, too! It turns out that Billy is working hard and getting smarter, because his most recent grade was much higher than some of his others, so he's doing the hard work, too! Let's give Rebecca and Billy a round of applause!"

After discussing how you, as the teacher, praise students, you should help them understand that they should praise themselves in the same fashion—by concentrating on the hard work and effort they used to earn a good grade. An example might be, "I'm proud of the hard work you did to do this well on a tough subject, and you should be proud of yourself for that effort!" or "Give yourself a pat on the back for completing those difficult problems. You worked hard and got them done!"

Helping students develop an internal sense that their hard work and persistence will pay off with increased intelligence and better grades is the essence of fostering a growth mindset (Waller, 2016). Thus, for at least one thirty-minute lesson, teachers should discuss self-praise with their students. One strategy for this is to literally go around the room having students practice such praise, with a strong emphasis on effort and persistence. Teachers might also want to develop a worksheet of examples of various types of praise—some examples that provide praise only for high grades and other examples that demonstrate praise for strong effort and hard study. Teachers can then discuss each example with the class.

The focus of this effort is to foster long-term intrinsic pride among the students in the class, and that will not be an overnight or one-lesson process. In order to reinforce this lesson, teachers should always praise students appropriately, and continually coach students to praise themselves in an appropriate fashion. This coaching should continue throughout the year.

Teach Students Basic Attribution Theory (Days 5 and 6)

Another training strategy used to foster growth mindset among students involves teaching students the basics of attribution theory—specifically, the difference between internal and external locus of control and how internal locus of control is more empowering for the student (Good, Aronson, & Inzlicht, 2003). First, a teacher should find a grade-appropriate video option for explaining the concept of locus of control. The following YouTube videos might be a good beginning.

- Locus of Control, Learned Helplessness, and the Tyranny of Choice by Khan Academy (www.youtube.com/watch?v=Vx1dnPMPhl0)
- Locus of Control and Examples of Internal and External Control (www.youtube.com/watch?v=EF6mRWSiwhY)
- Attribution Theory (www.youtube.com/watch?v=doMOHcTlK7o)
- Locus of Control (www.youtube.com/watch?v=CCgYWwdoogM)

Once the teacher has selected one or two age-appropriate videos, he or she should develop a participatory organizer to accompany each video. Definitions of *attribution* and *internal* and *external locus of control* should be discussed, along with the fact that internal locus of control empowers students over time. Students should be taught to distinguish between internal and external locus of control and consider how their own beliefs and attributions might impact their level of effort or study habits.

Next, depending on the age of the students, it can be interesting to have the students take an informal assessment of their own locus of control and then use those results as a basis for class discussion. Several informal measures may be found online (e.g., The Academic Locus of Control Scale: http://apexed.webstarts.com/uploads/TriceAcademicLocusofControlScaleKeyandExplanation.pdfV). By having students take such a measure and score themselves, the teacher can set up a good discussion of locus of control, and how it impacts one's persistence on challenging tasks.

In addition to teaching middle school students about brain functioning, Good and her colleagues (2003) taught middle school students attribution theory with an emphasis on developing an internal locus of control. That training did result in fostering a growth mindset and in improving academic scores (Good et al., 2003).

Teach Students to Celebrate Failure (Day 6)

Another aspect of the training involves teaching students to value failure as a step toward learning. Teachers can encourage increased effort and participation in class by offering some praise even for the effort behind incorrect answers in class. They might say something like, "That answer is close but not quite right. Still, kudos for trying that hard, and keep up that kind of hard work!" (Waller, 2016).

Also, teachers should show examples of where failure helped someone make progress. For example, legend holds that Thomas Edison tried hundreds of ways to make a lightbulb before succeeding. However, when asked about his failures, he replied, "I have not failed 700 times. I have not failed once. I have succeeded in proving that those 700 ways will not work. When I have eliminated the ways that will not work, I will find the way that will work." Then point out that Edison's hard work and persistence in that work changed the world.

While there is some question as to the accuracy of the Edison legend, it will help students understand the importance of failure—that failure is a step toward understanding. Teachers might emphasize this lesson by having students search online for other, similar examples, other successful failures. For example, the Apollo 13 moon mission was called a successful failure. That mission failed in the intended mission—to land on the moon—but succeeded in bringing back the crew alive, in the face of catastrophic system failure and nearly impossible odds. Students might develop brief reports of other failures that changed history in positive ways. The focus of these failed activities should be to help students see the value of failure, the value of taking risks or trying new, untested ideas. Students must be willing to fail and not be nervous about failure, as long as they subsequently learn from the failure.

Review: Combining This Information (Day 7)

Day 7 should be spent with a focus on how these various areas of knowledge now support each other. Attribution theory has been around for several decades, whereas the information on neurogenesis and the malleability of the human brain is much more recent (Sousa, 2010). Also, information about appropriate praise is only now developing (Finley, 2014; Waller, 2016), but the emerging literature on growth mindset is focusing on praise that develops the appropriate mindset for success, and all of these areas are coming together in the concept of growth mindset. Good and her colleagues (2003) showed that training that involved a combination of attribution theory training and teaching students about the importance of hard work in generating new neural connections was more effective than either approach alone. Thus, one lesson should be spent in review of this information and interpretation of these diverse areas in view of each other.

Assessment (Day 8)

As a final step, the teacher should develop a unit test based on the information taught in this growth mindset instruction. Definitions should be stressed (*dendrites, neurons, neurogenesis, malleability, locus of control, internal, external*) but also a deeper understanding of brain malleability, the value of internal locus of control, and how to effectively praise oneself to set up the expectation of success. After such an assessment, the teacher may choose to review one or more areas, depending on how the class does overall.

Long-Term, Continual Follow-Up

This step does not involve a specific thirty-minute lesson but is presented here to stress that teachers should continue the training to foster a growth mindset. This can be accomplished by continually emphasizing appropriate praise and self-praise and mentioning frequently how students have successfully grown their brains and how much students are empowered by developing an internal locus of control. Continual emphasis on these concepts will keep the students focused on a growth mindset and will, over time, create in those students the habits of learning that are likely to lead to a lifetime of success.

A Case Study: Teaching Growth Mindset

Mrs. Tremain, a fifth-grade teacher, had always loved mathematics and was very much aware that some of the young girls in her class had developed a negative attitude toward math. In particular, Mrs. Tremain was working with a young student, Amaris, who could not seem to master mathematics. She was having particular difficulty with word problems and any operations with fractions with unlike denominators. Mrs. Tremain had heard Amaris say many times, "I'm just no good in math!" Mrs. Tremain knew that Amaris was a capable student, and she wanted to help Amaris understand that she could be successful in these math areas if she made more effort.

In addition, Mrs. Tremain, along with all of the teachers in the school, were strongly encouraged by their administrator to implement action research projects and present data-based results from that research to the professional learning committee at the school. Thus, it seemed like a natural progression for Mrs. Tremain to develop and implement an action research project using the growth mindset strategy as an intervention with Amaris. Mrs. Tremain had read some of the research suggesting that improvements in growth mindset were possible among young girls (Good, Aronson, & Inzlicht, 2003), so she was motived to see how this might help her student.

She began her action research by deciding on a dependent measure for her individual work with Amaris. She quickly determined that the optimal variable for that was Amaris's grades on daily homework and classwork assignments rather than unit tests. Mrs. Tremain felt that a weekly average of daily assignment grades would more accurately capture a true picture of Amaris's performance over time. Mrs. Tremain then reviewed the previous three units and calculated an average weekly grade for those specific assignments and used those unit averages as a baseline.

In addition to this academic dependent measure, Mrs. Tremain developed two interview questions that she wanted to use as an informal survey with Amaris during the intervention. The two questions were:

1. Do you think you are working harder in mathematics after learning about your brain?

2. How do you feel when you succeed on a really tough math assignment?

While Mrs. Tremain recognized that these questions would not generate numeric data, she wanted to go beyond the numeric dependent measure and actually tease out Amaris's attitudes about her own success. Therefore, Mrs. Tremain planned to use these questions every week during the intervention period.

Mrs. Tremain then began an intervention by implementing the growth mindset lessons as described previously, doing a thirty-minute lesson either two or three times a week with the entire class. It took her four weeks to complete these eight lessons. During that time, she collected and saved the same performance data for Amaris as she had during the baseline. She also asked the interview questions weekly and made brief notes to capture the gist of Amaris's answers to those questions.

The data chart presented in figure 19.1 shows Amaris's performance data over the baseline and intervention periods and for several weeks after the intervention concluded. As these data show, Amaris accomplished mastery in various mathematics subjects, and some (not all) of the work during the intervention period did involve both word problems and fraction operations. These data showed improved academic performance during and after the training on growth mindset.

Also, Mrs. Tremain reviewed the interview questions and noted a change in the answers Amaris provided as the training moved forward. The change suggested that Amaris had begun to move much more toward a growth mindset. Thus, Mrs. Tremain concluded that her action research had been successful in changing Amaris's mindset and in fostering a growth-oriented mindset. Mrs. Tremain then determined to collect baseline data on a number of other girls and boys in her class during the following year.

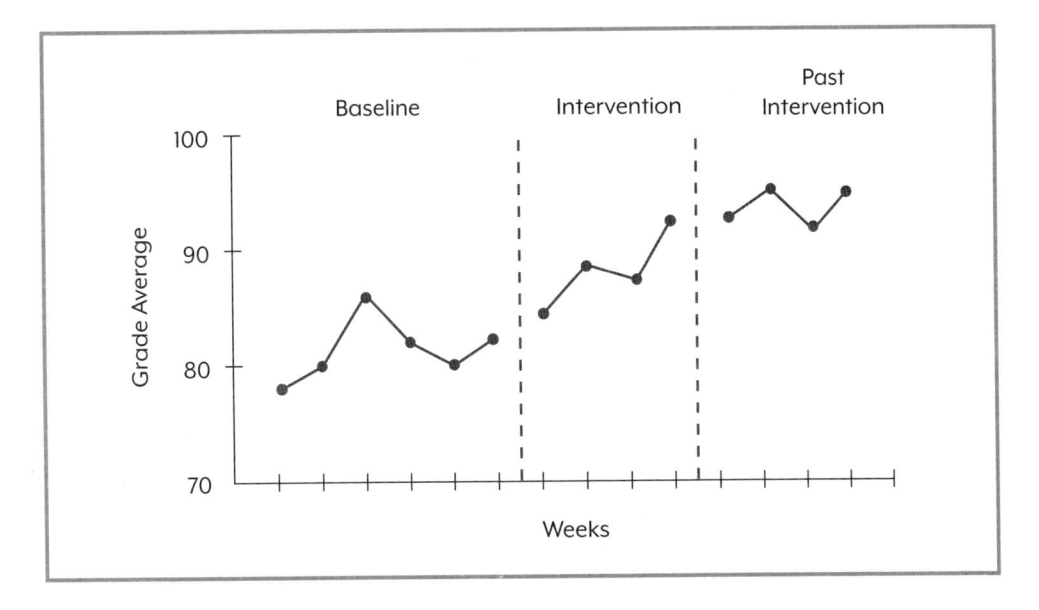

Figure 19.1: Amaris's baseline and intervention data.

Research on Growth Mindset

Research on the growth mindset concept is fairly recent and still ongoing, but the early research results are very positive (Aronson, Fried, & Good, 2002; Blackwell, Trzesniewski, & Dweck, 2007; Dweck, 2006; Good, Aronson, & Inzlicht, 2003; Ramsden et al., 2011). For example, Blackwell and her colleagues (2007) studied middle school students and compared students with a fixed mindset to students with a growth mindset. The results showed that students with a growth mindset were more motivated to learn and exerted more efforts in their studies. As a result, these students outperformed those with a fixed mindset in math.

In a subsequent study, Blackwell taught one group of students about growth mindset, emphasizing that persistence and hard work actually makes the brain grow and "makes you smarter" (Blackwell, Trzesniewski, & Dweck, 2007). The experimental group received eight lessons focused on brain functioning and neural transmission (how brain cells communicate with each other), the malleability of the brain over time, the dangers of stereotypes (avoidance of terms like *dumb* or *stupid*), and a strong emphasis on growing one's own brain and making oneself smarter. A comparison group was taught about the stages of memory. Results showed that three times as many students in the experimental group showed an increase in effort and engagement compared with the control group, and those experimental group students also improved their academic scores dramatically.

Other research has also shown positive effects of a focus on fostering a growth mindset (Aronson, Fried, & Good, 2002; Dweck, 2006; Good, Aronson, & Inzlicht, 2003; Ramsden et al., 2011). For example, research (www.mindsetworks.com) suggests that fostering a growth mindset results in increased prosocial behavior and less aggressive behavior, as well as reducing the achievement gap between boys and girls in mathematics (Good, Aronson, & Inzlicht, 2003). Other research showed a reduction in the achievement gap between students of different races, based on growth mindset training (Aronson, Fried, & Good, 2002). Clearly the existing research documents many benefits of fostering a growth mindset among our students.

Summary

Growth mindset, like other strategies discussed in this book, seems to be capturing the attention of educators around the world and with good reason; teaching that fosters a growth mindset does help students develop better attitudes, increases student engagement, and ultimately increases academic performance. Teachers should explore various approaches to fostering growth mindset, including both commercially available programs or the free instructional lessons described previously. In some ways, fostering a growth mindset, a set of work ethic habits that a student will carry throughout life, may be one of the most important things we can teach those in our charge, so teachers should certainly explore this innovative instructional approach.

Strategy 20

Goal Setting and Self-Monitoring for Increasing Attention Skills

Few strategies are more powerful for increasing students' engagement than self-monitoring to increase one's level of attention (Bedesem, 2012; Bender, 2013b; Hallahan & Sapona, 1983; Harris, Friedlander, Saddler, & Frizzel, 2005). Further, having individual students set a personal goal to pay attention more and then teaching them how will dramatically increase student engagement classwide (Elias, 2013; Freemark, 2014; Harris et al., 2005; Hattie, 2012; Marzano, 2009a). There are several aspects to this strategy, including the power of goal setting generally and the specific strategy for teaching students to pay attention.

From a broader perspective, setting goals and monitoring one's progress toward them is one hallmark of all successful individuals (Elias, 2013; Hattie, 2102). Therefore, it stands to reason that preparing students with these goal-setting and self-monitoring strategies should be a fundamental priority in every classroom, particularly when one considers how many students demonstrate problems with attention skills. This would include students with attention deficit hyperactivity disorders, learning disabilities, behavioral disorders, and many non-diagnosed students who merely have milder attention problems.

Of course, educators have long realized that setting goals can help in motivating students, and research bears out the proposition that personal goal setting is an effective strategy overall (Elias, 2013; Freemark, 2014; Hattie, 2012; Marzano, 2009).

Over the years, many terms have been used for this basic concept of setting goals and monitoring one's progress in relation to those goals: *self-monitoring, self-evaluation, self-regulation, progress monitoring,* and even *formative evaluation.* Marzano (2009), for example, describes this process as setting objectives and providing feedback relative to those objectives. In this instance, we will emphasize setting personal goals specific to one's on-task behavior, since this directly addresses the student engagement issue.

Regardless of the terms used by various educators, the idea remains relatively constant. Students do better academically and pay attention better when specific goals are stipulated and those goals are used in tandem with a simple self-evaluation process to monitor progress regularly (Bedesem, 2012; Bender, 2013b; Harris, Friedlander, Saddler, & Frizzel, 2005). This strategy is a tried-and-true way to increase academic performance and a variety of positive behaviors, including increased student engagement.

Teaching Goal Setting and Self-Monitoring

There are specific guidelines for setting individual student goals for increasing attention and for preparing students to self-monitor their own performance. First, setting an appropriate goal relative to one's own attention requires some guidance. Next, learning the habit of paying attention, the habits that will increase on-task time, is critical. Then, students must be taught to carefully monitor and honestly chart their own progress relative to their goal of increasing attention to task. Finally, teachers should ensure that the monitoring of progress toward increased attention is valued by the student.

Set Appropriate, Descriptive, Meaningful Goals

Because goal setting has not been stressed in some classrooms, students may need some instruction in identifying and setting appropriately descriptive goals for increasing attention. Specifically, students should be taught that effective goals must identify specific target behaviors and should emphasize some procedure for monitoring those target behaviors. For example, "I want to pay attention more" is not an effective goal for elementary students, since it is not specific in either sense—no target behavior is identified, and no procedure is suggested for monitoring that behavior. At best, that statement is merely a statement of intention or desire. However, that same goal for an elementary student might be stated as follows: "I will improve my on-task behavior by checking my on-task behavior whenever I hear a signal bell, marking whether I was on-task or not, and then returning immediately to work."

In that goal statement, several specific behaviors are identified, including checking on one's own attention to task, marking the behavior on a monitoring sheet, and returning to work. In this example, on-task time is used as the actual indicator of increased student engagement, such that this example is a measurable goal with specifics to help the student understand what is expected. Finally, teachers should always require students to write down their goals and devise ways to monitor them. Then students should chart the progress in improving their on-task behavior.

Teach Students to Pay Attention

Using that goal, teachers can use a procedure for self-monitoring on-task behavior first developed by Hallahan and his coworkers in the late 1970s (Hallahan & Sapona, 1983) and updated many times since (Bedesem, 2012; Bender, 2013b; Harris, Friedlander, Saddler, & Frizzel, 2005). Hallahan determined that many students with poor attention skills did not truly understand what paying attention meant, that they would need to be trained how to pay attention by developing a habit of routinely checking in with themselves about whether they were on-task or not (Hallahan & Sapona, 1983).

In that procedure, students are taught that paying attention means regular and periodic checking to see if one is looking at the task (reading a passage, math problem on the board, or a worksheet) and thinking about it (Hallahan & Sapona, 1983). That is what *attention* means.

To teach these skills, and make them a habit, the teacher needs a cue to check one's attention (usually a bell or ringtone) and a daily recording sheet (see figure 20.1).

Was I Paying Attention?	
Yes	No

Figure 20.1: Daily recording sheet for self-monitoring.

Initially, teachers used a teacher-developed twenty-minute audio tape that presented a ringtone that rang on average every forty-five seconds. (The length of time between the tones must vary, but should average forty-five seconds.) That ringtone was used to cue students to self-check their on-task behavior by asking themselves, "Was I paying attention?" or "Was I looking at the work and thinking about it?" They would then check on the daily recording sheet either the on-task or the off-task column and return to work. After twenty minutes, the students would rewind the tape and divide the number of on-task marks by the total number of marks to find out his or her percentage of on-task behavior.

Research showed that by doing this procedure over a ten- to fifteen-day period, students with attention problems could increase their engaged time and would actually develop the habit of paying attention in class that persisted long after the intervention (Hallahan & Sapona, 1983). The procedure would then be faded using a step-by-step procedure involving removal of the cue to record (ringtone) first and the daily question sheet next.

Of course, this description presents the original procedure and is probably still the best way to quickly explain this procedure to teachers unfamiliar with the process. However, technology has now been developed to make this self-monitoring procedure considerably easier. For example, Bedesem (2012) demonstrates the efficacy of the self-monitoring procedure using cell phone technology to replace the audio-tape ringtone and the daily recording sheet.

Monitor and Chart Progress

Goal setting to increase attention is virtually meaningless without reflective self-evaluation on one's performance relative to the goal of increasing on-task time. Students must be provided with a simple chart to let them know if they are improving their on-task behavior and thus improving their engagement with the subject matter. By charting the percentage of on-task behavior data generated in the previous procedure, students can develop a picture of their own engagement. An X-Y axis chart such as those presented previously in the case studies can provide an accurate portrayal of these data.

Help Students Value On-Task Behavior and Self-Monitoring

Finally, teachers must help students learn to value the goal setting and self-evaluation of the on-task behavior process. To encourage students to internalize higher levels of on-task time and make a habit of increased attention, teachers should undertake the procedure mentioned previously and do this self-monitoring training daily, while complimenting students on their increased percentages of on-task time.

Teachers should also point out that learning to pay attention in this fashion will help students increase their attention in all of their classes and will also increase their grades over time (Hallahan & Sapona, 1983).

Research on Goal Setting and Progress Monitoring

Research has shown that goal setting and reflective self-monitoring will increase students' on-task time, as well as achievement, and for that reason, this strategy is widely recommended in the educational literature (Bedesem, 2012; Elias, 2013; Freemark, 2014; Harris, Friedlander, Saddler, & Frizzel, 2005; Hattie, 2012; Moeller, Theiler, & Wu, 2012; Marzano, 2009). For example, in his meta-analyses on effective instructional strategies, Hattie's (2012) research showed that goal setting was number 48 on his list of the most effective 150 educational strategies overall, with an effect size of 0.50. Also, both Bedesem (2012) and Harris and her colleagues (2005) demonstrated that students can be trained to increase their engaged time using this simple procedure to learn how to pay attention better.

As one example, Moeller, Theiler, and Wu (2012) tracked the academic impact of goal setting and self-evaluation over a five-year period at twenty-three high schools in a quasi-experimental study using 1,273 students in Spanish classes. Results indicated that setting goals and monitoring one's progress toward those goals yielded an increase not only in engagement but also in academic achievement. Thus, the recent research strongly supports the original research—setting a goal to increase attention and then showing students how to do so will increase student engagement.

Summary

As this body of research shows, teaching students to pay attention and then to monitor their own levels of attention will increase student engagement. Further, developing the habit of focused attention is, in all probability, one of the more critical skills for success in life (Bender, 2012; Elias, 2013). Finally, like many of the effective strategies presented in this book, goal setting and self-monitoring of attention will build students' academic performance as well. For these reasons, this is a strategy that all teachers should implement across the grade levels.

Appendix

Meta-Analysis and Effect Size

Throughout this book, I've referred constantly to the meta-analytic work of two of the more important researchers in education today, Robert Marzano (2009, 2007; Marzano et al., 2001) and John Hattie (2012). These educational leaders have used the relatively recently developed meta-analysis technique to summarize research on effective instructional strategies, so for a book of this nature, their research had to be quite prominent.

While many teachers are quite fluent with this research, I wanted to provide some description of this meta-analytic technique for newer teachers or for those who may not be aware of what this important research tool provides. Thus, here is a brief explanation of what a meta-analysis is and how the effect sizes generated by that technique can be interpreted by educators in the classroom. I published one meta-analysis myself (Bender & Smith, 1990) when this research technique was still being developed, so I have some sense of the possibilities of this technique, as well as the inherent limitations and concerns.

Basically, a meta-analysis is a summarization of research data collected by many different researchers on the same question. The data is then mathematically pooled to create a large data set and to allow for certain comparisons. The original research question in all of the various studies might be something like, "How effective is reciprocal teaching compared to traditional instruction?" Because many different researchers have explored that question, there are many research studies available for a meta-analysis comparison, most of which report a mean and standard deviation for both an experimental group and a control group. Those data are necessary for the meta-analysis procedure.

Thus, using multiple studies on the same general question, the author of the meta-analysis can attack this question by combining those cumulative data and mathematically manipulating those data to draw some conclusions about the overall efficacy of reciprocal teaching. Further, the meta-analysis is a powerful technique, in that by combining data across studies, the meta-analytic research can generate extremely large experimental and comparison groups.

In a meta-analysis, the difference between groups is described as effect size, which can best be understood as the relative effect of a specific education intervention or strategy. This is done by a comparison of the distributions of the dependent measures between the experimental students and the control students across all of the studies.

Hattie (2012) describes an effect size as a scale that allows multiple comparisons independent of the original mode of scoring in the various studies, showing the relative comparison of various independent educational interventions on achievement. He reports that for his work, he completed over 800 separate meta-analyses. Further, Hattie (2012) notes that, whereas almost all education interventions work to some degree, an effect size allows the researcher to state which interventions work more effectively (Hattie, 2012; Marzano, 2007).

Effect sizes really measure how far the curve or distribution of the scores of students is moved by the specific intervention (in this case, reciprocal teaching). An effect size of 0.50 suggests that the distribution of scores of the students in the experimental groups was offset in a positive direction by half of a standard deviation, compared to the control groups. This demonstrates that the education intervention of reciprocal teaching is very effective, compared to the other treatments given to the control groups.

Advantages of Meta-Analyses

A combination of students across studies allows researchers to draw conclusions on the impact of a specific strategy based on very large samples of students. In that sense, meta-analyses such as those done by Hattie (2012) and Marzano and his coworkers (Marzano, 2007; Marzano et al., 2001) allow researchers to directly compare the efficacy of multiple treatments including treatments that were generated from different research studies. Therefore, researchers can make definitive statements on which teaching strategies might be more effective than others.

From the perspective of teachers, it is quite refreshing to read meta-analytic research that compares educational interventions to each other, even though there may be no available research studies that directly compare the two. For example, a meta-analysis allows one to state that reciprocal teaching is more effective than whole language instruction (Hattie, 2012). Thus, teachers seeking a new strategy should employ reciprocal teaching rather than whole language learning.

A meta-analysis can also allow researchers to state the percentage of gain in academic achievement associated with use of a particular educational intervention (Marzano, 2009, 2007, 2003; Marzano et al., 2001). This information, like the comparisons above, facilitates teacher decisions on what types of interventions to employ in the classroom. That is why this "percentage of achievement gain" figure has been reported for many of the educational interventions in this book.

Disadvantages of Meta-Analyses

With that noted, there are a number of assumptions that underlie any meta-analysis that are somewhat troubling. Most important, researchers using this technique have to determine that the differences between the various studies they include in their analysis are not substantive enough to make a meaningful difference in their overall conclusions. Here is an example.

As one might guess, there are typically many studies on the efficacy of a teaching strategy such as reciprocal teaching, particularly if the intervention strategy has been around for several decades. Further, while many different researchers have explored the question on the efficacy of reciprocal teaching, they would have explored that strategy in many different ways, so there would be many substantive differences in that research. For example, some researchers might use reciprocal teaching in an experimental design (i.e., experimental and control groups) by measuring the impact of six weeks of reciprocal teaching on students' academic achievement scores on unit tests in a seventh-grade science class. Another researcher might use reciprocal teaching in an experimental design to explore students' sense of their own learning in a fifth-grade class, as measured by student questionnaires (perhaps using a question like "How well did you learn in this reciprocal teaching lesson?"). Finally, yet another researcher seeking to expand the applicability of reciprocal teaching might use it in a second-grade class lesson on the water cycle only in one class period and using an end-of-class test score as the dependent variable.

In a meta-analysis, all of those studies would probably be included, even though the dependent measures (i.e., achievement scores on instructional units over time, scores on student surveys, and a one-time dependent measure score) are very different. The researcher has the responsibility in a meta-analysis to eliminate studies from the analysis that might confound the results. However, in most cases, editorial limitations (i.e., the number of pages allowed in a published research paper) often prohibit the researcher from providing much detail on the decisions he or she made, and that is a second disadvantage of this technique. When reading a meta-analysis, at least in many cases, the reader is flying blind regarding the specific assumptions made by the researchers.

Use of Meta-Analyses

As noted above, there are limitations and concerns with meta-analytic research, but this powerful tool does provide much guidance to educators. For that reason, I encourage educators to read these meta-analyses by various researchers, discuss them with your peers, your PLC, or your professional learning network, and then reflectively implement those instructional suggestions that seem to work best in your individual situation. As always, a reflective teacher, using his or her professional colleagues as sounding boards and willing to risk trying new instructional strategies, is the most powerful source for continually improving instruction, and I have every confidence that such teachers will continue to explore new strategies such as those presented herein.

References

Alabsi, T. A. (2016). The effectiveness of role play strategy in teaching vocabulary. *Theory and Practice in Language Studies, 6*(2), 227–234.

Albrecht, N. J., Albrecht, P. M., & Cohen, M. (2012). Mindfully teaching in the classroom: A literature review. *Australian Journal of Teacher Education, 37*(12), 1–13.

Aronson, J., Fried, C. B., & Good, C. (2002). Reducing the effects of stereotype threat on African American college students by shaping theories of intelligence. *Journal of Experimental Social Psychology, 38,* 113–125.

Arreaga-Meyer, C. (1998). Increasing active student responding and improving academic performance through classwide peer tutoring. *Intervention in School and Clinic, 24*(2), 89–117.

Artigliere, M. (2016). Leveraging technology in the classroom: Using Comic Life software to support literacy. *Journal of Teacher Action Research, 2*(2). Retrieved from www.practical teacherresearch.com/uploads/5/6/2/4/56249715/artigliere91-97.pdf

Ash, K. (2011). Games and simulations help children access science. *Educational Week, 30*(27), 12.

Anderson, S. (2014). *Let's build something together—Maker spaces and 20% time.* Retrieved from http://blog.web20classroom.org/2014/07/lets-build-something-together-maker.html

Barak, M., Ashkar, T., & Dori, Y. J. (2016). *Teaching science via animated movies: Its effect on students' learning outcomes and motivation.* Retrieved from http://telem-pub.openu.ac.il/users/chais/2010/after_noon/3_2.pdf

Barell, J. (2007). *Problem-based learning: An inquiry approach* (2nd ed.). Thousand Oaks, CA: Corwin Press.

Bedesem, P. (2012). Using cell phone technology for self-monitoring procedures in inclusive settings. *Journal of Special Education Technology, 27,* 33–46.

Bender, W. N. (2017). *20 strategies for STEM instruction.* West Palm Beach, FL: Learning Sciences International.

Bender, W. N. (2016). *20 disciplinary strategies for working with challenging students.* West Palm Beach, FL: Learning Sciences International.

Bender, W. N. (2013a). *Differentiating math instruction, K–8* (3rd ed.). Thousand Oaks, CA: Corwin Press.

Bender, W. N. (2013b). *Differentiating instruction for students with learning disabilities* (3rd ed.). Thousand Oaks, CA: Corwin Press.

Bender, W. N. (2012). *Project-based learning: Differentiating instruction for the 21st century*. Thousand Oaks, CA: Corwin Press.

Bender, W. N. (1985). Differential diagnosis based on task-related behavior of learning disabled and low-achieving adolescents. *Learning Disability Quarterly, 8*, 261–266.

Bender, W. N., & Smith, J. K. (1990). Classroom behavior of children and adolescents with learning disabilities: A meta-analysis. *Journal of Learning Disabilities, 23*, 298–305.

Bender, W. N., & Waller, L. (2013). *Cool tech tools for lower tech teachers: 20 tactics for every classroom*. Thousand Oaks, CA: Corwin Press.

Benson, R., Brack, C., & Samarwickrema, G. (2012). Teaching with wikis: Improving staff development through action research. *Research in Learning Technology, 20*(2).

Bergmann, J., & Sams, A. (2014). *Flip your classroom: Reach every student in every class every day*. Alexandria, VA: Association for Supervision and Curriculum Development.

Bharti, P. (2014). How to use augmented reality in the classroom. *Ed Tech Review*. Retrieved from http://edtechreview.in/trends-insights/insights/1210-how-to-use-augmented-reality-in-the-classroom

Blackwell, L. S., Trzesniewski, K. H., & Dweck, C. S. (2007). Implicit theories of intelligence predict achievement across an adolescent transition: A longitudinal study and an intervention. *Child Development, 78*(1), 246–263.

Blog Basics. (2012). *Teaching today*. Retrieved from http://teachingtoday.glencoe.com/howtoarticles/blog-basics

Bloom, J. S. (2015). Coding: The ultimate equalizer. *Huffington Post*. Retrieved from www.huffingtonpost.com/joel-s-bloom/coding-the-ultimate-equal_1_b_8032318.html?utm_hp_ref=education&ir=Education

Boss, S. (2011). *Immersive PBL: Indiana project reaches far beyond the classroom*. Retrieved from www.edutopia.org/blog/pbl-immersive-brings-clean-water-haiti-suzie-boss

Boss, S., & Krauss, J. (2007). *Reinventing project-based learning: Your field guide to real-world projects in the digital age*. Washington, DC: International Society for Technology in Education.

Bowman-Perrott, L. (2009). Classwide peer tutoring. *Intervention in School and Clinic, 44*(5), 259–267.

Breeden, J. (2015). *Review: MakerBot Replicator 3D Printer excels at enhancing classrooms*. Retrieved from www.edtechmagazine.com/k12/article/2015/06/review-makerbot-replicator-3d-printer-excels-small-and-durable-designs

Bruns, A., & Humphreys, S. (2007). *Building collaborative capacities in learners: The M/Cyclopedia project revisited*. Retrieved from www.academia.edu/2342321/Building_Collaborative_Capacities_in_Learners_The_M_Cyclopedia_Project_Revisited

Fuchs, D., Fuchs, L., & Burnish, P. (2000). Peer-assisted learning strategies: An evidence-based practice to promote reading achievement. *Learning Disabilities Research & Practice, 15*(2), 85–91.

Campbell, E. (2013). *Research round-up: Mindfulness in schools*. Retrieved from http://greatergood.berkeley.edu/article/item/research_round_up_school_based_mindfulness_programs

Caprino, K. (2014). 5 mindfulness steps that guarantee increased success and vitality. *Forbes*. Retrieved from www.forbes.com/sites/kathycaprino/2014/02/12/5-mindfulness-steps-that-guarantee-increased-success-and-vitality/

Cassady, J. C., Kozlowski, A., & Kornmann, M. (2008). Electronic field trips as interactive learning events: Promoting student learning at a distance. *Journal of Interactive Learning Research, 19*(3), 439–454.

Churchill, D. (2007). Web 2.0 and possibilities for educational applications. *Educational Technology, 47*(2), 24–29.

Class Tech Tips. (2014). *Creating augmented reality triggers with Canva*. Retrieved from http://classtechtips.com/2015/03/24/creating-augmented-reality-triggers-with-canva/

Cochrane Collegiate Academy. (2014). *How to engage underperforming students*. Retrieved from www.edutopia.org/stw-school-turnaround-student-engagement-video?utm_source=twitter&utm_medium=socialflow

Cox, J. (2015). *Classroom management meditation exercises for teachers*. Retrieved from www.teachhub.com/classroom-management-meditation-exercises-teachers

Cruz, B. C., & Murthy, S. A. (2006). Breathing life into history: Using role-playing to engage students. *Social Studies & the Young Learner, 19*(1), 4–8.

Curtis, C. (2015). Does Facebook really have a place in the classroom? *The Telegraph*. Retrieved from www.telegraph.co.uk/technology/facebook/10926105/Does-Facebook-really-have-a-place-in-the-classroom.html

Davis, L. C. (2015). When mindfulness meets the classroom. Retrieved from www.theatlantic.com/education/archive/2015/08/mindfulness-education-schools-meditation/402469/?utm_content=buffera4dba&utm_medium=social&utm_source=twitter.com&utm_campaign=buffer

Davis, V. (2015). *Year one with a 3D Printer: 17 tips*. Retrieved from www.edutopia.org/blog/year-one-with-3d-printer-vicki-davis?utm_content=blog&utm_campaign=year-one-with-3d-printer&utm_source=twitter&utm_medium=socialflow&utm_term=link

Deegan, P. C. (2015). *Implementing a schoolwide mindfulness program*. Retrieved from www.edutopia.org/blog/implementing-school-wide-mindfulness-program-patrick-cook-deegan?utm_content=blog&utm_campaign=implementing-school-wide-mindfulness-program&utm_source=twitter&utm_medium=socialflow&utm_term=link

De Gree, A. (2015). *Is 3D printing the next industrial revolution?* Retrieved from http://guff.com/is-3d-printing-the-next-industrial-revolution

De Pedro, X., Rieradevall, M., López, P., Sant, D., Piñol, J., Núñez, L., & Llobera, M. (2006). Writing documents collaboratively in higher education (I): Qualitative results from a 2-year project study. *Congreso Internacional de Docencia Universitaria e Innovación (International Congress of University Teaching and Innovation)*. Retrieved from http://uniwiki.ourproject.org/tiki-download_wiki_attachment.php?attId=98&page=UniwikiCongressos

Deters, F., Cuthrell, K., & Stapleton, J. (2010). Why wikis? Student perceptions of using wikis in online learning coursework. *Journal of Online Learning and Teaching, 6*(1).

Detroit Schools Choose Movie Maker to Fuel Creativity and Boast Test Scores. (2011, August 29). *eSchoolNews*. Retrieved from http://eschoolnews.com/2011/08/29/detroit-schools-choose-movie-maker-to-fuel-creativity-and-boost-test-scores

Doidge, N. (2007). *The brain that changes itself: Stories of personal triumph from the frontiers of brain science*. New York: Penguin Group.

Dredge, S. (2014). Coding at school: A parent's guide to England's new coding curriculum. *The Guardian*. Retrieved from www.theguardian.com/technology/2014/sep/04/coding-school-computing-children-programming

Dunleavy, M., Dede, C., & Mitchell, R. (2009). Affordances and limitations of immersive participatory augmented reality simulations for teaching and learning. *Journal of Science Educational Technology, 18*(1), 7–22.

Dweck, C. (2015). *Carol Dweck revisits the "growth mindset."* Retrieved from www.edweek.org/ew/articles/2015/09/23/carol-dweck-revisits-the-growth-mindset.html

Dweck, C. (2006). *Mindset: The new psychology of success*. New York: Random House.

Elias, M. J. (2013). Back to school: Goal setting with your students. *Edutopia*. Retrieved from www.edutopia.org/blog/back-to-school-goal-setting-students-teacher-maurice-elias

Epps, J., & Osborn, C. (2014). *Interactive project-based learning using 3D grant results*. Retrieved from www.youtube.com/watch?v=bfT1AqO1qi8

Evans, K. (2016). *How to start a blog from scratch in 20 minutes, step by step*. Retrieved from http://startbloggingonline.com/

Fears, S., & Patsalides, L. (2012). *The many benefits of teaching robotics in the classroom*. Retrieved from www.brighthubeducation.com/middle-school-science-lessons/17432-the-importance-of-teaching-robotics/

Ferriter, B. (2011). *Using Twitter in the high school classroom*. Retrieved from http://teacherleaders.typepad.com/the-tempered-radical/2011/10/using-twitter-with-teens-html?utm_source=feedburner&utm_medium=feed&utm_campaign=feed%3A+the_tempered_redical+%28The+Tempered+Radical%29

Ferriter, W. M., & Garry, A. (2010). *Teaching the iGeneration: 5 easy ways to introduce essential skills with web 2.0 tools*. Bloomington, IN: Solution Tree Press.

Finley, K. (2014). 4 ways to encourage a growth mindset in the classroom. Retrieved from www.edsurge.com/news/2014-10-24-4-ways-to-encourage-a-growth-mindset-in-the-classroom

Flanagan, L. (2015). *How turning math into a maker workshop can bring calculations to life*. Retrieved from http://ww2.kqed.org/mindshift/2015/11/19/how-turning-math-into-a-maker-workshop-can-bring-calculations-to-life/

Flipped Learning Network. (2014). *The four pillars of F-L-I-P*. Retrieved from www.flippedlearning.org/definition

Freemark, S. (2014). Studying with quizzes helps make sure the material sticks. *MindShift*. Retrieved from http://ww2.kqed.org/mindshift/2014/10/16/studying-with-quizzes-helps-make-sure-the-material-sticks/

Milwaukee Journal Sentinel. (2012). Game based learning catching on in schools. *eSchool News*. Retrieved from www.eschoolnews.com/2012/05/08/game-based-learning-catching-on-in-schools

Gardiner, B. (2014). Adding coding to the curriculum. *New York Times*. Retrieved from www.nytimes.com/2014/03/24/world/europe/adding-coding-to-the-curriculum.html?_r=0

Georgia district implements virtual world technology. (2012). *eSchool News*. Retrieved from http://eschoolnews.com/2012/03/28/Georgia-district-implements-virtual-world-technology

Ginsburg-Block, C. A., Rohrbeck, A., & Fanuzzo, J. W. (2006). A meta-analytic review of social, self-concept, and behavioral outcomes of peer-assisted learning. *Journal of Educational Psychology, 98,* 732–749.

Good, C., Aronson, J., & Inzlicht, M. (2003). Improving adolescents' standardized test performance: An intervention to reduce the effects of stereotype threat. *Applied Developmental Psychology, 24,* 645–662.

Graves, C. (2015). *Starting a school makerspace from scratch.* Retrieved from www.edutopia.org/blog/starting-school-makerspace-from-scratch-colleen-graves

Graves, E. A. (2008). *Is role-playing an effective teaching method?* Master's thesis, Ohio University.

Greenberg, M. T., & Harris, A. R. (2012). Nurturing mindfulness in children and youth: Current state of research. *Child Development Perspectives, 6*(2), 161–166.

Greenwood, C. R., Tapia, Y., Abbott, M., & Walton, C. (2003). A building-based case study of evidence-based literacy practices: Implementation, reading behavior, and growth in reading fluency, K–4. *The Journal of Special Education, 50,* 521–535.

Grisham, L. (2014). Teachers, students, and social media: Where is the line? *USA Today.* Retrieved from www.usatoday.com/story/news/nation-now/2014/04/09/facebook-teachers-twitter-students-schools/7472051/

Green, G. (2012). My view: Flipped classrooms give every student a chance to succeed. *CNN online.* Retrieved from http://schoolsofthought.blogs.cnn.com/2012/01/18/my-view-flipped-classrooms-give-every-student-a-chance-to-succeed/

Green, G. (2014). Flipped classrooms get results at Clintondale High School. *Techsmith.* Retrieved from www.techsmith.com/customer-stories-clintondale.html

Hallahan, D. P., & Sapona, R. (1983). Self-monitoring of attention with learning disabled children: Past research and current issues. *Journal of Learning Disabilities, 16,* 616–620.

Halleck, M. (2012). *ClassDojo action research.* Retrieved from https://prezi.com/jbcirteldtlh/class-do-jo-action-research/

Hamdan, N., McKnight, P., McKnight, K., & Arfstrom, K. (2013). *A review of flipped learning.* Retrieved from www.flippedlearning.org/review

Harris, K., Friedlander, B. D., Saddler, B., & Frizzell, R. (2005). Self-monitoring of attention versus self-monitoring of academic performance: Effects among students with ADHD in the general education classroom. *The Journal of Special Education, 39*(3), 145–157.

Hatten, S. (2014). *Engage elementary students with stop animation!* International Society for Technology in Education. Retrieved from www.iste.org/explore/articleDetail?articleid=128

Harris, E. A. (2015). Under stress: Students in New York schools find calm in meditation. *New York Times.* Retrieved from www.nytimes.com/2015/10/24/nyregion/under-stress-students-in-new-york-schools-find-calm-in-meditation.html?_r=1

Hattie, J. (2012). *Visible learning for teachers: Maximizing impact on learning.* London and New York: Routledge, Taylor, & Francis Group.

Heuvel, L. (2008). *Educators' use of Colonial Williamsburg electronic field trips and related web resources.* Williamsburg, VA: Colonial Williamsburg Office of Educational Outreach.

Hicks, J. (2015). *12 unexpected ways to use LEGO in the classroom.* Retrieved from www.edudemic.com/12-ways-use-lego-classroom/?utm_source=twitterfeed&utm_medium=twitter

Holland, B. (2014). How to start using augmented reality in the classroom. *Edudemic.* Retrieved from http://edtechteacher.org/how-to-start-using-augmented-reality-in-the-classroom-from-beth-holland-on-edudemic/

Horn, M. B. (2013). The transformational potential of flipped classrooms. *Education Next, 13*(3). Retrieved from http://educationnext.org/the-transformational-potential-of-flipped-classrooms/

International Society for Technology in Education (ISTE). (2010). *How can technology influence student academic knowledge?* Retrieved from http://caret.iste.org/index.cfm?useaction=evidence&answerID-12&words-Attention

ISTE Connects. (2015). *Wildly popular, then off the grid, virtual worlds are back in ed tech.* Retrieved from www.iste.org/explore/articleDetail?articleid=316&category=ISTE-Connects-blog&article=wildly-popular-then-off-the-grid-virtual-worlds-are-back-in-ed-tech&utm_source=Twitter&utm_medium=Social&utm_campaign=EdTekHub

Junco, R. (2011, March). Using Twitter to improve college student engagement. A presentation at South by Southwest (SxSW) Interactive, Austin, TX.

Kamps, D. M., Greenwood, G., Arreaga-Meyer, C., Baldwin, M., Veerkamp, M. B., Utley, C., Tapia, Y., Bowman-Perrott, L., & Bannister, H. (2008). The efficacy of classwide peer tutoring in middle schools. *Education & Treatment of Children, 31*(2), 119–152.

King, K., & Gurian, M. (2006). Teaching to the minds of boys. *Educational Leadership, 64*(1), 54–61.

Klatta, M., Harpsterb, K., Brownea, E., Whitea, S., & Case-Smith, J. (2013). Feasibility and preliminary outcomes for Move-Into-Learning: An arts-based mindfulness classroom intervention. *The Journal of Positive Psychology.* Retrieved from http://dx.doi.org/10.1080/17439760.2013.779011

Klopfer, E. (2008). *Augmented learning.* Cambridge, MA: MIT Press.

Klopfer, E., & Sheldon, J. (2010). Augmenting your own reality: Student authoring of science-based augmented reality games. *New Directions for Youth Development, 128*(Winter), 85–94.

Kodotchigova, M. A. (2001). Role play in teaching culture: Six quick steps for classroom implementation. In P. V. Sysoyev (Ed.), *Identity, culture, and language teaching.* Iowa City, IA: Center for Russian, East European, and Eurasian Studies.

Kuchimanchi, B. (2013). Role of animation in students' learning. *Ed Tech Review.* Retrieved from http://edtechreview.in/trends-insights/insights/367-role-of-animation-in-students-learning

Kunsch, C., Jitendra, A., & Sood, S. (2007). The effects of peer-mediated instruction in mathematics for students with learning problems: A research synthesis. *Learning Disabilities Research & Practice, 22*(1), 1–12.

Lamb, A. (2016). *Create virtual adventures.* Retrieved from http://eduscapes.com/sessions/virtual/create.html

Lampinen, M. (2013). *Blogging in the 21st-century classroom.* Retrieved from www.edutopia.org/blog/blogging-in-21st-century-classroom-michelle-lampinen

Larmer, J., Ross, D., & Mergendoller, J. R. (2010). 7 essentials for project-based learning. *Educational Leadership, 68*(1), 34–37.

Larmer, J., Ross, D., & Mergendoller, J. R. (2009). *PBL starter kit: To-the-point advice, tools, and tips for your first project in middle or high school.* San Rafael, CA: Unicorn Printing Specialists.

Le, D. (2016). *5 maker movement tools that are not 3D printers.* Retrieved from www.edudemic.com/maker-movement-tools/?utm_content=bufferf68a5

Lee, S., Wehmeyer, M. L., Sookup, J. H., & Palmer, S. B. (2010). Impact of curriculum modifications on access to the general educational curriculum for students with disabilities. *Exceptional Children, 76*(2), 213–233.

List, J. S., & Bryant, B. (2009). Integrating interactive online content at an early college high school: An exploration of Moodle, Ning, and Twitter. *Meridian Middle School Computer Technologies Journal, 12*(1). Retrieved from www.ncsu.edu/meridan/winter2009

Lyga, A. (2006). Graphic novels for (really) young readers. *School Library Journal.* Retrieved from www.schoollibraryjournal.com/article/CA6312463.html

Maben, S. (2016). *NASA taps North Idaho school for satellite project.* Retrieved from www.spokesman.com/stories/2016/feb/22/nasa-taps-north-idaho-school-for-satellite-launch/

Maclean-Blevins, A., & Muilenburg, L. (2013). Using ClassDojo to support student self-regulation. In Jan Herrington et al. (Eds.), *Proceedings of World Conference on Educational Multimedia, Hypermedia and Telecommunications* (pp. 1684–1689). Chesapeake, VA: Association for the Advancement of Computing in Education.

Madge, C., Meek, J., Wellens, J., & Hooley, T. (2009). Facebook, social integration and informal learning at university: 'It is more for socialising and talking to friends about work than for actually doing work.' *Learning, Media and Technology, 34*(2), 141–155.

Mak, B., & Coniam, D. (2008). Using wikis to enhance and develop writing skills among secondary school students in Hong Kong. *System, 36,* 437–455.

Markham, T. (2011). *Strategies for embedding project-based learning into STEM education.* Retrieved from www.edutopia.org/blog/strategies-pbl-stem-thom-markham-buck-institute

Marzano, R. (2015). *Student engagement: 5 ways to get and keep your students' attention.* Retrieved from www.marzanocenter.com/blog/article/5-ways-to-get-and-keep-your-students-attention/

Marzano, R. (2009). *Marzano's nine instructional strategies for effective teaching and learning.* Retrieved from www.ntuaft.com/TISE/Research-Based%20Instructional%20Strategies/marzanos%209%20strategies.pdf

Marzano, R. (2007). *The art and science of teaching: A comprehensive framework for effective instruction.* Alexandria, VA: Association for Supervision and Curriculum Development.

Marzano, R. J. (2003). *What works in schools: Translating research into action.* Alexandria, VA: Association for Supervision and Curriculum Development.

Marzano, R. J., & Haystead, M. (2009). *Final report on the evaluation on the Promethean technology.* Englewood, CO: Marzano Research Laboratory.

Marzano, R. J., Pickering, D. J., & Pollock, J. E. (2001). *Classroom instruction that works: Research-based strategies for increasing student achievement.* Alexandria, VA: Association for Supervision and Curriculum Development.

Maton, N. (2011). *Can an online game crack the code to language learning?* Retrieved from http://mindshift.kqed.org/2011/11/can-an-online-game-crack-the-code-to-language-learning/

McCarthy, J. (2015). *Igniting student engagement: A roadmap for learning.* Retrieved from www.edutopia.org/blog/ignite-student-engagement-roadmap-learning-john-mccarthy

McDaniel, K. N. (2000). Four elements of successful historical role-playing in the classroom. *History Teacher, 33*(3), 357–362.

McDowell, A. (2016). *Tech tip: Tech tools for elementary math instruction.* Retrieved from http://smartbrief.com/original/2016/08/tech-tip-tech-tools-elementary-math-instruction?utm_source=brief

Mergendoller, J. R., Maxwell, N., & Bellisimo, Y. (2007). The effectiveness of problem-based instruction: A comparative study of instructional methods and student characteristics. *Interdisciplinary Journal of Problem-Based Learning, 1*(2), 49–69.

Miller, A. (2015). *Makerspaces are making maker businesses.* Retrieved from www.makerspaces.com/makerspaces-are-making-maker-businesses/

Miller, A. (2012). *A new community and resources for games for learning.* Retrieved from www.edutopia.org/blog/games-for-learning-community-resources-andrew-miller

Mims, L. (2013). Classroom behavior? There's an app for that. *Edutopia.* Retrieved from www.edutopia.org/blog/classroom-behavior-classdojo-app-lisa-mims

Mindset Works. (2016). *Dr. Dweck's discovery of fixed and growth mindsets have shaped our understanding of learning.* Retrieved from www.mindsetworks.com/Science/Default

Miner, M. (2015). *Second Life lessons & classroom activities.* Retrieved from www.teachhub.com/second-life-lessons-classroom-activities

Moeller, A. J., Theiler, J. M., & Wu, C. (2012). Goal setting and student achievement: A longitudinal study. *The Modern Language Journal, 96*(2), 153–159.

Mongan-Rallis, H. (2006). *Virtual field trip guidelines.* Retrieved from www.duluth.umn.edu/~hrallis/guides/virtualfieldtrip.html

Moreno, R. (2009). Learning from animated classroom exemplars: The case for guiding student teachers' observations with metacognitive prompts. *Educational Research and Evaluation: An International Journal on Theory and Practice, 15*(9), 487–501.

Morris, R. V. (2003). Acting out history: Students reach across time and space. *International Journal of Social Education, 18*(1), 44–51.

Myers, A., & Berkowicz, J. (2015). *The STEM shift: A guide for school leaders.* Thousand Oaks, CA: Corwin Press.

National Education Association. (2015). *Research spotlight on peer tutoring.* Retrieved from www.nea.org/tools/35542.htm

Neilsen, L. (2014). *SetupanonymousbullyreportingwithCel.ly.* Techlearning.com. Retrieved from https://www.techlearning.com/Default.aspx?tabid=67&entryid=8325

Nhat Hanh, T. (2010). *Five steps to mindfulness.* Retrieved from www.mindful.org/five-steps-to-mindfulness/

Noel, M. (2007). Elements of a winning field trip. *Kappa Delta Pi Record, 44*(1), 42–44.

Noel, M., & Colopy, M. (2006). Making history field trips meaningful: Teachers' and site educators' perspectives on teaching materials. *Theory and Research in Social Education, 34*(3), 553–568.

Noonoo, S. (2012). Augmented reality apps transform class time. *T.H.E. Journal.* Retrieved from https://thejournal.com/Articles/2012/09/12/Augmented-Reality-Apps-Transform-Class-Time.aspx?Page=1

Nugent, G., Barker, B. S., & Grandgenett, N. (2012). *The impact of educational robotics on student STEM learning, attitudes, and workplace skills.* Retrieved from www.igi-global.com/chapter/impact-educational-robotics-student-stem/63415

Nussbaum-Beach, S. (2014). *Virtual field trips enhance learning and save time—action research from William Penn Charter School.* Retrieved from http://plpnetwork.com/2012/05/24/virtual-field-trips-enhance-learning-and-save-time-action-research-from-william-penn-charter-school/

Nyren, H. (2016). Top 5 coding games for kids that they'll want to play. *Edtechtimes.* Retrieved from http://edtechtimes.com/2016/01/19/top-5-engaging-coding-games-for-kids/?platform=hootsuite

Oaklander, M. (2015). Mini-meditators. *Time.* Retrieved from www.michigan.gov/documents/mdcs/WellnessArticle_482372_7.pdf

Pappas, C. (2013). *How to use wiki in the classroom. TechforTeachers.* Retrieved from www.techforteachers.net/wikis-in-the-classroom.html

Park, R. (2016). *Here's Rachel Park's overview of 3D printing and education.* Retrieved from https://all3dp.com/3d-printing-education-first-an-overview/

Politis, M. (2015). *Augmented reality—the coolest instructional technology you haven't heard of.* Retrieved from www.emergingedtech.com/2014/04/augmented-reality-emerging-education-technology/

Powel, M. (2014). *Robot teachers in the classroom.* Retrieved from http://iq.intel.com/robot-teachers-in-the-classroom/

Prescott, J. (2014). How professors are using Facebook to teach. *Washington Post.* Retrieved from www.washingtonpost.com/posteverything/wp/2014/07/10/how-professors-are-using-facebook-to-teach/

Pressly, A. (2014). *Easy tools for using robotics in the classroom.* Retrieved from www.iste.org/explore/articleDetail?articleid=93&category=ISTE-Connects-blog&article=Easy-tools-for-using-robotics-in-the-classroom

Ramsden, S., Richardson, F. M., Josse, G., Thomas, M., Ellis, C., Shakeshart, C., Seguier, M., & Price, C. (2011). Verbal and non-verbal intelligence changes in the teenage brain. *Nature, 479,* 113–116.

Rapp, D. (2008). *Virtual classroom: Second Life.* Retrieved from www.scholastic.com/browse/article.jsp?id=3749877

Rendina, D. L. (2016). *The value of guided projects in makerspaces.* Retrieved from http://renovatedlearning.com/2016/01/18/value-guided-projects-makerspaces/

Richardson, W. (2010). *Blogs, wikis, podcasts, and other powerful tools for educators.* Thousand Oaks, CA: Corwin Press.

Richardson, W., & Mancabelli, R. (2011). *Personal learning networks: Using the power of connections to transform education.* Bloomington, IN: Solution Tree Press.

Richtel, M. (2012). Blogs vs. term papers. *New York Times.* Retrieved from www.nytimes.com/2012/01/22/education/edlife/muscling-in-on-the-term-paper.html?-tx1

Ripp, P. (2015). *Some ideas for re-engaging students.* Retrieved from http://pernillesripp.com/2015/09/08/some-ideas-for-re-engaging-students/

Rosen, Y. (2009). The effect of an animation-based online learning environment on higher-order thinking skills and on motivation for science learning. *Journal of Educational Computing Research, 40*(4), 451–467.

Ruffini, M. F. (2009). Creating animations in PowerPoint to support student learning and engagement. *EDUCAUSE Quarterly, 32*(4). Retrieved from www.educause.edu/EDUCAUSE+Quarterly/EDUCAUSEQuarterlyMagazineVolum/CreatingAnimationsinPowerPoint/192966

Sadeghi, K., & Sharifi, F. (2013). The effect of post-teaching activity type on vocabulary learning of elementary EFL learners. *English Language Teaching, 6*(11), 65–76.

Sáez-López, J. M., Miller, J., Vázquez-Cano, E., & Domínguez-Garrido, M. C. (2015). Exploring application, attitudes and integration of video games: MinecraftEdu in middle school. *Educational Technology & Society, 18*(3), 114–128.

Schwartz, K. (2016a). *What changes when a school embraces mindfulness?* Retrieved from http://ww2.kqed.org/mindshift/2016/03/30/what-changes-when-a-school-embraces-mindfulness/

Schwartz, K. (2016b). *What ClassDojo monsters can teach kids about growth mindset.* Retrieved from http://ww2.kqed.org/mindshift/2016/01/19/what-classdojo-monsters-can-teach-kids-about-growth-mindset/

Schwartz, K. (2015b). *Beyond working hard: What growth mindset teaches us about our brains.* Retrieved from http://ww2.kqed.org/mindshift/2015/12/29/beyond-working-hard-what-growth-mindset-teaches-us-about-our-brains/

Schwartz, K. (2014). *Robots in the classroom what are they good for?* Retrieved from http://ww2.kqed.org/mindshift/2014/05/27/robots-in-the-classroom-what-are-they-good-for/

Schwartz, K. (2013). *Five research-driven education trends at work in classrooms.* Retrieved from http://blogs.kqed.org/mindshift/2013/10/five-research-driven-education-trends-at-work-in-classrooms/

Shapiro, J. (2014). *Using games for learning: Practical steps to get started.* Retrieved from http://ww2.kqed.org/mindshift/2014/09/05/using-games-for-learning-practical-steps-to-get-started/

Shah, N. (2012). Special educators borrow from brain studies. *Education Week, 31*(17), 10.

Sheely, K. (2011). *High school teachers make gaming academic.* Retrieved from http://education.usnews.rankingandreviews.com/education/highschools/articles/2011/11/01/high-school-teachers-make-gaming-academic?PageNr=1

Short, D. (2012). Teaching scientific concepts using a virtual world—Minecraft. *Teaching Science, 58*(3). Retrieved from www.academia.edu/1891072/Teaching_Scientific_Concepts_Using_a_Virtual_World_-_Minecraft

Singer, N. (2015). *Google virtual-reality system aims to enliven education.* Retrieved from www.nytimes.com/2015/09/29/technology/google-virtual-reality-system-aims-to-enliven-education.html?_r=0

Smith, D. F. (2015a). *Google Expeditions brings virtual reality field trips to schools across America.* Retrieved from www.edtechmagazine.com/k12/article/2015/11/google-expeditions-brings-virtual-reality-field-trips-schools-across-america

Smith, D. F. (2015b). *Skype connects classrooms with field trips around the world.* Retrieved from www.edtechmagazine.com/k12/article/2015/09/skype-connects-classrooms-field-trips-around-world

Smith, R. (2015). 3D printing is about to change the world forever. *Forbes.* Retrieved from www.forbes.com/sites/ricksmith/2015/06/15/3d-printing-is-about-to-change-the-world-forever/

Sousa, D. A. (2010). *Mind, brain, and education.* Bloomington, IN: Solution Tree Press.

Sousa, D. A., & Tomlinson, C. A. (2011). *Differentiation and the brain: How neuroscience supports the learner-friendly classroom.* Bloomington, IN: Solution Tree Press.

Sparks, S. D. (2011). Schools "flip" for lesson model promoted by Khan Academy. *Education Today, 31*(5), 1–14.

Spicer, J., & Stratford, J. (2001). Student perceptions of a virtual field trip to replace a real field trip. *Journal of Computer Assisted Learning, 17,* 345–354.

SRI International. (2014). Research on the use of Khan Academy in schools. Retrieved from www.sri.com/sites/default/files/publications/2014-03-07_implementation_briefing.pdf

Stansbury, M. (2013). Does research support flipped learning? *eSchool News.* Retrieved from www.eschoolnews.com/2013;07/30/does-research-support-flipped-learning/

Starting Point. (2016). *How to teach using role-playing.* Retrieved from http://serc.carleton.edu/introgeo/roleplaying/howto.html

Stillwell, T. (2011). Reading with pictures—supporting comics in the classroom. *Wired.* Retrieved from www.wired.com/geekdad/2011/02/reading-with-pictures-supporting-comics-in-the-classroom

Stoddard, J. (2009). Toward a virtual field trip model for the social studies. *Contemporary Issues in Technology and Teacher Education, 9*(4). Retrieved from www.citejournal.org/vol9/iss4/socialstudies/article1.cfm

Sweeney, J. (1998). *Me on the map.* Decorah, IA: Dragonfly Books.

Swett, A. M. (2015). *The effectiveness of virtual and on-site dairy farm field trips to increase student knowledge in science, social studies, and health and wellness standards.* Retrieved from http://docs.lib.purdue.edu/dissertations/AAI1573767/

Symonds Elementary School. (2015). Social and emotional learning: A schoolwide approach. *Edutopia.* Retrieved from www.edutopia.org/practice/social-and-emotional-learning-schoolwide-approach?utm_source=twitter&utm_medium=socialflow&utm_campaign=RSS

TeachThought Staff. (2015). *Education app spotlight: Contraption maker.* Retrieved from www.teachthought.com/apps-2/app-spotlight-contraption-maker/

TEEcontributor. (2011a). *5 ways to use Twitter in the classroom.* Retrieved from http://h30411/www3.hp.com/posts/1014985-5_ways_to_use_Twitter_in_the_classroom

TEEcontributor. (2011b). *5 more ways to use Twitter in the classroom.* Retrieved from http://h30411/www3.hp.com/posts/1118287-Five_more_ways_to_use_Twitter_in_the_classroom

TEEcontributor. (2001). *7 web 2.0 animation tools.* Retrieved from http://h30411/www3.hp.com/posts/1045052-7_web_2_0_animation_tools_tools?mcid=Twitter

Thacker, C. (2016). *How to use Comic Life in the classroom.* Retrieved from www.macinstruct.com/node/69

Thomas, L. (2016). *Mindful facilitation: Don't do something, just stand there.* Retrieved from www.edutopia.org/blog/mindful-facilitation-pbl-laura-thomas?utm_source=twitter&utm_medium=socialflow

Tizzard, R. (2010). Strategies that increase student engagement. In D. Gibson & B. Dodge (Eds.), *Proceedings of Society for Information Technology & Teacher Education International Conference 2010* (pp. 934–935). Chesapeake, VA: Association for the Advancement of Computing in Education.

Tomaszewski, J. (2012). Fresh ideas: Using wikis in the classroom. *Education World.* Retrieved from www.educationworld.com/a_lesson/using-wikis-in-the-classroom.shtml

Tomlinson, C. A. (2010). Differentiating instruction in response to academically diverse student populations. In R. Marzano (Ed.), *On excellence in teaching.* Bloomington, IN: Solution Tree Press.

Tomlinson, C. A. (2003). *Differentiation in practice: A resource guide for differentiating curriculum, grades K–5.* Alexandria, VA: Association for Supervision and Curriculum Development.

Tomlinson, C. A. (1999). *The differentiated classroom: Responding to the needs of all learners.* Alexandria, VA: Association for Supervision and Curriculum Development.

Tomlinson, C. A., Brimijoin, K., & Navaez, L. (2008). *The differentiated school: Making revolutionary changes in teaching and learning.* Alexandria, VA: Association for Supervision and Curriculum Development.

Topping, K. (2008). *Peer-assisted learning: A practical guide for teachers.* Newton, MA: Brookline Books.

Toppo, G. (2011). "Flipped" classrooms take advantage of technology. *USA Today.* Retrieved from www.usatoday.com/news/education/story/2011-10-06

Trentin, G. (2009). Using a wiki to evaluate individual contribution to a collaborative learning project. *Journal of Computer Assisted Learning, 25,* 43–55.

Tucker, B. (2012). The flipped classroom. *Education Next, 12*(1). Retrieved from http://educationnext.org/the-flipped-classroom/

National Council of Teachers of English. (2005). Using comics and graphic novels in the classroom. *The Council Chronical.* Retrieved from www.ncte.org/magazine/archives/122031

Vega, V. (2012). *Research-based practices for engaging students in STEM learning.* Retrieved from www.edutopia.org/stw-college-career-stem-research

Wallagher, M. (2015). *How blogging is being used in the classroom today: Research results.* Retrieved from www.emergingedtech.com/2015/09/the-state-of-blogging-in-the-classroom/

Waller, J. (2016). *6 strategies for teaching the growth mindset.* Retrieved from http://7mindsets.com/growth-mindset/

Walsh, K. (2011). *Facebook in the classroom. Seriously.* Retrieved from www.emergingedtech.com/2011/03/facebook-in-the-classroom-seriously/

Wheelock, A., & Merrick, S. (2015). *5 virtual worlds for engaged learning.* Retrieved from www.iste.org/explore/articleDetail?articleid=395&category=In-the-classroom

Welham, H. (2014). How to introduce mindfulness into your classroom: Nine handy tips. *The Guardian.* Retrieved from www.theguardian.com/teacher-network/teacher-blog/2014/jul/23/how-to-mindfulness-classroom-tips

Wolpert-Gawron, H. (2015). Project-based learning and gamification: Two great tastes that go great together. *Edutopia.* Retrieved from www.edutopia.org/blog/project-based-learning-gamification-go-great-together-heather-wolpert-gawron?utm_content=October15&utm_campaign=RSS&utm_source=twitter&utm_medium=socialflow%20

Yohana, D. (2014). *5 robots booking it to a classroom near you.* Retrieved from http://mashable.com/2014/08/29/robots-schools/

Yokana, L. (2015). Creating an authentic maker education rubric. *Edutopia.* Retrieved from www.edutopia.org/blog/creating-authentic-maker-education-rubric-lisa-yokana

Zepke, N., & Leach, L. (2010). Improving student engagement: Ten proposals for action. *Active Learning in Higher Education, 11*(3), 167–177.

Zhang, Y. A. (2012). Developing animated cartoons for economic teaching. *Journal of University Teaching & Learning Practice, 9*(2). Retrieved from http://ro.uow.edu.au/jutlp/vol9/iss2/5

Zimmerman, E. (2014). 3 free ways to add amination to your classroom. *T.H.E. Journal.* Retrieved from https://thejournal.com/articles/2014/03/25/3-tools-for-animation.aspx?=FETCLN

Index

3-D printing, 45–48, 53. *see also* makerspace

ABCya.com, 122*box*
Academy of MATH, 101, 103–104*box*
Academy of READING, 101, 103–104*box*
Albasi, T.A., 173
alternative reality game. *see* virtual worlds
animation
    case study, 123–124
    definition of, 119–120
    research on, 127
    tools for teachers, 122
    use in classroom, 120–122
Animation Desk, 122*box*
Apollo 13, 196
artifact, 36, 40–41, 41, 81, 82. *see also* project-based learning
attribution theory, 191–192, 195, 196, 197. *see also* growth mindset
augmented reality
    classroom setup, 60–61
    definition of, 57–58
    example of, 58–59
    options for, 59*box*
    research on, 61–62
avatar
    ClassDojo and, 185
    creating, 124–126
    definition of, 120–121

Ballestrini, Kevin, 68
Bank of America, 104
Bedesem, P., 204, 205
Bee-Bot, 92–93, 96*box*
Bergmann, J., 22, 23
Berkowicz, J., 38
BIE.org, 34*box*

Bill and Melinda Gates Foundation, 104
Blackwell, L. S., 199, 200
Blogger, 135
blogging
    definition of, 131–132
    example of, 133–134
    guidelines for, 135–137
    research on, 137
    use in classroom, 132–133
Boss, S. 32
brain malleability, 190–191, 193
Brainology, 192
brain plasticity. *see* brain malleability
Breeden, J., 46
Brimijoin, K., 20

Celly, 140*box*
ClassDojo, 185–186, 192
Clintondale High School, 30
CodeMonkey, 90*box*
Code Studio, 89*box*
coding
    classroom example of, 91–94
    definition of, 87, 87–88
    games, 90
    importance of, 88
    languages for young students, 89–90*box*
    research on, 98–99
    skills developed in, 90–91
    steps for teaching, 97–98
collaborative instruction
    peer tutoring as a strategy, 157
    student engagement and, 130
    Twitter and, 142–143
    wikis and, 147, 148, 149
Comic Life, 112–117
comic strips, 112

Common Core State Standards, 104*box*
conductive thread, 50
Coniam, D., 156
Contraption Maker, 50
creativity, 43, 44, 115, 120, 136–137
culminating project, 36. *see also* project-based learning
Curtis, C., 145
Cuthrell, K., 156

Dash and Dot, 96*box*
Davis, L., 46
Dede, C., 61
De Pedro, X., 156
desktop laser cutter, 49–50
Deters, F., 156
differentiated instruction
   definition, 11
   development of, 10
   forming groups in, 15–18
   guidelines for, 18–19
   increased achievement and, 11, 12
   models of, 12
   modification of traditional lesson plan and, 12
   research on, 19–20
   student engagement and, 17, 18
   versus traditional lesson plan, 14*box*
Discipline Tracker, 184*box*
Discovery Education, 79*box*
Doink.com, 122*box*
driving question, 34. *see also* project-based learning
drones, 50
Dunleavy, M., 61
Dweck, C., 189, 191, 192

Edison, Thomas, 196
Edmodo, 140*box*
Edublog, 135, 137
Edutopia.org, 32, 34*box*, 64
effect size, 208
Elford, Stephen, 70
emotional intelligence, 38
engagement. *see* student engagement
Epps, J., 53
Evans, K., 134
EZ-Robot, 96*box*

Facebook, 139–140*box*, 142, 145
failure, 196
Fast ForWord, 101, 103*box*
fixed mindset, 189. *see also* growth mindset
Flanagan, L., 53
flipped class strategy
   advantages of, 23–24
   case study, 28–29
   definition of, 21–22
   development of, 22
   example of, 24–26
   four pillars of, 23*box*
   increased achievement and, 22
   Khan Academy and, 108
   research on, 30
   steps for implementing, 26–28
   student engagement and, 22
   student responsibility and, 23, 24
flipped learning. *see* flipped class strategy

games
   classroom use, 63
   educational gaming sites, 65*box*
   example of, 66–67
   guidelines for, 72–73
   research on, 73–74
   standalone, 64
   student engagement, 73
gamification, 63–64. *see also* games
gaming. *see* games
Gardner, Howard, 13
genius hour, 43, 44, 44*box*, 50, 53
GEO Virtual Field Trips, 80*box*
goal setting and self-monitoring
   research on, 205
   success and, 201–202
   teaching, 202–205
GoAnimate.com, 122*box*
Gonzalez, Argos, 178, 179, 180
Good, C., 193, 196, 197
Google, 104
Google+, 140*box*
Google Cardboard, 76
Google Expeditions Pioneer Program, 76–77
graphic novels, 112
Green, Greg, 30
growth mindset
   attribution theory and, 191–192
   case study, 197–199

Index

curricula and, 192
definition of, 189–190
fostering a, 193–197
human brain malleability and, 190–191
research on, 199
Growth Mindset: The New Psychology of Success, 189

Hallahan, D. P., 203
Hamilton, Paul, 59*box*
Harris, K., 205
Hattie, J., 42, 73, 205, 207, 208
Hawn, Goldie, 179
Hicks, J., 49

individualized computer-driven instruction
curricula, 103–104*box*
introduction to, 101–104
Khan Academy and, 104–110
Internet searches, 40
Ivester, Eleanor, 91

Jumpstart, 46
Junco, R., 145

Khan, Sal, 104
Khan Academy, 26, 27, 101, 102, 104–110
KidBlog, 135
Klatta, M., 181
Kodable, 90*box*
Kodotchigova, M. A., 168

Lampinen, M., 137
Le, D., 49
Learning Sciences International. *see* LSI Tracker
lecture, effectiveness of, 10, 19
LEGOs, 48–49. *see also* makerspace
Levin, Joel, 69
Lightbot, 90*box*
Little, Elizabeth, 53
LSI Tracker, 38, 40, 184

Maclean-Blevins, 188
Mak, B., 156
MakerBot, 45–46. *see also* 3-D printing; makerspace
maker movement, 43, 44, 94. *see also* makerspace

makerspace. *see also* maker movement
definition of, 43–44
guidelines for, 50–52
materials and tools, 45–50, 51
research on, 53
resources for planning, 52
virtual world and, 50
Marzano, Robert, 20, 202, 207, 208
McDowell, A., 103*box*
Me on the Map, 92
Merrick, S., 71
meta-analysis
advantages of, 208–209
definition of, 207–208
disadvantages of, 209–210
use of, 209–210
microcontrollers, 50
mindfulness
classroom example of, 178–179
curricula, 179
definition of, 177–178
implementation of, 179–181
research on, 181
Mindful Schools, 179*box*
MindUP, 179*box*
Minecraft, 68–70. *see also* virtual worlds
MinecraftEDU, 69
minilesson, 21, 37*box*, 39, 40
Mitchell, R., 61
Moeller, A. J., 205
Moldenhauer, Jerry, 99
Morris, R.V., 173
Move Into Learning, 181
Myers, A., 38

NASA Virtual Field Trips, 80*box*
Navaez, L., 20
Ning, 140*box*
Noonoo, S., 62
North Idaho STEM Charter Academy, 32

OpenSim, 71*box*
open-source software programs, 50
ORIGO Stepping Stones, 103*box*
Osborn, C., 53

Park, Rachel, 44
PBL. *see* project-based learning
Pearson Education, 59*box*, 140*box*, 185*box*

peer tutoring
   case study, 158–160
   classwide, 160–162
   as a collaborative instruction strategy, 157–158
   research on, 162
percentage of achievement gain, 209
Pinterest, 79*box*
praise, 194–195, 197
Prescott, J., 145
professional learning network (PLN), 143
project anchor, 34, 37–38. *see also* project-based learning
project-based learning
   artifact, 36
   definition of, 31
   examples of, 32–35
   increased achievement and, 32
   project phases, 37–42
   project scope and, 32
   research on, 42
   structure and components, 34–36
   student engagement and, 42

Quest Atlantis, 70–71

RealWorldMath.org, 34*box*
Rendina, D. L., 52
response cost. *see* reward and response cost
Review360, 184–185*box*
reward and response cost
   definition of, 183
   tech-based options for, 183–185
Rich Kids 1.10, 184
Richtel, M., 131, 136
Ripp, P., 3
RobotBASIC, 89*box*
robotics
   classroom robots, 95–96*box*
   future impact of, 94–95
   prevalence in the classroom, 87
   research on, 98–99
   steps for teaching, 97–98
   teaching with, 95–96
RobotLab, 95, 96–97*box*
Rodrigo, Rebecca, 186, 188
role-play
   classroom example of, 166–167
   definition of, 165–166
   research on, 173
   steps for implementing, 167–172
   student engagement and, 165

Sammamish High School, 32
Sams, A., 22
SAS Curriculum Pathways, 104*box*
Schwartz, K., 94, 99, 182
Scott, Susan, 66
Scratch, 89*box*, 97
Scrivner-Limbaugh, Allison, 166
self-monitoring. *see* goal setting and self-monitoring
Short, D., 70
Shoup, Jessica, 149
simulations, 63
Sketchup, 47*box*
Skype, 77
social networking
   tools for, 139–140*box*
   Twitter as a tool for, 140–145
SpaceChem, 90*box*
SRI International, 108
Stansbury, M., 119
Stapleton, J., 156
storyboarding
   Comic Life and, 112–117
   definition of, 111–112
   and virtual field trips, 83
student engagement
   and achievement, 1, 3
   avatars and, 120, 127
   blogging and, 131, 137
   ClassDojo and, 185–187
   and coding and robotics, 98–99
   collaborative instruction and, 130
   and Comic Life, 117
   creativity and, 43
   definition, 1–2
   flipped class strategy and, 22
   games and simulations and, 63, 73
   goal setting, 201
   goal setting and self-monitoring, 205
   and learning, 3
   learning styles and, 10, 18
   lecture and, 10, 19
   makerspace and, 51, 52
   mindfulness and, 180
   Minecraft and, 69

peer tutoring and, 163
publication and, 116, 126, 147
rewards and, 183
role-play and, 173
social networking and, 141, 145
strategies for, 3–6
and technology, 5–6
and traditional lesson plans, 13–15
virtual field trips and, 84
wikis and, 156
SuccessMaker, 101, 103*box*
Symonds Elementary, 178

Teachers, 2
TeacherTube, 26, 61
teaching
    3-D printing tips, 46–47*box*
    with a class robot, 95
    coding and robotics, 97–98
    games and simulations and, 64–65
    goal setting and self-monitoring, 202–205
    and student engagement, 3–5
    tips, 4–5
    with virtual field trips, 79–81
TedEd, 26
The Academic Locus of Control Scale, 196
The Foos, 89*box*
Theiler, J. M., 205
The JASON Project, 79*box*, 80
Thingiverse, 46
Tomaszewski, J., 155
Tomlinson, C., 10, 11, 13
Toontastic, 122*box*
traditional lesson plan
    versus differentiated lesson, 14*box*
    example of, 13–15
    modification of, 12–13
    phases of, 12*box*
    student engagement and, 13–15
Tumblr, 135
twenty percent time, 43, 44*box*
TwHistory, 142
Twitter, 140–145

Unity, 71*box*
University of Minnesota, 94

Virtual Field Trips, 79*box*
virtual field trips
    activities, 76, 80, 82
    case study, 77–78
    citing sources, 84
    definition of, 75
    guidelines for creating, 81–84
    guidelines for teaching with, 79–81
    predeveloped, 76
    presentation platform, 83
    research on, 84
    sources, 79–80*box*
    storyboarding and, 83
    student-developed, 76
    teacher-developed, 76
    technology tools for, 76–77
virtual worlds
    as complex gaming, 67–71
    makerspace, 50
    most common, 71
Voki, 124–126. *see also* avatar
Voki Classroom, 121, 125

Wallagher, M., 135, 137
WeDo, 95–96*box*
Weebly, 135
Wheelock, A., 71
Wikipedia, 40, 148
wikis
    classroom example of, 149–151
    definition of, 148
    research on, 156
    setting up, 151–156
    as tool for collaborative instruction, 147, 148, 149
    using class wiki, 148–149
Wikispaces, 150, 152
Wonderworkshop, 96*box*
WordPress, 135
World of Warcraft, 71*box*
Wu, C., 205

YouTube, 26, 41, 61, 82, 97, 124, 135, 148, 193